The Big All-Year Book of
Holidays & Seasonal
Celebrations

preschool/kindergarten

Issues 14-18

Teaching & Learning Company

1204 Buchanan St., P.O. Box 10
Carthage, IL 62321-0010

This book belongs to

_____

Edited and compiled by Donna Borst

Cover photos by Images and More Photography; Rubberball Productions; Corel; Image Ideas, Inc.

Cover design by Sara King

Illustrations by
Janet Armbrust	Mary Galan Rojas
Chrissy Schofield	Gary Hoover
Veronica Terrill	Vanessa Schwab
Becky Radtke	

Copyright © 2002, Teaching & Learning Company

ISBN No. 1-57310-339-X

Printing No. 987654321

Teaching & Learning Company
1204 Buchanan St., P.O. Box 10
Carthage, IL 62321-0010

At the time of publication every effort was made to insure the accuracy of the information included in this book. However, we cannot guarantee that agencies and organizations mentioned will continue to operate or to maintain these current locations.

Table of Contents

Fall 7

Winter 78

Spring & Summer 186

Dear Teacher or Parent,

Welcome to another edition of our popular *Best of Holidays & Seasonal Celebrations* series. It's been another exciting adventure for me as I go through the back issues and remember all of the fun we had putting those magazines together. It's always a little tricky trying to make sure that we cover all of the major holidays while not ignoring some of the lesser-known celebrations, but I love a challenge! And then, of course, there are some events that nobody may have heard of but they are just so fun we have to share them with you. I know I have learned a lot over the years and hope that you have, too. As a matter of fact, I now pride myself at being the Queen of Holidays—I think I pretty much know about every holiday and celebration there is. I can tell you when Dental Health Month is without blinking an eye. I can give you the dates for Kwanzaa, Women's History Month, Dairy Month, Book Week and Aquarium Month without missing a beat. This is not really a life-altering achievement, but I'm pretty proud of it. Most importantly, I hope that you have also gleaned something from *Holidays* and that your students have had fun while learning about all of the different holidays and celebrations that are featured in every issue. You can be sure that we certainly do our best to provide a magazine (and "Best-of" book) that is just a little different and a whole lot of fun.

In this book we cover the usual (Christmas, Thanksgiving, Valentine's Day and Easter) but there is also so much more. We have snowball celebrations, a menorah relay race, winter activities, a lesson on the bald eagle and tips for successful preschool crafts. We've included fun with mittens, creative bird snacks, activities for chocolate lovers and Purim fun. Pigs, shamrocks, wind, weather, trees and pets—we have it all. And that doesn't even include our regular features of "Seasonal Science, Snacktivities, Make-in-a-Minute Crafts and KidSpace.

So when you flip through this book, think of all the fun that lies between these pages. The fun that we had in putting it together and the fun that is just waiting around the corner for you and your students. And if you ever need a reason to celebrate, or just want to know when Lei Day is—you know who to call!

Donna

Donna Borst, Editor

Swishing and Wishing

The leaves are falling from the trees,
all orange, red and gold.
I love it when the autumn comes
and days are getting cold.

My feet go walking through the leaves.
A-swish, a-swish, a-swish.
A million more would fall around
if I could have my wish.

They'd fall and fall and get so deep
they'd nearly reach my chin.
Yahoo! A swimming pool of leaves!
I'd laugh and jump right in.

by Irene Livingston

Bag of Ice Cream

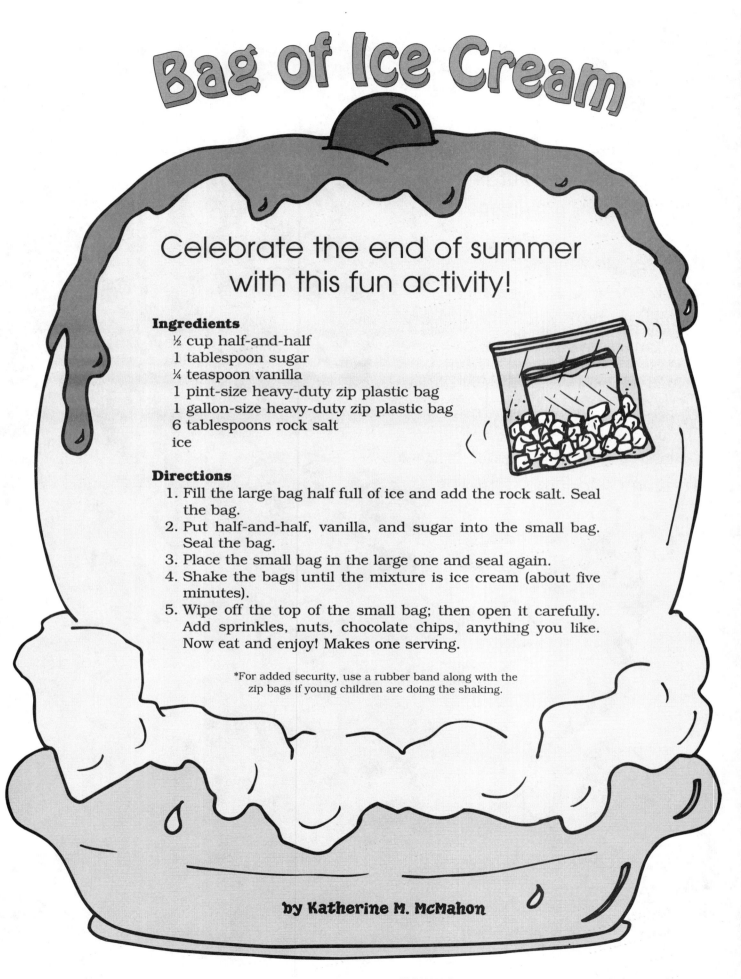

Celebrate the end of summer with this fun activity!

Ingredients
- ½ cup half-and-half
- 1 tablespoon sugar
- ¼ teaspoon vanilla
- 1 pint-size heavy-duty zip plastic bag
- 1 gallon-size heavy-duty zip plastic bag
- 6 tablespoons rock salt
- ice

Directions
1. Fill the large bag half full of ice and add the rock salt. Seal the bag.
2. Put half-and-half, vanilla, and sugar into the small bag. Seal the bag.
3. Place the small bag in the large one and seal again.
4. Shake the bags until the mixture is ice cream (about five minutes).
5. Wipe off the top of the small bag; then open it carefully. Add sprinkles, nuts, chocolate chips, anything you like. Now eat and enjoy! Makes one serving.

*For added security, use a rubber band along with the zip bags if young children are doing the shaking.

by Katherine M. McMahon

Making Friends

New school year, new class, new friends . . . Invite your youngsters to learn more about themselves, each other, and their new surroundings with activities that celebrate Friendship Day.

Classroom Community

Talk with your children about what the term **friendship** means to them. Prompt them to include ideas about sharing, cooperation, and helping each other, as well as having fun together. To illustrate the concept of the class being a group of friends, have the children help to paint a large Friendship Tree on butcher or craft paper. Include several branches. Hang the tree on a wall after the paint dries. Now, take photographs of individual children and label each with the child's name. Hang the photos among the tree branches. Remember to include a photograph of yourself! Variation: Make a school-wide community Friendship Tree by also including photographs of school personnel, such as the principal and the nurse.

by Marie E. Cecchini

Understanding Trust

A friend is a person you trust. Demonstrate the meaning of the word **trust** to your children by using chairs, tables, boxes, and baskets to set up an obstacle course in an open area of the classroom. Let the children pair up with a partner, then let one of the partners close their eyes and have the other partner lead this child safely through the course. Explain that the leader is a friend who will help you through the obstacles without getting hurt. Continue the game until each child has had a turn to play both roles.

Connections

A simple way to invite children to make new friends is to encourage the building of connectors, such as roads and bridges, between individual structures in the block center. This way, children can still maintain their separate constructions while learning to work together to plan and share the connections.

Our New Friends

Invite each child to draw a self-portrait at the top of a sheet of paper. After the children have become familiar with each other, have class members contribute ideas of what they like about each child in the class. Try to elicit comments about kindness, cooperation, sharing, and so on. Write these contributions below each child's self-portrait. Continue this project for several days, if necessary, to include each class member.

When the pages are complete, compile them into a class friendship book for your library center, or display the pages on a bulletin board.

Friendship Ribbon Chain

The class can make a year-round decoration for their classroom using pieces of wide ribbon, permanent markers, and a stapler. Collect odds and ends of ribbon pieces, each about 8" long. Have the children each choose one, then help them to write their names on their ribbons with permanent marker. Loop the ribbon pieces in an interlocking chain of friendship that includes the names of all class members, then hang to display. Should you have any new class members throughout the year, their names can easily be added. Should any class members move away, their name ribbons can easily be removed for them to keep as a memento.

Clean-Up

A little exercise in creative dramatics can help children understand the value of cleaning up and putting things back where they belong. Invite each child to pretend to be a favorite toy. Let the children tell the class what they are pretending to be. Now, have the "toy children" gather in a special area of the room. This area is to be considered the toy box. One by one, remove the "children toys" from this toy box and place them around the room. When all of the toys are out, play music and allow the children to dramatize their toys. Stop the music to indicate when playtime is over. Exclaim at the mess of having the toys all over the room. Tell the children that as you tap their heads, they will put themselves back in the toy box. Note the difference between a floor space crowded with toys and one cleared of the mess. Would they know where to find the toys when it was time to play again?

One by One

You can use clothespins, yarn in several colors, and an empty bleach or milk jug to demonstrate the importance of taking turns to your children. Tie a different color length of yarn to one end of each clothespin. Drop the clothespins into the plastic jug, leaving the yarn ends hanging out through the top. Invite several children to pull one piece of yarn to lift a clothespin. The children will observe that the clothespins become jammed at the neck of the jug. Ask for ideas on how to solve this problem. Help the children conclude that the solution is as easy as pulling one string at a time, or taking turns.

Materials
    poster board for clown, hat, shoes, and balloons (variety of colors)
    yarn (balloon string)
    colored cotton balls (clown hair)
    construction paper (cut-out letters)

Directions
1. Cut out a clown from poster board and color him.
2. Glue colored cotton balls to the clown for his hair.
3. Cut balloon shapes from various colors of poster board. Print a student's name on each balloon.
4. Mount the clown and balloons on the board.
5. Attach yarn to each balloon. Gather the yarn into the clown's hand and attach it securely.
6. Cut letters for the caption from construction paper and mount them on the board.

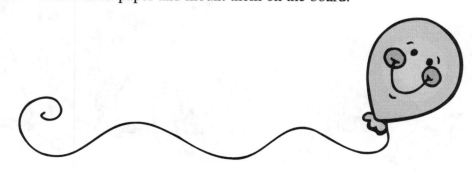

by Marcia Jeffries

12

Go Ahead—Smile!

Use these ideas during National Smile Week, the second week in August, to emphasize the importance (and fun) of smiling.

"Wear a Smile" Song

Sing this song with your children to the tune of "Row, Row, Row Your Boat."

Smile, smile, wear a smile
Everywhere you go.
If you're happy, wear a smile
So everyone will know!

Smiley Masks

Give each child a paper plate, crayons or colored markers, some glue, and a craft stick or tongue depressor. Let each child draw a smiling, happy face on the plate. Glue a craft stick or tongue depressor to the back of the plate for a handle. As children sing the song, they may hold their smiley masks in front of their faces. (You may want to help them cut out eyeholes so they can see through their masks.)

Make Me Smile!

Seat children in a circle. Explain that you want them to be as serious as they can be. Choose a child to be "it" and go around the circle, doing everything he or she can to make the other children smile. As soon as a child smiles, he or she must be "it." You may want to make a few rules before you play the game, such as "it" may not touch anyone (such as to tickle them) to make the children smile.

by Mary Tucker

Smiling Faces

Bring an instant camera to class and take a picture of each child smiling. Arrange the photographs on a bulletin board in the shape of a big smile. Print on a long strip of paper *What Makes You Smile?* and attach it across the top of the board. Ask the children to share what kinds of things make them smile. If they need help thinking of ideas, suggest some (a kiss from my puppy, a hug from my mom, chocolate ice cream, somebody smiling at me). Print their ideas on colored index cards and let the children sign their names on the cards. Place some blank index cards and a marker in an envelope and attach it to the corner of the bulletin board. Encourage visitors who come into your class (parents, the principal, the janitor, and so on) to add their own ideas to the board.

You Smile and I Smile

Encourage children to smile at everyone this week and to notice how often people smile back at them. Ask them how they feel when they smile at someone who does not return their smile. How do they feel when their smile makes another person smile?

Sights and Sounds of Autumn

Autumn Nights

When the sky turns as black
As a bat's wing,
The woodland creatures
Begin to sing.

Tree branches stretch,
Thin fingers high,
And try to pluck
The moon from the sky.

Scarecrows dance with
The shadows of the night,
And Jack-o'-lanterns grin
In toothy delight.

by Ann K. Smiley

It's All in Fall

Purple berries,
Yellow leaves,
Red apples
With brown seeds,

Blue skies,
Gray skies
White moon,
Pink sunrise,

Orange pumpkins,
Black cats,
Green witches
With pointed hats.

Every color—
They are all
Part of what
We call fall.

by Katharine McKnight McMahon

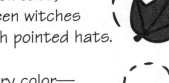

Autumn Noise

"Screech,"
cries a crow
as it flies through the trees.
I reach
for my hat
in the cool autumn breeze.
Crunch,
go the leaves
under my feet.
I munch
on an apple—
an afternoon treat.

by Elizabeth Giles

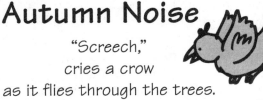

Colorful Fall

The days get shorter in the fall, and the green leaves turn colors. Why? The trees no longer make chlorophyll (green coloring matter). This allows the yellow pigments (coloring matter) which have been in the leaves all along, to become more visible.

Red leaves show when light and temperature changes make sugar in the leaves. Some trees, such as sugar maples, first show yellow, then orange, and finally red colors. The dogwoods and black gums turn ruby red, while ashes, poplars and paper birches show golden yellow colors. The oaks remain green longer than other trees, making a nice contrast to the bright colors. Eventually they turn brown.

Here are some activities you can do to bring fall inside your classroom.

Dry Arrangements

1. From the fields and woods, collect a variety of dried flowers, seed pods, thistles, grasses, leaves, and anything else you can find.
2. Cover an empty cereal box, plastic bottle, or jar to use as a vase.
3. Put a fairly thick layer of Styrofoam™ or florist foam inside the bottom of the container.
4. Insert the stems into the foam and make an attractive arrangement.
5. For additional weight, you can add small pebbles or stones.
6. Place it on a table for all to enjoy.

by Judy Wolfman

Make a "Real" Tree

1. Draw the trunk and branches of a tree on paper.
2. Color or paint the trunk and branches.
3. Paste on real leaves. If the leaves are too large, cut them into smaller bits.

Create a Fall Scene

1. Using curved lines, draw several rolling hills across a piece of white paper.
2. With a black crayon or marker, draw several trees with branches.
3. Dip a damp sponge piece into red paint and blot randomly on the trees.
4. Do the same thing using yellow, orange, green, and brown paints.
5. If you wish, you can frame your colorful rolling hills.

Make a Leaf Shape Book

1. Collect leaves from different trees.
2. Pin a leaf to a piece of paper.
3. Using a small amount of paint, stroke the paintbrush from the middle of the leaf outward onto the paper.
4. Let the paint dry; then carefully remove the leaf.
5. Do the same thing using different leaves and colors. Compile the pages into a book with an attractive cover.
6. Be sure to give your book a title and put your name on it as the author.

Fall

Outdoor Learning Discoveries for Little Ones

Welcome little ones back to school with an outdoor picnic on a warm and sunny day. Spread a blanket, eat a lunch, then go exploring. You won't need to venture far to find these busy little insects. They will find you. Follow them back to their home and learn a little along the way.

An Ant's Home Is His Castle

Ants work together to build underground nests with many rooms and tunnels. These social insects work hard to help one another survive. If we were able to visit an ant colony, what we would see would resemble a miniature castle. The queen ant rests in the throne room, laying eggs and being groomed. The worker ants are very busy. Their jobs are to do all the housekeeping, maintenance, nursery duties, grooming and feeding each other, and of course, collecting food.

Build Your Own Ant Town

You Need
• sandbox or sandy area
• shovels, spoons, or digging utensils

Directions
1. Divide the children (worker ants) into groups of four.
2. Give each group a space in the sandbox or sandy area in the school yard.
3. Using the tools provided, have each group of worker ants build an ant's home. (Their home will have to be horizontal in the sand so the rooms can be seen.)
4. After the workers have completed their homes, they can give tours to the other worker ants and compare building strategies.

Did You Know . . .

• There are more ants than any other creature on Earth?
• A colony can have hundreds, thousands, or even millions of ants?
• Most ants are black, brown, red, or yellow?
• Ants are the longest lived insect? Worker ants can live 1-7 years and the queen can live 15-20 years.
• A colony can uproot and relocate quickly when they are threatened?
• The smallest ant measures 0.8 mm long and the largest ant is 1⅝ inches long?

by Robynne Eagan

On the Food Trail

Watch the ants as they march along on their search for food!

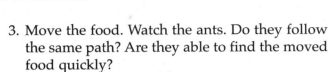

You Need
- apple or other food
- white paper
- anthill

Get Ready
1. Put the apple or another piece of food that an ant will like on a piece of paper near an ants' nest.
2. Wait for some ants to find the food. Observe them. Watch the ants as they communicate. As they rub together or lick each other, the first ant is passing the smell and taste messages to the others, explaining that she has found food. As that first ant walks the trail back, she lets her abdomen drop down to the ground several times, leaving a scent trail for the others to follow.

3. Move the food. Watch the ants. Do they follow the same path? Are they able to find the moved food quickly?
4. Now rub out the ant trail by sprinkling it with soil. Again observe the ants. They are confused for a while, but they will eventually find the right trail again.
5. Scatter different sized pieces of bread on the soil. Watch how ants cooperate to share the work of bringing large pieces of food back to the colony. Observe them as they share the load of lifting up to 50 times their own weight!

Some ants inflict painful stings. Be cautious and aware of the ants in your area!

Let's Study a Scurrying Squirrel

Autumn is a time to enjoy the beauty of the season and a time to begin preparations for the winter months ahead.

It is easy to spy on a squirrel, since they are active during the day. We are able to watch them work and play. They are constantly on the look-out for food. Squirrels are vegetarians. They eat a wide variety of plants, but mostly enjoy eating fruits and of course, nuts! In the fall, squirrels are very busy finding and burying nuts.

Did you know a squirrel can bury up to 50 nuts per hour? Here's how! For each nut, the squirrel digs a hole three to four inches (10-12 cm) deep using its front paws. The nut is edged into place with its nose, and is also marked with a scent gland which is located near the mouth. The Earth is then pushed back into place. Soft and gentle patting from the front paws tops off each site. Later, when the squirrel is hungry and wants to find its buried treasure, either the scent which it left or the smell of the nut will guide it to the exact spot. Memory plays only a small part. Not all buried nuts are found and the result is new trees.

19

Find the Nut

A game of hot and cold.

You Need
- acorns (or other nuts)
- wide open space

Get Ready
1. One person is the squirrel and closes his or her eyes.
2. The remaining students hide the acorn.
3. The "squirrel" opens his or her eyes and starts to look for the hidden cache. The students who hid the food guide the "squirrel" by shouts of "warmer" (if the squirrel is getting closer to the nut) or "colder" (if the squirrel is going farther away from the nut).
4. The students can take turns being the "squirrel."

Warm-Up Movements

Play a game of Squirrel Says on a crisp fall day and stay warm while doing all the actions.

Play Follow the Head Squirrel. Don't forget to act like a squirrel searching for nuts, getting ready for those cold days to come.

 # Staying Warm

When the weather gets very cold, squirrels seek shelter in underground tunnels under the snow or tree cavities and sleep for a few days. They also stay warm by sleeping inside heaps called "middens." Middens are formed when a squirrel bites through the bracts (the outerpart) of a spruce or pinecone to get to the seeds. The bracts fall to the ground and accumulate in heaps.

Getting Ready for Cold Winter Months

Red squirrels, gray squirrels, and flying squirrels do not hibernate. They remain active all winter. Squirrels are busy in the fall storing food which they will need for the winter. These hiding places are called "caches." Squirrels also take advantage of bird feeders and enjoy eating food left out for the birds.

Let's Make a Squirrel Feeder

An easy treat for students to make and squirrels to enjoy.

You Need
- string
- cobs of corn (one per child)

Directions
1. Husk some of the corn to leave a 1 inch (2.54 cm) piece of stalk at the end of the cob.
2. Tie string firmly around the end of the stalk so the corn will hang. This may take several knots and rounds of string.
3. Hang the corn from a tree or other overhanging area where the squirrels can feast and you can watch.

Seasonal Science

Invite your youngsters to explore the wonders of the world around them with these back-to-school-time activities and projects.

Color Match

Activity

Fall offers an excellent opportunity for children to observe changes in nature firsthand. Invite them to contribute ideas about changes they have observed. Note the cooler temperatures, how the sun sits lower in the sky, the shorter days, and any changes in color. Discuss how shorter days provide less sunlight. Combined with lower temperatures, this affects a plant's ability to make its own food, thereby changing the color of some leaves and letting the plants know it's time for a rest. Prepare to take the children on a color nature walk by gluing several squares of colored paper down the left-hand side of a plain sheet of paper. As the children spot one of these colors while they are walking, have them point out their discovery so you can mark the color they have found. When you return to the classroom, let the children help count the tally marks next to each color. Which colors did they find the most/least of in nature during this season?

Project

Prepare a simple color match game for the children to use independently by collecting paint chart colors (2 of each) from a local hardware store. Cut the color swatches apart if necessary, then challenge the children to correctly match them. For older students, choose a color theme such as green, and challenge them to match the various shades.

by Marie E. Cecchini

Seasonal Sort

Activity

Scientists are better able to study natural phenomena through the use of organization and classification. Help your children learn about the seasonal changes in nature using this process. First, talk with the class about the meaning of the words *weather* and *season*. Are they the same thing? How are these concepts related? Let the children define the word *season* in their own words. Next, have the students name the four seasons. List these words on the board. Discuss types of weather and activities people do for each season. Let the children cut magazine pictures depicting clothing, activities, and weather for each season. Finally, place the names of the seasons on a bulletin board. Have students put their magazine pictures into seasonal categories and hang them in the correct sections. Can the class name the season during which school begins?

Project

Show the children how to fold a sheet of white construction paper into four sections. Number the sections 1-4. Have the students draw a picture for fall in the first section; then proceed through the remaining sections, drawing pictures for winter, spring, and summer. Let each child cut the sections apart, arrange them in numerical order, and add a cover page to make a mini book. Staple the pages together.

Feeling Fine

Activity

Family Health and Fitness Day in September reminds us to keep an eye on how we take care of ourselves. Fall is also the beginning of a long season of colds and flu. Talk with the children about how we feel when we are healthy, as compared to how we feel when we are unhealthy. Germs are what cause us to get sick. Germs love to live in warm, dirty places. One way we pick up germs is with our hands. How can we clean germs from our hands? Experiment with washing dirty hands using water alone, then with warm water and soap. Which method did a better job? We also pick up germs from the air around us. When people do not cover a cough or sneeze with a tissue, they spray germs into the air for others to breathe in. Experiment to see how this works. Let children hold tissues or paper towels in front of their faces. Have them cough, then pretend to sneeze at the paper. What happens? Why? Where are the germs?

Project

Help the children to trace and cut right- and left-hand shapes from tagboard. Glue each pair of hands together so they overlap slightly. Glue a small, decorative soap to one hand in each pair, and a yarn hanger to the back. Let the children take their hand plaques home to hang near their bathroom sinks as a reminder to keep those hands clean, clean, clean.

Exploring Differences

Activity

Invite students to explore the differences and similarities of apples in honor of Apple Month this October. Display and name several varieties of apples, such as Granny Smith, McIntosh, and both Red and Yellow Delicious. Have the children tell how they are the same (they are all apples; each has a tough covering—the peel; each has a stem; and so on) and how they are different (color, size, and so on). Slice each variety and put it on a different plate for children to observe and taste. Again, how are they the same/different (color, taste, texture)? Graph each child's choice of a favorite. Which variety is the most popular? Note that the apple flesh no longer covered by the peel turns brown when exposed to air. Watch and see which variety turns brown first and which stays white the longest.

Project

Have the children stuff paper lunch bags with crumpled newspaper to make giant apples. Gather the top of each bag together and tape it to make a brown stem. Let the children paint their apples red, yellow, or green according to the variety they wish to make. When the paint dries, let them draw and cut a green paper leaf to glue near the stem.

Animal Care

Talk with your children about the differences between wild and domestic animals. Note that during the late fall, wild animals prepare for winter by storing food, migrating, or readying nesting areas for hibernation. Domestic animals, such as farm stock or household pets, do not find these rituals necessary as they are provided with food and shelter on a daily basis. However, fur-covered domestic animals do grow thicker coats to protect their bodies from the colder temperatures of winter. Talk with the class about the basic needs all animals have—food, water, and shelter. Discuss the various types of body coverings different animals have, such as fur, scales, skin, shells, and feathers. How do these body coverings help the animals? Let the children use a magnifying glass to examine body covering samples.

Project

Animal Shelter Week falls in the month of November. Can the children explain the purpose of shelters for animals? Help the children make posters to hang throughout the school building, encouraging everyone to donate old blankets, towels, and animal food for a local shelter. Collect these supplies in your classroom or the main lobby at school. Enlist parent volunteers to assist in transporting the items to the shelter. Can the children tell why this is a worthwhile project?

Harvesttime

Activity

The celebration of Thanksgiving is a traditional expression of our gratitude for a bountiful harvest. During this season we are exposed to a wide variety of foods, some of which we will taste for the first time. Collect a sampling of fruits and vegetables, foods that are harvested from around the world. Have the children contribute ideas on how these edibles are similar/different. Note that each is a living thing that needs food and water to grow. Challenge the children to tell one thing that is the same about all of the samples and all living things. Help them conclude that all living things contain water. Experiment to find the water in your collection. Cut each sample into two or more pieces. Try hand squeezing, spoon pressing, and fork squashing fruit and vegetable pieces. Note that juice is extracted from each sample, more juice from some than others. Juice is mostly water.

Project

Provide the children with plastic sandwich bags and the following ingredients for making their own snack mix: dry cereal circles, dry cereal squares, raisins, chopped walnuts, and small chocolate or fruit-flavored candies. Pour each ingredient into a different container. As each food is poured, discuss whether the sound is soft or loud.

by Marie E. Cecchini

Make -in-a- Minute Crafts

Leafy Place Mat

Enjoy autumn colors in all their splendor while sharing a snack with family and friends.

Materials
- colorful autumn leaves
- crayons with paper peeled off
- 11" x 17" white paper (27.9 x 43.2 cm)
- clear adhesive vinyl

Directions
1. Gather flat, flexible autumn leaves.
2. Select crayon colors similar to the colors of the leaves.
3. One by one, slip the leaves vein-side up under the paper. Gently rub the side of a crayon back and forth across the surface of the paper over the leaf. An image of the leaf will appear.
4. Repeat the process with leaves of various shapes and colors until the page is full of colorful leaves.
5. Cover the place mat with clear adhesive vinyl or have it laminated.

Autumn Glory Bracelet

A keepsake of an autumn hike in the woods

Materials
- roll of wide masking tape
- nature items

Directions
1. Attach a loop of wide masking tape, sticky side out, around the wrist of all the students.
2. Talk about all the items they may find on their walk which they can use to make their autumn glory bracelet. Consider baby pinecones, leaves, pebbles, seed pods, tiny wild flowers, moss, or whatever catches their eye.
3. As the students walk, they can pick up pretty bits of nature and stick them on the tape. Each will return with an interesting and appealing autumn glory bracelet.

by Robynne Eagan

Sandpaper Pictures

A gift for grandparents to proudly hang in their homes

Materials
- fine sandpaper
- crayons
- string

Directions
1. Have students use crayons to draw a picture on the sandpaper. Encourage a simple design with many colors.
2. Place the drawing on a cookie sheet and put it in a 225°F (110°C) oven for 30 to 60 seconds until the wax melts into a paint-like finish.
3. Attach string to the picture for hanging. Give the sandpaper picture to a special grandparent for Grandparents' Day.

Super Loop Glider

*Have some fall fun! Design, then let go!
How far can she fly? How many loops and spins?*

Materials
- plastic straw
- paper cut in two strips, 1½" x 8½" and 1½" x 7½" (4 x 21 cm and 4 x 19 cm)
- tape
- markers or crayons

Directions
1. Color or make designs on the two strips of paper.
2. Form each strip of paper into a loop.
3. Close each loop with a piece of tape.
4. Tape the large loop to one end of the straw.
5. Tape the small loop to the other end.
6. Toss the glider into the air, with the smaller loop in front.
7. Watch it go! Measure the distance, have a race, have some fun!

Paper Plate Monster

Chomp, chomp! These zany monsters are sure to give a laugh, not a fright!

Materials
- white paper plate
- poster board
- scissors
- glue
- chenille stems (pipe cleaners)
- crayons or markers
- ribbon

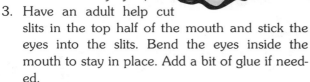

Directions
1. Fold a paper plate in half to make a giant mouth.
2. Cut out a few 3" (7 cm) long, arch-shaped eyes from poster board. (Monsters can have many eyes.)
3. Have an adult help cut slits in the top half of the mouth and stick the eyes into the slits. Bend the eyes inside the mouth to stay in place. Add a bit of glue if needed.
4. Make antennae or horns and attach them to the mouth in the same way.
5. Cut out arms, legs, or tentacles. Glue them to the underside of the mouth so that they stick out.
6. Color the monster. Let your imagination soar! Glue ribbon inside the mouth for the monster's tongue.
7. This paper plate monster can sit up and guard the little one's Halloween treats.

Egg Carton Spiders

Silly, spooky, or scary, these spiders are sure to delight! Hang these spiders in the classroom.

Materials
- foam egg carton cup
- black paint and paintbrush
- scissors
- chenille stems (pipe cleaners)
- black marker
- needle
- black thread

Mummy Pin

The little ones will enjoy making a pin to wear, then they can make another to give to their own mommy to wear!

Materials
- wooden craft stick
- white embroidery thread
- glue
- 2 googly eyes
- jewelry pin
- scissors

Directions
1. Wind the white embroidery thread around the craft stick over and over. The more thread you wind on, the fatter your mummy will be. Be sure to wind more near the top for the head.
2. Attach the thread to the back of the mummy with glue.
3. Glue two googly eyes to the front, and the jewelry pin on the back.
4. Wear your mummy pin to the classroom Halloween party.

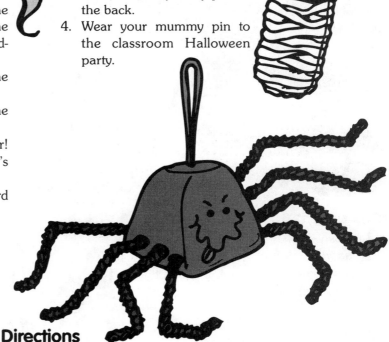

Directions
1. Cut out an egg cup from a foam egg carton.
2. Paint it black.
3. Draw or paint the spider's face on one of the sides. Do you want it to be scary, friendly, or even silly?
4. Poke four black chenille stems through one side and out the other. Bend them so that the spider can stand up.
4. Have an adult sew a thread up through the inside of the spider's head for hanging.

Snacktivities

Invite children to enjoy the taste of fall with snack activities that suit the occasion.

Golden Fruit Treats

September—Honey Month

Ingredients
- 1 cup golden raisins
- 1 cup chopped walnuts
- 10 graham crackers, crushed
- ¼ cup honey

Measure all of the above ingredients into a mixing bowl. Mix well with a fork or slotted spoon. Provide each child with a small amount of the mixture to roll into bite-size balls for a sweet treat that's ready to eat.

Apple-Spice Mix-Up

October—Apple Month

Ingredients
- 2 cups applesauce
- 1 ½ cups milk
- ½ tsp. vanilla
- ½ tsp. cinnamon
- ¼ tsp. ground cloves
- nutmeg

Measure all of the ingredients except the nutmeg into a blender. Mix well. Pour the beverage into individual serving cups. Sprinkle the top of each drink with nutmeg.

Sailboat Salad

October—Columbus Day

Ingredients
- cored apple halves (one for each child)
- applesauce
- cottage cheese
- triangle-shaped crackers
- raisins

Have the children place their apple halves, flat side up, on a plate. In a mixing bowl, combine a little applesauce with the cottage cheese. Fill the core hollow in each apple half with this mixture. Set raisin people into the cottage cheese-applesauce mixture. Add a triangle-shaped cracker for a sail.

by Marie E. Cecchini

Star Pizza

October—Pizza Month

Ingredients

    triangle-shaped crackers
    spaghetti sauce, warmed
    parmesan cheese

Have the children count out five crackers each. Challenge them to arrange their crackers into a five-pointed star shape on a plate. Dollop each star cracker with spaghetti sauce. Sprinkle parmesan cheese over the sauce.

Party Spiders

October—Halloween

Ingredients

    prepared cupcakes (remove papers)
    black licorice strings
    chocolate icing
    small gumdrops

Let the children spread frosting over their cupcakes to cover them. Cut strings of black licorice into pieces for spider legs. Have the children each count out eight pieces (legs). Help them insert one end of each of their licorice pieces around the outside of their cupcakes. Use a knife inserted into the top of each cupcake while inserting the legs. Add two gumdrop eyes to each spider.

Sweet—Treat Popcorn

October—Popcorn Poppin' Month

Ingredients

    popcorn kernels
    cinnamon
    ¼ cup sugar

Add cinnamon to the sugar to taste. Set aside. Pop the corn kernels and place the popped corn into a large bowl. While the popcorn is still warm, sprinkle it with the cinnamon-sugar mixture. Toss lightly, then serve.

Airplane Sandwich

November—Aviation History Month

Ingredients

hard-boiled eggs

mayonnaise

hot dog rolls

cheese slices

Peel and chop the hard-boiled eggs. Mix in a small amount of mayonnaise. Help the children spread this egg mixture over one half of an open hot dog roll. Let the children cut wing shapes from the cheese slices. Place the wings into the egg mixture at the sides of the hot dog roll. Top with the second half of the roll; then eat.

Fall Fun Pops

November—Fall

Ingredients

four 3-oz. packages orange-flavored gelatin

2½ c. boiling water

non-dairy whipped topping

yellow food coloring

Put gelatin powder into a mixing bowl, add the boiling water, and stir until dissolved. Pour the mixture into eight 5-oz. paper cups and chill until firm, at least 4 hours. When solid, peel the paper cup from the gelatin chunks; then cut the gelatin to make thick slices (about 2-3 inches). Slide a craft stick into each slice to make a pop. Tint the whipped topping with the food coloring. Dip each pop into the topping before eating.

Fruity Feline Roll-Ups

November—Cat Week

Ingredients

pita bread

kiwi fruit

strawberries, halved

bananas

cream cheese, softened

maraschino cherries

seedless green grape halves

Slice each pita bread into two rounds, one round for each child. Help the children spread softened cream cheese over their pita circles. Let the children add strawberry half ears, grape half eyes, a cherry nose, and banana strip whiskers. Peel and slice the kiwi. Cut each slice of kiwi in half to make half circles for the children to use as the cat mouth. Help the children roll up their cat faces with the fruit inside. Cut each pita roll in half if desired.

by Marie E. Cecchini

Fall Fun

Fall Centerpiece

Materials

2 paper plates
glue
twigs, leaves, pinecones, acorns
large candle

Directions

1. Glue the two paper plates together to form a sturdy base.
2. Glue an assortment of leaves, twigs, and so on around the plate, leaving a circle in the center to place the candle.
3. Place the candle in the middle of the centerpiece.

by Sherry Timberman

Collecting Colors

Materials

paper lunch bags
crayons
paper
pretty fall day

Directions

Let children decorate lunch bags with fall pictures and colors. Then take them outside on a color hunt, taking their decorated bags along. Encourage them to observe the world around them and gather nature items, such as green grass, brown acorns, and red berries in their bags. When you get back to your classroom, have children draw what they saw but were unable to bring back with them.

by Katharine M. McMahon

Why Is Mary Ann So Happy?

Mary Ann skipped happily down Main Street with her ponytails swaying back and forth. Her backpack was stuffed with books, and her sweater was buttoned all the way up to her neck. A very wide grin stretched across her face and her baby blue eyes seemed to sparkle with delight.

"Hello," she said to Mr. Hooper, who was sweeping up all of the leaves that had fallen in front of his fix-it shop.

"Hello, Mary Ann," he said as he stopped sweeping long enough to let her walk past.

Mary Ann's arms swung back and forth at her sides as she strolled farther down the street.

At the corner of Main Street and First Avenue, Mr. Edwards, the crossing guard, was helping children safely cross the street, just as he did every afternoon.

Mary Ann smiled at him and said, "Hello."

"Good afternoon, young lady," he said to her as he tipped his hat.

Mary Ann walked through the park. *Crackle crunch!* went the fallen leaves under her feet. She bent down to pick up some acorns and pinecones and filled her pockets with them.

Miss Anderson was sitting on a green bench feeding seeds to the birds. She noticed how happy Mary Ann looked and asked? "Why are you wearing such an enormous grin?"

"When I left for school this morning, the air was cool and crisp. I had to button my sweater all the way up," Mary Ann said. "And as I walked past Mrs. Smith's yard, I noticed lots of pumpkins growing in her garden. Then as I walked across the school yard, the wind started to gently blow the leaves off the trees. They drifted down to carpet the the ground with colors of red, orange, brown, and yellow!"

"Yes, Mary Ann," said Miss Anderson. "That's exactly what is supposed to happen this time of year."

"I know! That is why I am so happy," Mary Ann said. "Because my favorite season is finally here!"

Can you guess Mary Ann's favorite season?

by Suzanne Connolly

Name _____

Autumn Shapes

Draw a line from the autumn shape to its shadow.

Fun with Finger

 Time for School

Summer is over.
School has begun.
I'll never forget
My summer fun!
(Clap hands while saying this rhyme.)

The Traffic Light

I hurry to school,
(Walk quickly in place.)
Don't want to be late.
(Shake head no.)
I reach the corner
(Stop walking.)
And have to wait.
(Stand still.)
The light is yellow.
I look at the top.
(Point up to top of light.)
Now it's turned red.
That tells me to stop.
(Stretch arm out with palm away from you.)
Don't want to be late,
(Shake head again.)
That light is so slow!
(Step from one foot to the other nervously.)
Look, now it's turned green!
(Point to light.)
I can safely go.
(Smile, nod head, and walk quickly in place.)

Colorful Leaves

Colorful leaves float quietly down.
(Gently flutter hands downward.)
They make a carpet on the ground.
(Indicate carpet on ground.)
Then *swish*, the wind comes swirling by
(Swish hands in front of you.)
And sends them dancing to the sky.
(Flutter hands upward.)

Leaves, Flowers, and Birds

Watch the leaves as they fall gently to the ground.
(Hold hands high and let them fall gently.)
See the flowers nod their heads, looking all around.
(Nod head and turn it gently around.)
Little birds flap their wings high above the trees.
(Flap arms.)
As they head for the south, away from the cold breeze.
(Continue to flap arms.)

by Judy Wolfman

plays

Scarecrow Man

I'm a funny scarecrow man.
(Point to self.)
I flop around like a scarecrow can.
(Flop around loosely.)
I move my arms
(Move arms around.)
And my wrists.
(Shake wrists.)
I move my legs
(Shake legs one at a time.)
And shake my fists.
(Shake fists.)
I bend way down,
(Bend backwards.)
That scares the crows.
Does it scare you?
(Point to others.)

Three Little Pumpkins

Three little pumpkins were sitting on a wall
(Show three fingers.)
When a witch came riding by.
(Swoop one arm down.)
She laughed, "Hee, hee, hee, I'll take you all
(Indicate everyone.)
And make a pumpkin pie!"
(Rub tummy and lick lips.)
(Note: Use a "witchy" voice for
line 3.)

Rosh Hashanah
Happy New Year

The shofar's sound I love to hear,
With notes that are so loud and clear.
(Cup one hand around an ear and listen.)
To all, its meaning is very dear
As it calls out, "Happy New Year!"

Time to Say "I'm Sorry"

If I have hurt someone,
Or made him feel real sad,
(Hang head down and look sad.)
Yom Kippur is the time to say,
"I'm sorry; I won't be bad."
(Hold up right hand as a promise.)

Yummy Sandwich

Let's make a sandwich. Here's how it's done.
(Show hands, palms up.)
Spread mustard on bread; add a slice of meat.
(Use a finger to "spread" mustard on palm of other hand.)
If you don't want bread, you can use a bun.
It sure looks yummy and good enough to eat!
(Slap hands together and pretend to take a bite.)

Turkey in Hiding

The fat turkey gobbler runs about,
(Tuck hands under armpits and run around.)
To find a place to hide.
(Stop and hide.)
If you listen, you can hear him shout,
(Put hand to ear and listen.)
"You won't get me inside!"
(Shake head.)

Pilgrim Children

Pilgrim children worked hard each day
(Pretend to scrub, wash, hoe.)
At home and in the sun.
(Continue to work.)
They made up different games to play
(Pretend to throw a ball, jump, etc.)
So they could have some fun.

The Leaf That Wouldn't Leave

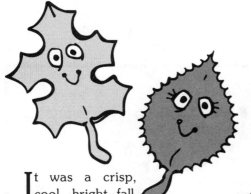

It was a crisp, cool, bright fall day. In the air was a feeling that winter would soon be on its way. By this time, all the leaves had changed into their pretty autumn colors; some red, some orange, some yellow and brown. One by one they floated merrily down to the ground where they gathered together in a big pile beneath the old maple tree. But one lone leaf still hung there, afraid to let go. His name was Redford.

Redford held on ever so tightly to the big branch where he lived. Every day the other leaves below called up to him, "Come down, come down here with us! Any day now the children will come to play."

Redford had heard all about the children's happy faces as they played in the leaves. It sounded like so much fun to him. But he was afraid to let go.

"Will it hurt when I fall?" he asked the leaves in the pile.

"No," they told him. "Besides, we'll be right here to catch you. Don't be afraid."

But Redford was afraid. The pile seemed so far away from the high branch where he hung. His long slender stem shook with fear every time he looked down.

"What if I get carried away by the wind?" he asked the leaves on the ground.

"Don't worry, the ground is covered with many friendly leaves," they said, "But if you let go right now, you'll land down here with us."

Redford looked around, up, and down. He realized he would have to let go someday. So, finally he said, "Okay, I'll do it; but I'm not looking!"

The leaves below let out a big cheer. They all counted together. "One, two, three . . ." Redford closed his eyes and held his breath.

He let go, but he didn't feel anything. Had he left the tree? Was he stuck? Redford didn't know what to think. So he opened one eye first, then he opened the other. He couldn't believe what was happening. He was floating, and it was fun! He twirled and swirled. He swooped and looped. He spun and grinned as he drifted closer and closer to the huge pile below. Then ever so gently he landed in the arms of his friends. Everyone was happy for Redford, including Redford himself.

Then one of the leaves said, "Hey, do you hear something?" All at once, they stopped to listen. In the distance they could hear the sound of happy children heading down the street toward them. They were coming to play! It was the moment all the leaves had waited for.

As the sound of the children's footsteps drew near, Redford smiled a big smile. He was happy to be with his friends again. He was happy the children were on their way. And he was glad he'd let go when he did, for he'd made it to the ground just in time!

by Jill N. MacGregor

Grandparents

Bulletin Board

We Think Our GRANDparents Are GRAND!

My grandparents are fun!
Melanie

My grandparents love me a lot.
Sara

My grandpa makes me laugh.
Amy

My grandparents take me to church.
Drew

My grandma is a good cook.
Devon

Grandparents are the greatest!
Ask any one of us.
They're patient, kind, and loving,
And they hardly ever fuss.
Every kid should have at least
One of them, or two,
'Cause no one knows how to love
Just the way grandparents do.

My grandma gives me big hugs.
Steven

My grandpa tells good stories.
Chad

I like to hear my grandparents talk.
Emily

I like to stay with my grandma.
Mary

My grandparents take me fun places.
Mike

My grandpa takes me fishing.
Aaron

My grandma sings to me.
Luis

If you plan to invite grandparents to your class before or after Grandparents' Day, have children help you put this special bulletin board together before the visit.

1. Cover the bulletin board with colorful wrapping paper as a background.
2. Print the poem on the computer or print it with a dark marker on light colored construction paper and mount it at the center of the board.
3. Cut letters for the caption from dark colored construction paper and mount them across the top of the board.
4. Have each child think of something he or she wants to say about grandparents. Print their comments on small construction paper rectangles of various colors.
5. Mount the students' comments around the poem. (If there's space, add some photos of children with their grandparents.)
6. Blow up a couple of bright colored balloons and tie them closed. Attach a length of curly ribbon to each balloon.
7. Attach the balloons to the top edges of the board.

by Mary Tucker

TLC10339 Copyright © Teaching & Learning Company, Carthage, IL 62321-0010

Fun with Grandpa

Teacher: Copy this page for each child. Explain that they should look for items beginning with the letter "f" in the picture. They should find at least five "f" items. Then let them color the picture.

Name _____

Dog Week Poster

Let's celebrate Dog Week. Think of ways to take good care of a dog and write or draw your ideas in the paw prints. Color the picture.

I take my dog for a walk.

Name _____

NAME THAT DOG!

Spot　　　Tiny　　　Digger　　　Happy　　　Whitey

Teacher: Celebrate Dog Week the last week of September. Give each child a copy of this page. Read each dog's name aloud. Have children draw a line from the name to the dog they think it goes with.

BY MARY TUCKER 41

October 16—World Food Day

Food Fun

Literature

Add books about food and world cultures to the classroom library or reading space and read them aloud for story time. Don't forget other areas of the classroom. Add books about food to the dramatic play center, a snack table, a cooking area, or a sand/water table. Give children a visual clue that hands need to be clean and dry before handling books. Put books that accompany the sand or water table in a plastic bag and place the bag on a paper or cloth towel. Try some of these books about food and world culture:

Bread, Bread, Bread by Ann Morris, HarperCollins, 1989
Chicken Soup with Rice by Maurice Sendak, HarperCollins
Everybody Cooks Rice by Norah Dooley, First Avenue Editions, 1992
How My Parents Learned to Eat by Ina R. Friedman, Houghton Mifflin, Co., 1987
Pancakes, Pancakes by Eric Carle, Aladdin Paperbacks, 1998

Cooking
Bread, Bread, Bread

Collect a variety of breads from the bakery, grocery store, and if possible, from individual families. You may also choose to bake one or two loaves of bread in the classroom. Slice the breads and label each different variety. Provide butter, peanut butter, and jelly or jam for children to try on the breads. Discuss how the breads are similar or different as children sample them. A chart or graph should culminate the activity. Showing each child's favorite type of bread. Read Ann Morris' book *Bread, Bread, Bread* during the activity.

Art
Soup Label Collage

Collect paper labels from soup cans. Provide children with construction paper (9" x 12" or 12" x 18"), scissors, and glue. Have children cut and trim labels and glue in a random, overlapping fashion to create a colorful collage. Read *Chicken Soup with Rice* by Maurice Sendak before or after this activity. Arrange the soup label collages in and around a large paper soup bowl on the bulletin board.

by Carol Ann Bloom

Food Packaging Puzzles

Collect empty food boxes in the classroom to assure that puzzles will reflect the eating habits and traditions of your children. Try to include a broad selection of food packaging: taco boxes, Oriental rice boxes, pasta boxes, matzo boxes, tea boxes, and couscous boxes. Remove the front of the box in one piece. Use a pencil to divide the plain side of the piece into several puzzle sections. Cut the pieces apart, following the pencil lines. The result is a puzzle that, when put together, forms a food picture. Store each puzzle in a separate envelope, paper pocket, or plastic bag. Or make a book of food packaging puzzles by filling a three-ring binder with pocket folders, place a puzzle in each folder and print the food name on the folder. You may want to provide younger children with a duplicate box front (uncut) for them to use as a guide when putting together puzzles.

Math

Egg Carton Count

Cut several egg cartons in half; use the six-sectioned containers for this counting activity. Number the sections from 1 to 6. Provide a variety of counting objects in separate cups: be mindful of the choking hazards presented by items that are small. Children can also practice counting by twos, fives, tens, and even hundreds by assigning a value of two, five, ten, or one hundred to each object. Label the egg carton sections accordingly such as 2 to 12, 5 to 30, 10 to 60 or 100 to 600.

Music

Fruit Shakers

Have children draw and color fruits on the backs of small paper plates. Stress that they draw the fruits large enough to fill the center of the plate. Draw the same fruit on two plates. Place the plates with matching fruits, front sides together, and staple halfway around. Put several small objects in the plate pairs and staple the rest of the way around. Try different objects to make different sounds: buttons in one set of plates, pebbles in another, paper clips in a third. Again, be aware of choking risks. Pass out fruit shakers for children to play during a sing-along. Try songs about food. Use the same technique to make veggie shakers.

Is Anybody Hungry?

Make the concept of hunger the focus of group time by beginning with a discussion of what it feels like to be hungry. Make short lists along the way, posing questions such as:

Have you ever been hungry?
How did it make you feel?
How did your stomach feel?
What did you do?
What do you like to eat when you are hungry?
What is your favorite food?

Many children, through exposure to news and television, have an awareness, however slight, of world hunger. Find out how much the children in your classroom know about world hunger by asking questions such as:

How would you feel if you were hungry,
but had nothing to eat?
Do you think there are any places in the world where this happens? Anywhere in America?
Anywhere in our community?
How and why might this happen?

Encourage children to think about possible reasons for hunger:

- the absence of well-stocked supermarkets and grocery stores in many parts of the world
- not enough money to buy food
- shortages of food
- adverse weather conditions where food is grown (floods and droughts)

Is there anything we can do to help?

This may also be a good time to discuss appreciating the food we have and not wasting it.

If there is a local food bank or homeless shelter in your community, initiate a food collection in the classroom in honor of World Food Day. Make a list of the types of food that can be donated. Have children assist in making the list and preparing a sign to alert parents about the collection.

Motor

Food Charades

Cut a number of paper strips and write an action that occurs during the eating or preparing of food on each strip. Include actions such as:

- stirring in a bowl
- chopping fruits/vegetables
- slicing bread
- using a rolling pin
- kneading dough
- flipping pancakes or burgers
- turning on the stove or oven
- peeling fruits/vegetables
- opening a can
- washing hands
- licking an ice cream cone
- biting an apple
- sipping through a straw
- pouring milk into a glass
- using a napkin

Place the strips of paper in a large stew pot or salad bowl. Have children choose a slip, read it (or for nonreaders, teachers can whisper the words), and perform the action. Ask other players to guess the action being performed.

Name _____

Fantastic Fire Fighters

Fire fighters are very important people in our community! They put out fires and keep us safe. Talk to an adult about how you can practice fire safety in your home! Look carefully at these two pictures of Frank the Fire Fighter. Then find and circle five things that are in the top picture but not the bottom.

by Becky Radtke

Donny Dalmatian

Donny Dalmatian lives at the fire station in town. As you help him find his way home, read the important fire safety rules that are along the way!

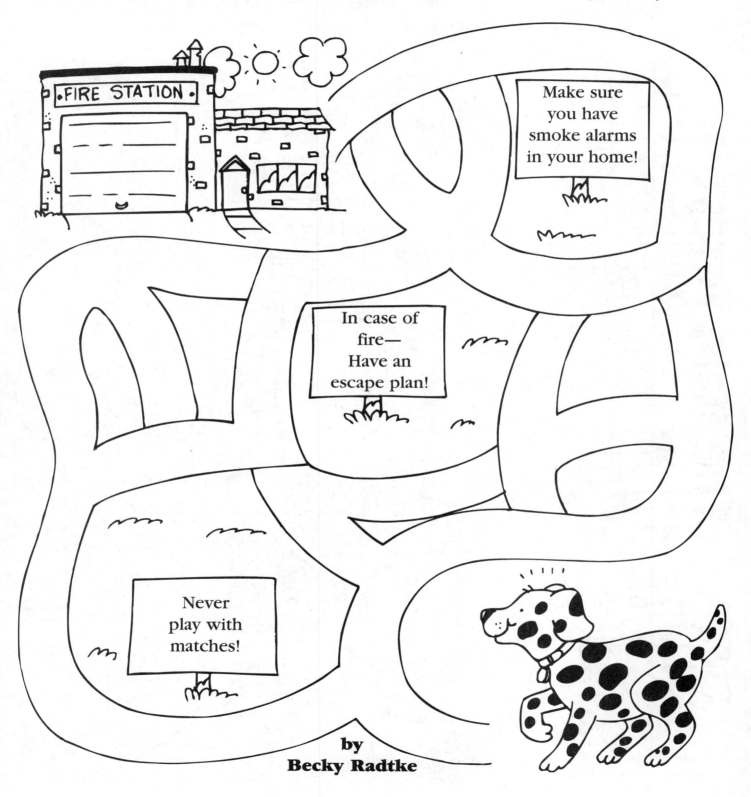

Make sure you have smoke alarms in your home!

In case of fire— Have an escape plan!

Never play with matches!

by
Becky Radtke

by Janet A. Armbrust

The Rain Forest

There are six butterflies in this rain forest. Circle them. Color the picture.

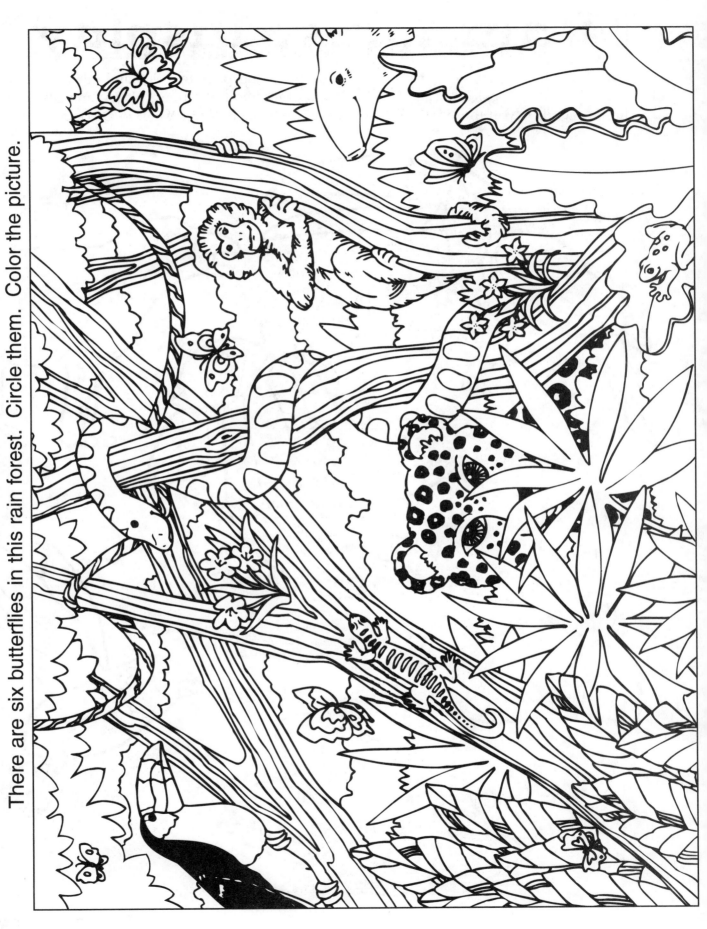

Name _____

Rain Forest Display

Give each child the patterns on this page and the following page to color and cut out. Mount the pieces on the bulletin board in a rain forest display. Talk about the trees, plants, animals, and birds that can be found only in the rain forest to observe World Rain Forest Week in October.

by Mary Tucker

48

Rain Forest Patterns

The Smallest Pumpkin in the

Pumpkin Patch

Sammy was the smallest pumpkin in the pumpkin patch. No matter how hard he tried, he just couldn't grow any bigger than he already was. It was almost Halloween, and he was sure no one would pick him to take home. He looked around at all the other pumpkins. "How did they get so big?" he wondered. Sammy decided to ask them.

Diana, the prettiest pumpkin in the pumpkin patch, was contentedly drying herself in the early morning sun. "Good morning, Diana," Sammy said shyly, waiting a moment before he continued. "I was wondering . . . how did you get to be so big?"

"Well," said Diana, shining like the copper-colored leaves around her, "every morning before the sun comes up, I bathe in the dewdrops left by the morning mist. The dewdrops splash all over me and fall gently upon my skin. I guess that's what makes me grow bigger." Diana gazed proudly at her glowing skin. "Maybe if you bathe in the dewdrops before the sun comes up, you will get bigger, too."

"Wow!" thought Sammy. "Maybe that will help me grow bigger." That night, Sammy was so excited, he could hardly sleep. He waited for the morning mist to come.

When morning finally arrived, Sammy sat as quietly as he could, feeling the dewdrops trickle down his skin. But he did not grow any bigger. Sammy was very sad. It was almost Halloween.

Later that day, Sammy noticed Tommy, the coolest pumpkin in the pumpkin patch, sitting in the afternoon sun. "Good afternoon, Tommy," Sammy called out. "I was wondering, how did you get to be so big?"

"Well," said Tommy, looking cool in his sunglasses, "every afternoon I sit in the sun until I'm nice and warm." Tommy casually glanced over at Sammy, pushing his sunglasses to the top of his head. "Maybe if you sit in the afternoon sun until you're nice and warm, you will get you bigger, too."

**by Lola De Julio
De Maci**

"Cool!" thought Sammy. "Maybe that will help me grow bigger." When the afternoon sun appeared, Sammy sat until he became nice and warm. Soon the sun started to fade into evening, but Sammy still did not grow any bigger.

Sammy was very unhappy. Bathing in the morning dewdrops didn't help him grow bigger. Sitting in the afternoon sun didn't help him grow bigger. What was he going to do?

Tonight was Halloween and Sammy was still the smallest pumpkin in the pumpkin patch. One by one, all the other pumpkins were picked from the vines, and Sammy sat there all by himself. He wouldn't be celebrating Halloween like the other pumpkins.

Daniel, the oldest and wisest pumpkin in the pumpkin patch, had listened to all the advice the other pumpkins had given Sammy. Daniel gently whispered in Sammy's ear, "You are just as special as all the other pumpkins. We are all special in our own way, so each one of us can give something beautiful to the world." Daniel smiled warmly at Sammy. "You are a special pumpkin; you'll see."

Sammy listened to what Daniel had to say, but he still had a hard time figuring out why he was special. Diana was picked as a beautiful centerpiece for a dinner table, and Tommy was picked as a Jack-o'-lantern to sit on some-one's front porch. Sammy knew why they were special.

"You are a special pumpkin," Daniel repeated. "You'll see."

When nighttime came, the pumpkin patch was dark and lonely. Daniel had gone to sleep and Sammy was all alone. It was a beautiful night. The stars twinkled brightly in the dark sky and the moon glistened like a giant crystal ball. Suddenly, beams of moonlight fell over the pumpkin patch right where Sammy lay. Sammy, the smallest pumpkin in the pumpkin patch, suddenly looked bright and magical in the moonlight's glow.

Just then a car came rumbling up the road toward the pumpkin patch. "Grandma! Grandma!" the little boy in the car cried, looking out the window at Sammy. "I want that little pumpkin! I want to take it home!" Grandma stopped the car, and the little boy ran over to Sammy and picked him up.

"What a splendid pumpkin!" exclaimed Grandma. "It's just the right size for you."

So in the magical glow of the moonlight, Grandma and the little boy took Sammy home with them. Sammy was very happy. It was a beautiful Halloween night, and Sammy felt very special indeed.

Halloween
Projects and Activities

Spooky Forest

Have children cut tree silhouettes with thick trunks and thin branches from black paper. Provide stencils, if necessary. Glue trees on gray paper (9" x 12" or 12" x 18").

Cut eyes (ovals, triangles, circles, and other spooky shapes) from a variety of colors of paper. Add circular eyeballs of different colors. Glue the eyes on the tree trunks.

Stretch out cotton balls into long, thin wisps. Glue the cotton wisps across the trees to add a spooky, foggy look.

Night Scenes

Children will have fun making this Halloween night paper to use as a background on which to display a variety of three-dimensional art.

Have children use a white wax candle (small birthday candles work well) to draw stars all over 9" x 12" (or larger) pieces of white poster board. Paint over the poster board with blue watercolor paint or blue tempera paint that has been thinned with water. Use a large brush or a sponge for painting.

The wax stars will "shine" through. Let the paint dry.

Try any of the following displays or one of your own ideas:
- Add gold and silver star stickers.
- Glue on black paper witches, brooms made with craft sticks, and crescent moons.
- Glue or tape on paper ghosts or ghosts made with tissues or white paper towels.
- Stencil the words *boo, trick-or-treat,* or *Happy Halloween.*
- Use markers and cut paper to make spooky eyes. Cut out and glue on the night sky.
- Glue on black paper bats.
- Glue on owls and the word *whoo-ooo-ooo.*

Paper Chain Skeleton

Use the idea of a traditional paper chain to make a life-size skeleton to decorate a wall, a door, or a Halloween party. Cut a skeleton skull, two hands, two feet (trace your own!), and two long bone shapes from white paper. Cut long, wide strips of white construction paper, form them into circles and connect the circles to make five long chains (two arms, two legs, and a body). Combine the chains with the bones and skull. Add the hands and feet to complete the Paper Chain Skeleton.

by Carol Ann Bloom

52

Pasta-tively Scary Skeleton

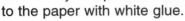

Provide children with black paper, glue, and a variety of pasta shapes: macaroni, ziti, penne, bows, and spaghetti of different thickness and length. Encourage children to experiment with the pasta on the paper until they have made a skeleton from head to bony toes.

When they are pleased with the skeleton, glue the pasta to the paper with white glue.

Paper Bag Owl

Have children loosely stuff brown paper lunch bags half full of crumpled newspaper. Bring the top of the bag together and fold the two outer corners in toward the center to form a point. Tape.

Fold the point down over the lower half of the bag and glue or tape in place. Cut orange paper beaks, black and yellow paper eyes, and black or brown paper feet. Glue in place: the triangular beak on the bag point; eyes on either side of the point; and feet under the front of the bag.

Window Clings

Give each child a foot-long piece of plastic wrap. To make the wrap easier to work with, tape each corner to the table.

Have children use permanent markers to draw and color a Halloween scene: Jack-o'-lanterns, witches, moons, bats, ghosts, children in costume, and so on.

Children may draw free-hand or use stencils. Or place pictures under the clear plastic wrap so that children can duplicate the picture on the plastic wrap. When the markers are dry, place the decorated plastic wrap on window-panes.

Each child can make his or her own window cling or make one large classroom project. Children can work in groups of three to six on longer lengths of plastic wrap.

Tattoos with Nature's Glue

Cut Halloween shapes (cats, moons, stars, pumpkins, ghosts) or any design (flowers, hearts, lightning bolts, fish, birds, animals) from colored tissue. To adhere the tissue shapes to the skin and create a tattoo, use a natural glue—potato starch. Cook a potato until it is fork-tender (in boiling water or in an oven) and cut the potato in half.

Place the colored tissue paper design on the surface of the cooked potato so that it will absorb some of the potato starch. Then place the tissue design on the skin. Remove skin tattoos with soap and water or cold cream.

Images of Halloween

Jack-o'-Lanterns

One Jack-o'-lantern in the night
with a candle shining bright.
(Hold up your hand, then wiggle your hand so it's like a flickering candle.)

Two Jack-o'-lanterns, big and round,
close together on the ground.
(Put fists side by side.)

Three Jack-o'-lanterns by the tree,
smiling wide for all to see.
(Smile wide and put a finger on each side of your mouth.)

Four Jack-o'-lanterns in a row,
grinning in the moon's soft glow.
(Make a circle with your arms over your head and smile.)

Five Jack-o'-lanterns sit and wait
for trick-or-treaters by the gate.
(Put elbows on your knees and your chin in your hands, then make a funny face.)

by Elizabeth Giles

Images of Halloween

The air is crisp, the night is black,
A toothy grin from spooky Jack.
Dots of light move down the street
As children run to trick-or-treat—
Scarecrows, clowns, and black cats, too.
From far away an owl calls "Whoo-o-o."
It seems that all these things must mean
That once again it's Halloween!

by Joan Welch Major

Halloween

One *(Hold up 1 finger.)*
Jack-o'-lanterns with a toothy grin.
(Point to your teeth.)

Two *(Hold up 2 fingers.)*
bony skeletons are looking thin.
(Bend elbows and wiggle your hands.)

Three *(Hold up 3 fingers.)*
friendly monsters with a lot of hair.
(Rub the top of your head.)

Four *(Hold up 4 fingers.)*
wispy ghosts floating in the air.
(Wave your hands above your head.)

Five *(Hold up 5 fingers.)*
little scarecrows, the best ever seen.
(Clap hands.)

They're all getting ready
for Halloween!
(Put hands to mouth and shout "Halloween.")

by Elizabeth Giles

54

Pumpkin Piñata

Turn your next Halloween party into a Mexican fiesta with this exciting Latin American art project. Make and break a pumpkin piñata with your students. It's fun, creative, and functional.

Materials
- round balloon
- newspaper
- 1 cup flour
- 2 cups water
- bowl
- orange paint
- craft glue
- black construction paper
- orange and green tissue paper
- 2 pieces of string (4 feet long)
- scissors
- candy and small toys
- broom handle

Directions

1. **Prepare materials.**
   Blow up a balloon. In a bowl, mix flour and water into a glue-like paste. Cut newspaper into one-inch strips.

2. **Complete papier-mâché.**
   Dip paper strips into the paste and remove excess. Spread wet strips onto balloon and flatten until smooth. Cover entire balloon with one or two layers of paper. Let dry. Repeat two times.

3. **Decorate paper-covered balloon.**
   Paint paper orange and let dry. Repeat if necessary. Apply glue to the paper and sprinkle on small pieces of orange tissue paper (approximately ½ inch by ¼ inch). Let dry. Cut out eyes, nose, and mouth from black construction paper and glue onto piñata.

4. **Prepare pumpkin piñata.**
   Cut a four-inch hole at the top of the piñata. Remove balloon. Fill piñata with candy and small toys. Make a small hole on either side of the large hole. Lace string through each hole and tie securely. Stuff green tissue paper into the hole and shape into a stem. Hang piñata from the ceiling or from the end of a broom handle.

5. **Have a piñata party.**
   Take turns hitting the piñata with a broom handle until it breaks and the goodies fall out. Share the treats!

by Glen Arnould

Name _____

STARTING SOUNDS

Say the name of each picture.
Then circle the letter that makes the beginning sound.

p   r   t

s   c   d

l   r   b

g   h   m

a   c   n

b   v   m

TLC10339 Copyright © Teaching & Learning Company, Carthage, IL 62321-0010

Definitely Different

Find the picture in each line that is different from the others.
Draw an X through it.

by Becky Radtke

How Many Are There?

Write the number of items in each group inside the box.

by Becky Radtke

Story Time

Add sparkle to Halloween with ideas from *The Halloween Book* by Sharon McKay and David MacLeod (Somerville House Books, 1994). This handy book features creative ideas for sensational decorations such as a scarecrow pumpkin and a pumpkin totem pole. Party games and recipes for tasty Halloween treats are also included, as well as safety tips for young trick-or-treaters.

Holiday! Celebration Days Around the World

by Deborah Chancellor
Dorling Kindersley, 2000

Take a fun-filled journey around the world to discover a year of special festivities. Bright, colorful photographs, and interesting text create excitement for holidays such as Chinese New Year, Halloween, Diwali, Christmas, and Kwanzaa.

Trick or Treat Countdown

by Patricia Hubbard
illustrated by Michael Letzig
Holiday House, 1999

Halloween is coming, so let's get ready! Here's a lively counting book that will help teach your young goblins to count from 1 to 12 with a host of zany monsters and colorful Jack-o'-lanterns. Counting has never been this much fun!

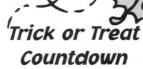

P.B. Bear, Catch That Hat!

by Lee Davis
Dorling Kindersley, 1997

One windy fall day P.B. Bear and his friends, Hilda and Patsy, are enjoying one of the most popular pleasures of the season—playing in a big pile of colorful, crunchy leaves—when a big gust of wind suddenly whistles by and P.B. Bear's hat flies away. All ends well, though, as P.B. Bear's friends team up to help him find his lost hat.

Sergeant Sniff's Halloween Mystery Treat

by Valerie Garfield
illustrated by Julie Durrell
HarperFestival, 2000

Calling all detectives! Here's a Halloween mystery just for you. Everyone is enjoying Officer Owl's Halloween party, when suddenly Captain Cat's treat is missing. Can you help the super sleuth Sergeant Sniff find the missing treat? Just follow the scratch-and-sniff clues scattered throughout the book!

by Mary Ellen Switzer

My Monster Mama Loves Me So
by Laura Leuck
illustrated by Mark Buehner
Lothrop, Lee & Shepard, 1999

There's nothing better than a mother's love—even a monster mama's love! In this endearing rhyming story, a young monster tells about the special things its mother does to show her love. From combing cobwebs from the little monster's bangs to baking delicious cookies filled with bugs, this monster mom is top-notch.

Scarecrows
by Lola M. Schaefer
Pebble Books, 1999

Three cheers for those magical straw people standing tall in the pumpkin patches every autumn! Children will marvel at the appealing, colorful photographs of scarecrows in this sensational fall book. The simple text gives a description of scarecrows and their purpose. A vocabulary list, book list, and internet sites on the subject are also included. Other book titles in this Fall Fun series include *Masks, Costumes,* and *Jack-o'-Lanterns.*

Whooo's Haunting the Teeny Tiny Ghost?
by Kay Winters
illustrated by Lynn Munsinger
HarperCollins, 1999

This lighthearted and entertaining ghost story is sure to get everyone in the Halloween mood. It's all about a tiny ghost and his teeny, tiny cats who have a BIG problem. It seems that someone is haunting their teeny, tiny house. Can you guess "whooo's" there?

Fall Rhyme Time
Strike up the band! Here are some positively perfect poetry books on parade for the fall season!

Shake dem Halloween Bones
by W. Nikola-Lisa
Houghton Mifflin Company, 1997

Rattlebone Rock
by Sylvia Andrews
HarperCollins, 1995

The Bug in Teacher's Coffee:
And Other School Poems
by Kalli Dakos
HarperCollins, 1999

There's a Zoo in Room 22
by Judy Sierra
Gulliver Books, 2000

The Animal Fair
Animal Verses compiled by Jill Bennett
Viking, 1990

Little Dog Poems
by Kristine O'Connell George
Clarion Books, 1999

Surprises
Poems selected by Lee Bennett Hopkins
Harper & Row, 1984

Bats!
by Roger Generazzo
illustrated by Greg Harris
McClanahan Book Company,
2000

Did you know that a brown bat can catch and eat 1200 mosquitoes in an hour? Learn all about these incredible flying mammals this Halloween. Bats have become a familiar symbol during the Halloween season, so let's discover the inside story on them. This handy book features fascinating facts about bats, including a diagram of their body parts and a map showing the locations where different bats live. *Bats!* is a new paperback in the great new Know-It-All Series, featuring informative books on animals.

60

Pooh's Fall Harvest
by Isabel Gaines
illustrated by Mark Marderosian and Ted Enik
Mouse Works, 2001

Colorful pumpkins on the vine, shiny red apples glistening in the sun! Fall harvest season has come to Hundred-Acre Wood. Winnie the Pooh and his friends gather in Rabbit's garden to help gather the fresh fruits and vegetables. When they are finished, Rabbit decides on the perfect way to thank his friends for their hard work—he invites everyone to a harvest celebration.

Turkey Ticklers: And Other A-maize-ingly Corny Thanksgiving Knock-Knock Jokes
by Katy Hall and Lisa Eisenberg
illustrated by Stephen Carpenter
HarperFestival, 2000

Knock-knock. Who's there? A lively group of students treating readers to a very corny selection of knock-knock jokes this Thanksgiving season. The children serve up lots of humor as they prepare for their school Thanksgiving play.

Our Thanksgiving (My First Hello Reader)
by Kimberly Weinberger
illustrated by Diane deGroat
Scholastic, 1999

Join a happy family as they busily prepare for a festive Thanksgiving dinner. Is the turkey ready yet? Better hurry; the guests are on their way. Will the dinner be ready on time?

Youngsters will also enjoy playing vocabulary games using the game cards included in the book. Other short Thanksgiving games are also featured, such as Rhyme Time and A Thanksgiving Feast.

by Mary Ellen Switzer

Books Are Good Friends

"Wouldn't you like to have a friend who teaches you how to make or cook things? Or describes places all over the world? Or tells you about different people and how they live? Or shares wonderful stories with you?"

A book does all of these things—and more. A book can be a best friend. National Children's Book Week in November gives us a chance to think about books and how to take care of them.

Where Are Books Found?

Books are in schools, libraries, stores, and homes. Plan a field trip to one or more of these places and see what different types of books are available.

Why Are Books Important?

Books tell us about new places, people, and cultures, teach us how to do and make things, and help us find new information. As a class, decide on something the children would like to learn, make, or do. Gather books on the subject and allow everyone to discover how books can help. Books also entertain us with a variety of stories. Talk about the different types of stories there are, and read several to the children.

Treat Books with Care

Talk about taking care of books. Discuss ideas such as keeping books in a safe place, carrying books, holding books, protecting books from the weather, turning pages carefully, handling books with clean hands, not writing in books, using bookmarks, and not eating while reading. Allow each child to demonstrate these skills, using his or her own book.

by Judy Wolfman

How Are Books Made?

Explain that books are printed and put together by big machines called printing presses at printing companies. After the pages are printed, machines fold, gather, and cut them. Then they are sewn together, trimmed, and covered. Books can be big or little, thick or thin, hard-cover or paperback. No matter what the size or shape, you must look inside to know how good the book is. Show examples of each. If possible, visit a printer so children can see a printing press in action.

Make a Book

Use two pieces of cardboard for each cover. Have each child glue paper over the cardboard and decorate it; then cut sheets of paper the same size as the cardboard for the pages. Help children punch two holes along the side of the pages and the cardboard covers. Then tie a ribbon through the holes. Have children write or draw whatever they want in their books.

Make a Bookmark

Cut a strip of construction paper or cardboard about two inches wide and a little shorter than a book for each child. Let them draw pictures or designs to decorate their book-marks. Teach them to slip them between the pages of books in places they want to mark. Discuss why a book-mark is important and how it should be used.

Make a Bookplate

Discuss what a bookplate is (a label that tells people that the book belongs to you). Give each student a piece of wide brown paper tape or a wide self-adhesive label. Have them print their name in the middle and draw a design around it. Show children how to wet the back of the paper tape or peel the adhesive off the self-sticking label and place the bookplate on the inside cover of a book they own.

Enjoy Books

Encourage students to look at and read as many books as they can. They will enjoy looking at the pictures, making discoveries, and learning stories. Talk about collecting books and putting them in safe places at home and school. Encourage children to share their books with others and ask others to share theirs throughout the year.

Five Little Turkeys

Let children act out this poem with their fingers or the finger puppets below. If you use the puppets, you'll need five turkey puppets and one farmer puppet for each child. Let the children color the puppets.

Five little turkeys were waiting for their lunch,
(Hold up one hand and wiggle fingers or turkey finger puppets.)

So the farmer came along and gave them a bunch!
(Pretend to scatter corn with the other hand or farmer finger puppet.)

They gobbled up the corn with a snippy, snippy, snap;
(Put fingers of the "turkey" hand together, opening and closing them as you pretend to gobble corn from the ground.)

Then they all settled down to take a little nap!
(Press both hands together and rest head on one side of them as if sleeping.)

by Nancy Garhan Attebury

Giving Thanks

My Mom, as she dishes
The dinner all out,
Says, "Think of some things
To be thankful about."

"Well—TV and presents
And warm beds and cars.
And turkey and snowmen
And wishes on stars."

I'm getting so hungry,
I twitch in my seat.
"I'm thankful for everything!
Now, can we eat?"

by Irene Livingston

Activity: After reading the poem, let children make an "I Am Thankful" collage by cutting out pictures from magazines and gluing them on a sheet of poster board. Discuss each item pictured.

Name _____

Fabulous Feast

Eating from a feast of delicious foods is a wonderful way to celebrate Thanksgiving!
Count each group of items. Then color the plate to the right that shows that number.

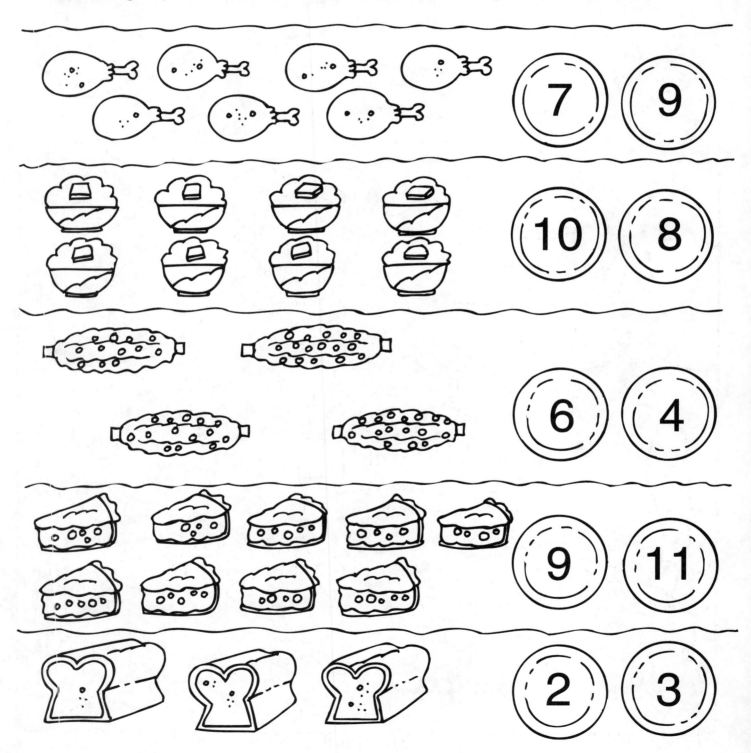

by Becky Radtke

Horn of Plenty

Look at this horn of plenty. It reminds us that we have plenty of reasons to be thankful when Thanksgiving comes! See if you can find and color the shapes below in the picture.

by Becky Radtke

Name _____

Thanksgiving Wish

These turkeys have gathered to give you a holiday wish!
Draw a line from each one to his or her shadow.

by Becky Radtke

Turkey Trot

Give a hop to the left,
And then to the right.
Flap your elbows
With all your might.

Stick out your neck
And gobble loud!
Hold up your head
And strut real proud.

Wiggle your tummy
With all you've got,
And that's how you do
The turkey trot!

by Ann K. Smiley

Holiday Newsletter

Entering school for the first time can be both frightening and exciting for young children. One way to reduce the anxiety is to visit the school and take a look around before the first day. Meet your child's teacher if you can. It is also a good idea to begin your school year schedule at home before school starts. Earlier bedtimes, getting up at the same time every day, and setting aside time each evening to read stories or practice writing letters, numbers, and your child's name (homework) are good school year rituals. Finally, if you are enthusiastic and excited about school and learning, your child will most likely be also. So keep a positive attitude and you will be off to a great start.

Simple Science

September is International Solar Month in honor of the heat and light the sun provides for living things on Earth. Experiment with your child to discover the power of the sun. You will need a paper plate, waxed paper, old crayons, a blunt knife, yarn, newspaper, scissors, tape, and an iron. Have your child place a piece of waxed paper on the paper plate; then use the blunt knife to shave pieces from several different crayon colors. Place each color group of shavings separately on the waxed paper and place the plate in a warm, sunny window. Observe what takes place as the shavings absorb the warm sunlight. Do some colors melt faster than others? (Dark colors absorb sunlight; light colors reflect it.) Experiment with a different source of heat. Let your child cut two identical shapes from waxed paper. Place one shape on a sheet of newspaper and sprinkle it with crayon shavings. Place the second waxed paper shape on top of the first. With the iron set at a low temperature, smooth it over the waxed paper to melt the shavings, adhering the waxed paper shapes to each other. When it's cool, tape a yarn loop to the back of the shape to hang this colorful decoration.

On the Move

Fall means football. Let your child practice the necessary coordination skills for kicking the ball with this simple project. Cut two ovals from brown felt and glue the edges together, leaving a small opening for stuffing. Allow the glue to dry, then fill the football shape with dry beans or rice. Glue the opening closed. When the glue has dried, tie one end of a length of rope or cord around the middle of the football beanbag. Fasten the opposite end of the rope or cord to an outdoor tree branch so the football beanbag is close to, but not touching, the ground. Let your child practice kicking this football, using one foot at a time. How high does the football fly?

Creative Kitchen

Exercise those fine motor muscles by molding colorful cream cheese biscuits for fall. You will need 1 cup of butter and 6 oz. of cream cheese, both softened to room temperature, 2 cups of flour, and food coloring of your choice. Put the cream cheese in a mixing bowl and stir in several drops of food coloring to tint. Add the butter and flour, stir, then knead with your fingers. Shape into golf ball size rounds and place them on a cookie sheet. Flatten the tops slightly, then bake for 12 to 15 minutes at 350°F until golden brown. Cool slightly, but serve warm with your favorite jam or jelly.

The Reading Room

Books can open up new worlds to children and broaden their interests. Celebrate Literacy Day this September with a trip to the library. You may want to look for a few of the following.

A Halloween Happening by Adrienne Adams, Aladdin, 1991.

Abuela's Weave by Omar S. Castañeda, Lee and Low Books, 1995.

Best Halloween Book (ABC Adventures) by Patricia Whitehead, Troll, 1998.

Clean Your Room, Harvey Moon by Pat Cummings, Aladdin, 1994.

Do You Want to Be My Friend? by Eric Carle, HarperCollins, 1995.

Shoes from Grandpa by Mem Fox, Scholastic, Inc., 1992.

Will I Have a Friend? by Miriam Cohen, Aladdin Paperbacks, 1989.

by Marie E. Cecchini

Poetry in Motion

Your child's class will learn about fire safety during Fire Prevention Week in October. Ask your child to repeat what he or she learns to reinforce the concepts presented; then share the following finger counting rhyme:

Five Brave Firemen

Five brave firemen ready for a run,
The first one's driving engine number one.
The second one carries a roll of water hose;
The third one puts a mask upon his nose.
The fourth one wears a fire hat and boots;
The fifth one says, "We're ready. Let's scoot!"

Mathworks

Let an autumn nature walk help your child learn about the concept of measurement. Walk together and collect items such as leaves, twigs, stalks of grass, and so on in a bag. Collect different lengths of each item (nothing longer than a dinner spoon). Indoors, have your child sort the items into like piles of leaves, twigs, and so on. Challenge your child to arrange one pile of objects in size order from largest to smallest. Glue each arrangement on a sheet of paper and hang them in his or her room.

Communication Station

Newspapers can be a good source of material for encouraging language experiences. Celebrate Newspaper Week this September with these activities. Have your child search large print newspaper headlines and cut out letters to spell his or her name. Glue these letters in order on a sheet of paper. Help your child search the newspaper for all the letters of the alphabet. Glue these in alphabetical order on a long strip of paper to make an alphabet banner to hang in your child's room. Finally, divide a sheet of paper into three sections. Have your child glue small cut-out letters in one section, middle-size letters in a second section, and large letters in the third section to make a "sizes" collage.

From the Art Cart

Celebrate Friendship Day with an art project. Help your child draw and cut an apple shape from construction paper; then cut the apple in half. Help write your child's name on one of the halves and the name of a best friend on the other. Punch a hole at the top of each half. Thread and knot yarn through each hole to create friendship necklaces. Decorate the apple halves with glue and glitter. The object of the friendship necklaces is that each child wears the other's name.

It's Back to School

Happy Columbus Day!

AUTUMN

Grandparents' Day is Coming Soon!

Help Fight Fires

Happy Halloween to All!

Date:
To:

From:

You've Earned ☐ Bone-us Points

Happy Halloween

WOW!

_____
(child's name)

has taken off to a Great Start!

_____
(teacher's signature)

Take Note...

Welcome to my Class!

Hang Out and Read!

Tackle a Book

You're Scoring Big in

_____
(skill or subject)

From Your Teacher:

TLC10339 Copyright © Teaching & Learning Company, Carthage, IL 62321-0010

Clip Art for Thanksgiving

Give Thanks, Dude!

Snowman Smiles

Do you see my snowman? We built a happy snowman,
Who stands in our yard by the evergreen tree.
1, 2, 3 big snowballs created this snow doll.
Two eyes and a mouth: he is smiling at me!

We poked on some buttons, stick arms and wool mittens.
We wrapped a long scarf, and stuck on a nose.
Our snowman can watch us, but he cannot catch us
When freezing for freeze tag while the winter wind blows.

The snow is so white, reflecting sunlight,
That we squint and we blink, but the snowman just stares.
"His cheeks don't get red or rosy," I said.
"His toes don't get numb, but look what he wears!"

We wear layered clothing. He wears almost nothing.
His jacket of snow is all that he needs.
The snow drifts and swirls as the snowman stands still.
We have sledding races and go at great speeds.

A red bird flies quickly to rest on the pine tree.
A rabbit and mouse come to cuddle and stay.
Snowman is not lonely, he is not the only
One to be outside all night and all day.

We play until supper, and the snowman keeps smiling.
Darkness is falling. Soon daylight will end.
Goodnight, Mr. Snowman. We'll see you tomorrow.
We'll build a snowlady to be your best friend!

by Amy Houts

Outdoor Learning Discoveries
for Little Ones

Bring on the Snow!

Winter offers a wonderland of preschool learning activities and ideas and the opportunity for little ones to move, speak, sing, dance, play, and learn more freely. Winter activities are enhanced by the snowy playground that occurs in many places, but many children never get the chance for snow day fun. No snow? No problem! If you live in a warm climate and never get snow, bring the chilly winter of other climates to you. Turn your Kid Space—or your classroom—into a winter playground with the following activities.

Snowball Factory

You Need
- scrap paper
- large laundry baskets

Bring on the Snow

You Need
- ice shavings from an indoor ice rink

Get Ready
Invite parents to help make large quantities of ice, or collect shavings from the local rink. Shovel the ice shavings into a shady corner of Kid Space.

Directions
1. Invite students to help you crumple white scrap paper into tidy little balls.
2. Collect the snowballs in laundry baskets until you need them.
3. Place the snowballs in one area. Invite children to have a friendly snowball fight. (Remind them that real snowballs can be dangerous.)
4. Pour the snowballs out and place the basket about 6 feet (3 m) away. Have children try to throw the snowballs into the laundry basket.

Bring on the Ice

You Need
- crushed ice, ice cubes, shaved ice
- wading pool

Get Ready
Fill the wading pool with ice or other snowy materials.

Let's Play
Bundle students into winter wear and invite them to make snowmen, snowballs, and snow forts before the snow melts. Snow inspires children to use large and fine motor skills while gaining some scientific understanding of the phenomena they play with.

by Robynne Eagan

Snowmaking "Machine"

If you aren't able to bring real snow to your Kid Space, make some imitation snow and let the fun begin!

You Need

- 1 large furniture or appliance box
- white latex or spray paint and painting materials
- lots of white scrap paper
- white pillowcase

Preparation

Paint the box white, inside and out, using a roller and latex paint or white spray paint. Allow it to dry for at least two days before bringing it into the classroom.

Directions

1. Place the box with the open side up. Invite students to help with a mystery project. They can sit inside the box and shred or cut paper. The paper can be kept in a white pillowcase or smaller white box.
2. Once you have enough paper pieces to fill the big box you are ready to announce the big surprise "We are going to have a snow day in our classroom!" Send home a note announcing the big event. Request that students bring in warm clothes, rubber boots, hats, and mittens if possible.

Snow Day

Bring winter into your classroom!

Get Ready

- Turn the air conditioning on to make your classroom chilly.
- Freeze water in a variety of shapes and forms.
- Add ice to the sand/water center.
- Hang paper snowflakes from the ceiling.
- Paint your windows with spray-on snow.
- Add winter wear and sports gear to your housekeeping and dramatic play centers.
- Set up snow crafts at your craft center.
- Supply winter theme books at your reading center.
- Invite students to dress for winter, even if they don't need to. Don't let them get overheated.

Snowstorm

Make a snowstorm in your classroom.

You Need

- scraps of white paper prepared by students (see Snowmaking Machine)
- paper bags (white if possible)
- large fans (2 or more)

Preparation

1. Put paper scraps into enough plastic bins or paper bags for each pair of children.
2. Set up fans in safe locations at either end of the area.

Directions

1. Invite children to join you in a designated area for a snowstorm.
2. Hand out bags of snow to each pair of children.
3. When you shout "Jack Frost," children are allowed to throw "snow" into the air to create a snowstorm. When the bag of snow is empty, have children pick up snow off the ground and throw it into the air again. The fans will blow the snow around. When everyone has had enough fun, move on to making a snow fort (see page 8).

Mitten Match

You Need
- a pair of mittens for each two children

Preparation
Have someone hide the mittens around your Kid Space before you take students outside.

Directions
1. Invite students to search around your Kid Space for a lost mitten.
2. When children have found a mitten, they can assist others in doing the same.
3. Once all children have a mitten, the group can return to the gathering spot.
4. Have children place the mitten on the hand it fits.
5. Now children must find the friend who has the matching mitten.
6. Have children join their mitten hands together to play a pairs game of follow-the-leader. The teacher or an extra helper should be the leader.

Ice Fishing

Turn your water table into an ice fishing center.

You Need
- water table
- ice cubes made with food coloring
- slotted spoons, tablespoons, ladles, etc.
- small buckets or plastic tubs

Directions
1. Float the colored ice cubes in the water.
2. Let children use various items to fish for the cubes.
3. They can place the items in the buckets and when finished, place them back in the water.

Snow Fort

You Need
- paper snow
- white box used for Snowmaking Machine
- craft glue and glue sticks

Preparation
Cut a rounded door shape in one end of the box, large enough for children to pass through it. Turn the box upside down.

Directions
1. Invite four children at a time to paste the paper scraps to the outside of the box.
2. Remaining scraps of paper can be swept up by snow sweepers and thrown in the snow bin.
3. Children can play in the snow fort for weeks to come.

Counting Snowmen

A simple outdoor song and game.

Directions
1. Choose 10 children to be "snowmen."
2. Have the entire group sing the song that follows to the tune of the song "Ten Little Indians."
3. As each number is called, tap one more snowman on the head. When tapped on the head, a snowman rises from the snow to stand up until ten snowmen are standing.
4. As you count backwards, touch each child on the head and have them melt back into the snow.

One little, two little, three little snowmen,
Four little, five little, six little snowmen,
Seven little, eight little, nine little snowmen,
Ten little frosty friends.

Ten little, nine little, eight little snowmen,
Seven little, six little, five little snowmen,
Four little, three little, two little snowmen,
One little frosty friend.

TLC10339 Copyright © Teaching & Learning Company, Carthage, IL 62321-0010

Snow Much Fun

Snow Factory

Snow isn't always white. When the flakes fall through the Earth's atmosphere, they hit all sorts of impurities like dust and pollen. These impurities can actually color the snow so it looks dirty. This process does, in turn, help clean the air of some of these impurities.

All snowflakes are different. The snow crystals can form an infinite number of shapes as they join together. Snowflakes can also change shape as they fall by picking up water crystals from clouds and water vapors in the air, by joining other snowflakes or by melting. Perfectly symmetrical snowflakes are very uncommon.

The English language has only one word for snow—*snow*. But the Eskimo language has over 40. Each one describes a different type of snow. *Sitilluquq* is hard snow, *maujaq* is soft snow, and *aumannaqtq* is very soft snow. Since snow is an important part of their lives, they have many words for it.

Catch the Falling Snowflakes

Give children white paper and let them spend a little time cutting out snowflakes. When you have accumulated quite a few, place them in a basket or bucket. Tell them that you are going to make it snow and you want them to catch as many snow flakes as they can. They cannot pick up any once they hit the floor. As they gather round, toss the snowflakes up into the air. When all of the flakes have fallen, let everyone count his or her catch to see who has the most.

My Snowman

Provide each child with three white paper circles, a sheet of blue or black paper for the background, and an assortment of paper punch-outs. Supply glue and let children design their own personal snowpersons.

Snowball Slushies

Freeze white grape juice or other light-colored juice in ice cube trays. When frozen, put them into a blender and mix until they are slush. Use an ice cream scoop to make snowballs. Put each one in the top of a paper cup.

by Sherry Timberman

Snowflake Hat

Materials
- large paper plate
- confetti
- pattern on page 44
- glue
- scissors
- glitter glue or sequins (optional)

Directions
1. Cut the paper plate as illustrated, without cutting through the outer edge of the plate.
2. Decorate the snowflake pattern on page 44 with confetti (and any optional trims).
3. Cut out the snowflake and glue it to the center of the prepared plate.

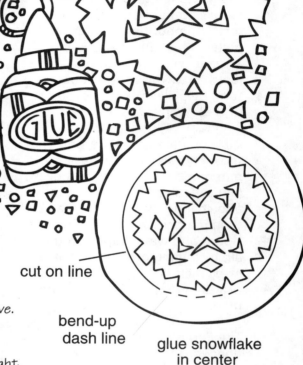

cut on line

bend-up dash line

glue snowflake in center

Song

The Itsy Bitsy Snowflake
To the tune of "The Itsy Bitsy Spider"

The itsy bitsy snowflake came falling from above.
Down, down it fell, then landed on my glove.
Out came the sun and made it glisten bright;
Then the itsy bitsy snowflake melted out of sight.

Activity
Make a snowflake necklace to go along with your snowflake hat. Cut two paper snowflakes; then glue them together after placing a looped 20-inch length of ribbon or yarn in the center. You may want to add glitter glue or even glue some salt or sugar to your snowflake to make it sparkle.

Books
The Big Snow by Berta and Elmer Hader, Simon & Schuster, 1967.
Owl Moon by Jane Yolen, Philomel Books, 1987.
Katy and the Big Snow by Virginia Lee Burton, Sandpiper, 1974.
The Snow Speaks by Nancy White Carlstrom, Little Brown & Co., 1995.

by Dyan Beller

Dot-to-Dot Fun

Starting with number 1, connect the numbers and see something you can make in the winter.

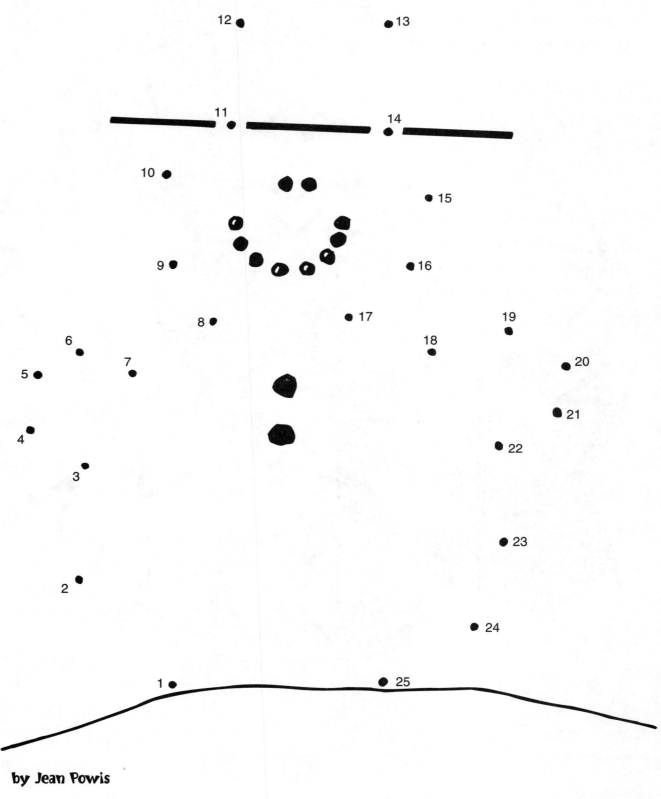

by Jean Powis

Snowgirl Friend

I built a brand-new snowgirl
Then stared at her and said,
"Did you just shiver from the cold
With nothing on your head?"

Some snow fell off her forehead.
It looked a little odd,
And as I patted on more snow
I thought she gave a nod.

I clapped my hands. She heard me!
Oh, what a nice surprise!
She's come to life, I'm thinking,
Right here before my eyes.

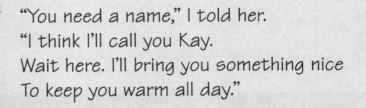

"You need a name," I told her.
"I think I'll call you Kay.
Wait here. I'll bring you something nice
To keep you warm all day."

I brought my old red jacket,
A thick one with a hood.
I'm pretty sure she smiled and said,
"Oh, thank you! That feels good!"

You might not think I heard it.
Okay. Well, I don't mind.
But lots of awesome things can happen
Just from being kind.

by Irene Livingston

Georgie's First WINTER

Georgie sat quietly in the falling snow, watching the snowflakes dance around him. He had never seen snow before. This was his first winter.

"Georgie!" called Mama from the front door of their burrow, "Come in. It's time to go to sleep now. Winter is here!"

"But I don't want to go to sleep," Georgie cried. "I want to play in the snow."

"Okay," said Mama, sticking her head out of the doorway. "Just five more minutes. Then you'll have to come in." Georgie just couldn't understand why groundhogs had to sleep all winter long. He wanted to stay up and have fun.

Georgie quickly ran over to the frozen pond where girls and boys were ice-skating. They were twisting and twirling and skating on one foot. "Wow!" exclaimed Georgie. "That looks like fun. I want to skate, too." So after the girls and boys left, Georgie stepped onto the ice. He tried twisting and twirling and skating on one foot. But the ice was so smooth and slippery that Georgie landed right on his bottom. Smack! "Ouch!" he cried. "I don't think skating is fun. I don't ever want to skate again. Ever!"

Georgie crawled to the edge of the pond and stood up. Then he headed for the top of a snowy hill where girls and boys were snowboarding. They raced down the hill, screaming and laughing and having lots of fun. "Wow!" exclaimed Georgie. "I want to go snowboarding! I want to have lots of fun." When the girls and boys disappeared over the next hill, Georgie found a piece of driftwood to use as a snowboard. He raced down the hill, screaming and laughing. Swoosh! But he did not have any fun. He flew so fast that he landed face first in a big pile of snow. "Yikes!" Georgie yelled. "I can't see! I don't think snowboarding is fun."

Lola De Julio De Maci

"This isn't any fun!" exclaimed Georgie. "It's too hard! I'm tired. I want to go home and go to sleep." So Georgie hobbled back to his burrow where his brothers and sisters were already sleeping. Mama was waiting for him at the front door.

"Did you have fun in the snow?" Mama asked, hugging Georgie tightly.

Georgie got up and dusted himself off. "I don't ever want to go snowboarding again. Ever!"

Suddenly Georgie noticed a little girl making a snowman in her front yard. "I want to make a snowman," Georgie said. "I think it would be fun." Georgie watched the little girl make a snowball. She pushed it and rolled it in the snow, making it bigger and bigger. Soon it was big enough to make a snowman.

Georgie got very excited. He gathered snow in his small furry paws and pushed it and rolled it and pushed it and rolled it. Ughh! But no matter how hard he tried, he could not make a snowball.

Georgie snuggled in Mama's arms. "Playing in the snow isn't so much fun," he murmered softly. "It's too hard. I want to go to sleep." Mama carried her little groundhog into the burrow. And by the time she put him to bed, Georgie was already dreaming of pink-colored peach blossoms poking their heads out of winter's snow. It wouldn't seem long until spring.

Winter Day

Clothes for the Weather

Help children understand how the weather affects what we wear both inside or outside. Buy several different colors of felt, including a square of "skin color." Cut out a simple boy and/or girl and a variety of clothing with which to dress him or her. Include underwear, shirt, pants, dress, socks, shoes, boots, raincoat, umbrella, winter jacket, scarf, hat, and mittens. Ask a child to dress this "weather friend" appropriately for the day's weather. Then ask children how they would dress themselves in various kinds of winter weather.

Winter Walk

Pick a day that is sunny, not blustery cold or windy. The warmest winter hour will be around 2 p.m. Before going on a walk, bundle yourself and the children in boots, coats, hats, scarves, and mittens. While on your walk, look for clues. Who has been here? If there is snow on the ground, you might see tracks from other people's boots, or prints from birds, dogs, cats, or wildlife. Find something smooth; find something rough; look for something green, blue, white, and so on. Stop and listen to sounds. Do the children hear birds singing? An airplane? Cars? Ask questions: How does the snow feel? Is it easier or harder to walk in the snow? How is walking in boots different? Challenge children to remember something from their walk. Come back in a reasonable time, depending on the temperature.

Snowflake Shapes

Children can help make snowflakes by folding square pieces of paper in half, then again, and cutting out shapes such as triangles (for diamond shapes), semi-circles (for circles), and squares (for rectangle shapes). Round off the edges and make cuts into the edges; then unfold the papers to reveal beautiful paper snowflakes. Point out the diamonds, circles, rectangles, and other shapes in each snowflake. Count how many of each shape, and how many shapes there are all together. Hang the snowflakes in the window.

by Amy Houts

Activities

Winter Scene

Ask children to create a winter scene based on what they saw on the walk. Use dark colored construction paper such as black or blue and colored chalk to create snow pictures.

Snow and Water Experiment

Scoop snow into three containers. Put one container in the freezer, one in the refrigerator, and leave one out on the counter. Check periodically to see which one is melting fastest. Also look to see if the melted snow is dirty or clean. If you live in a climate without snow, fill three containers with water. Place one in the freezer, one in the refrigerator, and one on the counter. If you are using a closed container, be sure to leave space for the ice to expand. Have children observe what happens to the water, using their senses of touch and vision. Write down what they observed. Post their observations on a bulletin board.

Winter Matching Game

Buy winter stickers such as snowmen or snowflakes and 3" x 5" index cards. Make sure you have at least two of each type of sticker. Instruct children to put one sticker on each card. Then turn the cards over and lay them all out on a table. Let students take turns to see if they can match two cards turning over only two cards at a time. If they match, the student keeps the two cards. If the cards do not match, they must be turned face-down again. This is a good memory game!

Freeze Game

This game is fun when played with two or more persons. Play music on a CD or tape player. Tell children to dance or move while the music is playing, but to stop or "freeze" when the music stops. You may want to direct this activity by telling children specific movements to make such as: hop, run in place, stomp your feet, clap your hands, and so on.

Winter
Outdoor Learning Discoveries
for Little Ones

Winter provides many opportunities for helping children learn the differences between their left and right hands and their left and right feet. This activity will make it easier for you to get little ones into their gear and out the door. It is not so important for children to be able to name left and right at this stage—but it is helpful for them to recognize matching the shape of their hands and mittens or their feet and boots.

The Right-Left Lesson

You Need
- two sheets of poster board
- collection of stray mittens

Directions

1. Help children trace their right hands on one sheet of poster board and their left hands on another. Print their names inside their handprints.

2. Encourage children to recognize how all the hands on one poster share similarities, while all the hands on the other poster share similar traits. Which way does the thumb point? Which side of the hand is the baby finger on?

3. Discuss differences between the two hands. Help children recognize the distinct shape of each hand.

4. Hang the hand posters on a bulletin board. Hold up a mitten. Ask children to study the shape of the mitten and the shape of the hands on the poster. Which poster would this mitten belong to? Pin the mitten over a hand on the poster. Do this exercise over and over to reinforce this concept. Stray mittens may be easily claimed from the right-left board.

Try This

Repeat a similar exercise using feet. Feet can be traced on a plank on the floor. Children can practice laying shoes or boots over the tracings. Does the boot bottom match the foot shape?

What Is Snow?

Snow is a wondrous wintry thing. It is white, fluffy, and beautiful. It floats in the air. But what is it? Believe it or not, a snowflake starts as a tiny droplet of water. The droplet freezes to form crystals. Frozen crystals join together to form the flakes that fall from the clouds through the sky and down to you.

by Robynne Eagan

The First Snow

There is nothing like a first snow to create a winter wonderland of fun.
Bundle your students up and take them out to experience the joy of it all!

Let Snow Inspire Language

Walk with your students. Encourage them to put the experience into words. Ask questions. Listen. Encourage students to share ideas with one another.

- Can you smell the snow?
- How does it feel on your face?
- Why does the snow melt when it lands on your face or hands?
- Where does the snow come from?
- What happens when you step on the snow?
- What will happen to your footprints if the snow keeps falling?

Let Snow Fill Your Imagination

You Need
- large sheet of cardboard or an old blanket

Directions
1. Invite your students to lie on the board or blanket and stare up into the falling snow.
2. What do they see? What do they hear? What do they feel?
3. What does this snowfall make the children think about?

Simple First-Snow Pleasures

- Make a snow angel.
- Roll a snowball.
- Make tracks.
- Follow the leader.
- Pull a friend on a sled, or sled down a hill.

Make Figures in the Snow

Directions
1. Invite children to make snow angels by lying in the snow and moving their arms and legs in and out. It is a bit tricky to get up without ruining the image.
2. Now ask children to use their imaginations. What else can they make? A star? A moon? A snake?

Snowball Celebrations

When the weather is just right for rolling snowballs, head for the hills!

Pass the Snowball

Directions
1. Organize your group into a simple circle.
2. Have students gently pass a snowball from child to child.
3. How many times can the snowball go around the circle before it falls apart?
4. Add more snowballs to be passed around at the same time.
5. Try some variations. How quickly can the snowball go around the circle and stay in one piece?

Melting Snowball

With a little music and some packing snow, you can play a chilly version of Hot Potato.

Directions
1. Have students form a circle.
2. Explain that the snowball will be passed around until the music stops. When the music stops, everyone must freeze in position. The child holding the snowball will move on to another activity.
3. The last child in the game will be called Snow Queen or King.

Fill the Bucket

You Need
- large bucket
- 1 small cup for each participant
- timer with a signal bell

Directions
1. Challenge students to work together to fill the bucket with snow before the times runs out. Who is fast? Who can fill his or her cup quickly?
2. Have children get ready with their cups. When you signal the race to begin, children may start to fill the bucket, using only their cups.

Snow People with Pizzazz

You Need
- classroom dress-up clothes

Directions
1. Arrange children into groups of four to six.
2. Help each group make a simple three-snowball snowman.
3. Once the body has been formed, get ready for some fun.
4. Bring the classroom dress-up kit outside for some creative snow characters.
5. Take photos of the characters to be displayed in classroom.

Letters in the Snow

You Need
- alphabet cards
- well-bundled helpers

Directions

1. Have the children form pairs. Ask children to be very careful not to walk on the letters that are made during this activity.
2. Give each pair one alphabet card and have them tromp that letter into the snow.
3. When the letter has been made (and inspected), the group can make another letter.
4. Continue to hand out alphabet cards until all the letters have been made.
5. When all the letters have been made, gather students around you.
6. Sing the alphabet song together. Hold up each letter as you sing its name.
7. Now start going through the alphabet in the snow, letter by letter—who can find the letter A . . . B . . . and so on.

Waiting & Anticipating

Preschoolers aren't patient waiters! They don't have a clear understanding of time. Tomorrow, next week, five months from now, all mean about the same thing to little folks. Doctors sometimes even warn expectant parents to delay sharing the news with small siblings-to-be, unless they wish to be asked daily, "When is the baby coming?" While waiting is hard, anticipating is fun and exciting. The secret is to find a happy medium. We can take a hint from the animals. During the winter lots of animals are sleeping. Use the following fingerplays to share their stories with your students when you talk about waiting for spring.

Brown Bears

In winter all the brown bears
Into their caves do creep.
(Curve one hand to make cave; other hand "hides" in cave.)
Their coats grow thick and furry
Before they go to sleep.
(Hands together as a pillow for sleeping.)
Shh, they're sleeping!
(Finger to mouth, anticipatory pause.)
At last the waiting's over.
The snow has gone away.
(Fingers coming down as snow.)
"It's springtime! It's springtime!"
(Hands up in the air twice.)
All the brown bears say.

Raccoons

In winter all the masked raccoons
(Hands make masks around eyes.)
To hollow logs do creep.
(Hands make circle.)
They eat a great big supper
(Rub tummy.)
Before they go to sleep.
(Hands together as a pillow for sleeping.)
Shh, they're sleeping!
(Finger to lips, anticipatory pause.)
At last the waiting's over.
The snow has gone away.
(Fingers coming down as snow.)
"It's springtime! It's springtime!"
(Hands up in the air twice.)
All the raccoons say.

by Ellen Javernick

96

Smelly Skunks

In winter all the smelly skunks
(Hold nose.)
To cozy nests do creep.
(Hold hands like nests.)
They snuggle with their brothers
Before they go to sleep.
(Hands together as a pillow for sleeping.)
Shh, they're sleeping!
(Finger to lips, anticipatory pause.)
At last the waiting's over.
The snow has gone away.
(Fingers coming down as snow.)
"It's springtime! It's springtime!"
(Hands up in the air twice.)
All the skunks say.

Groundhogs

In winter all the groundhogs
To their burrows creep.
(Make hole with one hand and have other hand dive in.)
They dig themselves a bedroom
(Digging motion.)
Before they go to sleep.
(Hands together as a pillow for sleeping.)
Shh, they're sleeping!
(Finger to lips, anticipatory pause.)
At last the waiting's over.
The snow has gone away.
(Fingers coming down as snow.)
"It's springtime! It's springtime!"
(Hands up in the air twice.)
All the groundhogs say.

Turtles

In winter all the turtles
(Put one hand over the other to make shell; thumb of bottom hand is turtle's head.)
Off to the pond do creep.
(Make hand turtle "walk.")
They dig down in the squishy mud
(Claw hands as if digging in mud.)
Before they go to sleep.
(Hands together as a pillow for sleeping.)
Shh, they're sleeping!
(Finger to lips, anticipatory pause.)
At last the waiting's over.
The snow has gone away.
(Fingers coming down as snow.)
"It's springtime! It's springtime!"
(Hands up in the air twice.)
All the turtles say.

Children

In winter all the children,
(Point to children in room.)
The Earth's whole family,
(Hold hands in circle over head.)
Are waiting for springtime,
Waiting patiently.
Shh, they're sleeping!
(Finger to lips, anticipatory pause.)
At last the waiting's over.
"It's here! It's here!" they say.
"It's springtime! It's springtime!
Hooray, Hooray, Hooray!"
(Raise hands three times.)

Ice Skate Ornament

Materials

1 piece of paper
red or green felt
2 jumbo paper clips
beads (or buttons)

glue
scissors
yarn
decorations (lace, rickrack, etc.)

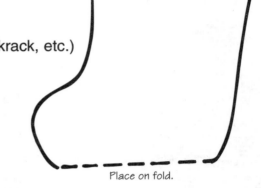

Place on fold.

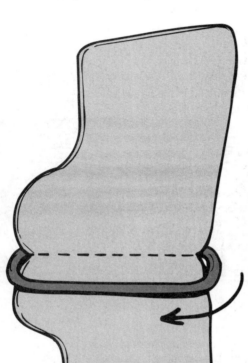

Directions

1. Trace the pattern on paper and cut it out.
2. Fold the felt in half, place the pattern on the fold, and cut it out. Repeat for the other skate.
3. Slide a jumbo paper clip over the felt to the fold on each skate.
4. Fold over each skate and glue it together.
5. Decorate both skates with lace and beads. Glue on the decorations.

6. Poke a hole in the corner of each skate and thread yarn through. Tie the skates together with yarn and make a bow.
7. Hang the skates on your Christmas tree. Glue a paper label with your name and the date on the back of the skates for a keepsake.

by Laura Moore

Creative Bird Snacks

Cookie Cutter Bird Treats

Materials

- cookie cutters
- bread
- peanut butter
- raisins, popcorn, cereal
- shoestring licorice

Directions

1. Let children use cookie cutters to cut shapes from bread slices.
2. Show them how to lightly dip raisins, popcorn, and cereal in the peanut butter, then stick them on the bread shape to decorate it.
3. Help each child push a shoestring licorice piece through the top of the bread for a hanger.
4. Hang the bird treats in trees near your classroom so children can watch the birds eat them.

Cereal Wreath Bird Feeder

Materials

- Cheerios™ (or other circle cereal)
- shoestring licorice

Directions

1. Show children how to string cereal onto shoestring licorice.
2. When the shoestring licorice is filled with the cereal, tie the two ends together to make a wreath.
3. Hang the wreath in a tree or on a fence for birds.

by Sally Stanley

Seasonal Science

Each new year begins a new cycle of seasonal changes. Invite your children to explore the changes winter brings to the world around us by observing the results of a few simple experiments.

Seasonal Weather Cycle

Activity

Help children define the word season. Name the four seasons and briefly discuss the changes in nature during each. Talk about how people respond to seasonal change, noting activities and clothing chosen. With the children's help, make a list on chart paper of words that tell about the winter season.

Project

Make *My Favorite Things* booklets. Each child will need five sheets of paper. On the cover page the child will write the title, *My Favorite Things*, then add his or her own name below. On each successive page the child will write the name of a season at the top and draw a picture of his or her favorite seasonal activity below. Help the children caption with "I like to . . . ," then staple the completed pages into individual booklets.

Cold & Flu Season

Activity

Demonstrate how uncontained coughs and sneezes spread germs. During the winter months people are confined to smaller spaces, which enables germs to travel faster from one person to another. When we cough or sneeze, our bodies force out air. This air is filled with the germs that cause us to cough or sneeze. If we do not "catch" our germs in a tissue, they spread through the air for others to breathe in, and what happens when you breathe in other people's germs? Sprinkle a little powder or cornstarch on a sheet of paper for the children to see. Hold the paper away from the children and pretend to sneeze on it. Again, show the paper to the children. What happened to the powder? Why?

Project

Have the children make "Mr. Sneeze" stick puppets. Let each one draw and color a face on a small paper plate, gluing on yarn hair and a loose tissue over the nose. Tape a craft stick handle at the back of each plate. Encourage the children to tell a short story about Mr. Sneeze.

by Marie E. Cecchini

Winter Air Movement

Activity

Demonstrate how warmer temperatures cause air to expand and occupy more space, while colder temperatures cause the volume of air to shrink. You will need two pans of water, one warm, one cold; one small, empty soft drink bottle; and a small balloon. Display the bottle. Talk about how it contains air even though we cannot see it. Cap the mouth of the bottle with the end of the balloon, making sure it completely covers the bottle top and is secure. The balloon will hang over the side of the bottle. The air is now "captured" in the bottle. Set the bottle in cold water for about five minutes. What happens? The children will observe no change, though the air within the bottle is now chilled. Set the bottle in the pan of warm water and observe. As the water warms the bottled air, it will expand. The expanding air has only one place to go, so the balloon will fill with warm air. Return the bottle to the cold water and the balloon will deflate (cool air occupies less space).

Project

Have children make paper "Happy New Year" balloons to suspend from the classroom ceiling. Let each one draw, cut and color a large balloon shape from construction paper. Show them how to write *Happy New Year* on both sides of their balloons. Attach a length of yarn to the bottom of each balloon. Fix a string at the top of each and hang them throughout the room.

Winter Temperatures

Activity

Demonstrate the effect temperature has on water. After it snows, have the children work to make two small snowpeople. Leave one outside, and bring the second one indoors in a dishpan. Build both as close to the same size as possible. Throughout the day, observe both snow figures. Take several photographs of the indoor snow figure to form a sequential story. What happens to the indoor snow figure as time passes? Ask children to contribute ideas as to why the indoor snowperson changes more rapidly than the outdoor one.

Note: If you live in an area that does not receive snow, use plastic containers to make two identical giant ice cubes. Leave one in a tub in the refrigerator and place one in a tub in the classroom. You will achieve the same results.

Project

Let the children cut out magazine pictures depicting the opposites—hot and cold. Prepare a large sheet of poster board by creasing it down the center, separating the sides with a marker line, and labeling the columns *Hot* and *Cold*. Have children glue their pictures to the appropriate side of the chart. When the project is completed, create a stand-up display by bending the poster board along the crease line.

Sounds

Activity

Experience the relationship between molecules and sound. Holiday meal preparation requires the use of various appliances, utensils, and containers. Collect magazine pictures of appliances. Have the children name them and tell how they are used. Collect various hand-powered utensils. Have the children name and demonstrate the use of each. Collect containers made of various materials, such as wood, glass, metal, plastic, and heavy ceramic. Talk about the material that makes up each and how these materials are all made up of molecules (small particles) bonded together in different ways. Very lightly tap the side of each container with a wooden spoon. Note the different sound each material makes. Materials like metal with tightly bonded molecules make a loud sound, while plastic with looser molecule bonding creates a softer sound. The more loosely packed molecules can absorb some of the sound.

Project

Provide bookmark-size rectangles of white paper or fabric, and several types of berries, such as strawberries, blueberries, and raspberries. Help the children cut the berries in half; then gently press the cut end of the berries onto their rectangles to make prints. Allow the bookmark prints to dry before using the bookmarks. Fabric rectangles can be glued to cardboard pieces of the same size to make sturdier bookmarks.

Scents

Activity

The holiday season allows us to explore scents as well as sounds. Try this simple experiment to demonstrate how molecules, small particles that make up materials, can move from one substance to another. Prepare hot/warm cocoa with the children. Have them stir their cocoa with candy canes. Note that the stirring end becomes white and thinner. Invite the children to contribute ideas on why this happens. Briefly talk about how everything is made up of tiny particles called molecules. Water and/or heat, as in the hot cocoa, can cause the molecules to break away from each other. They break away, but do not disappear. To find out where the candy cane molecules went, taste the cocoa. Part of the candy cane has dissolved into the cocoa.

Project

Have the children make scented hot cocoa pictures. First have them draw and color a mug on a sheet of paper. Draw a candy cane shape at the top of the mug. Next spread glue over the open end of the mug. Sprinkle cocoa powder over this glue. Now spread glue over the candy cane. Sprinkle with crushed peppermint.

102

Fun with Mittens

Here's a game to play in the classroom when the weather is cold and wintry.

Directions

1. Have one child sit in a chair with his back facing the other students. Place a mitten on the floor behind his chair. Tell the child he can't turn around.

2. One of the other children quietly gets up, grabs the mitten, and hides it near him or her (puts it in his or her desk or sits on it).

3. After the child has hidden the mitten and the classroom is again quiet, say the following rhyme with the children:

   Mitten, mitten, who's got the mitten?
   Could it be an orange and white kitten?

4. The child who had the mitten taken stands up and faces his or her classmates, and answers:
   I don't think it's an orange and white kitten,
   I think it's . . . (guess one of the classmates).

5. Give the child several tries (3 to 5). If the child guesses correctly, the classmate who hid the mitten takes his or her place on the chair. If the child doesn't guess correctly, he or she remains on the chair and the game continues.

by Sally Stanley

103

Sammy the Snowman

Sammy the snowman needs some mittens.
Draw some mittens on his hands.

TLC10339 Copyright © Teaching & Learning Company, Carthage, IL 62321-0010

Mitten Count

Help! The kittens have lost their mittens. Count the
number of mittens in each box and circle the correct number.

2   1   3

3   4   5

1   2   4

105

Mitten Matchup

Mitten, mitten, where are my mittens? Match the mittens that belong together by drawing a line to connect them.

Creative Coloring

Color this pair of mittens.

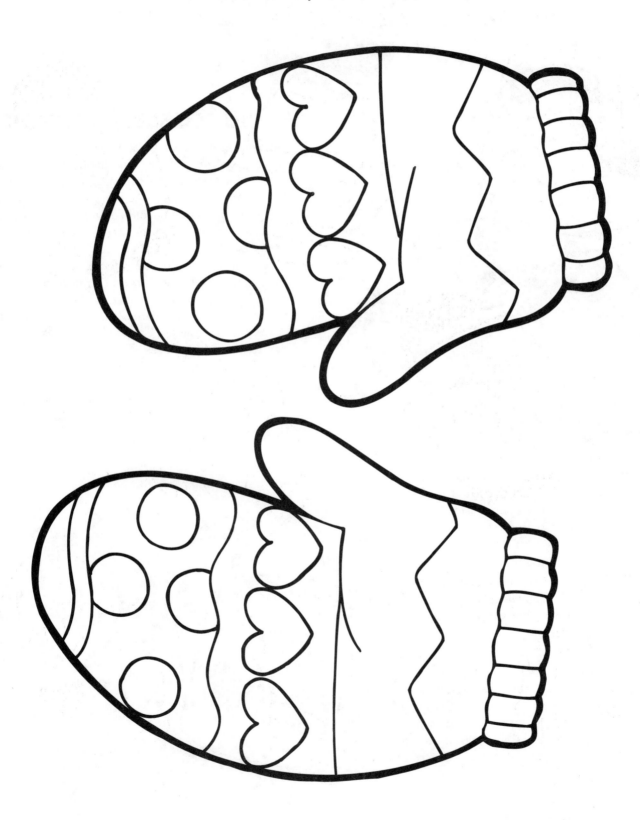

Tips for Successful Preschool Crafts

Six Successful Secrets

1. Select a craft activity that is appropriate for the ability level, group size, time allotment, and relevance to a particular theme or topic of interest.

2. Create a model to help you better instruct students and recognize potential difficulties. Your model will serve as a visual aid to those making the craft.

3. Plan how the activity will be set up and presented. How will instructions be offered, if at all? How many students will work on the craft at one time? How much time will be needed? How will you identify or mark pieces? Where will finished works go to dry? What cleanup will be expected? What will happen to unfinished pieces?

4. Establish simple, safe, and effective instructions for making the craft and cleaning up.

5. Be an active educator. Reinforce concepts as children work, recognize efforts, encourage creativity, be flexible, and enjoy the activity along with your students.

6. Plan a follow-up display and a system for storing and transporting pieces home.

Magic Materials

Safe

Preschool craft materials should be non-toxic and at least 1-inch in diameter. Products that pose any danger should be used only when one-to-one supervision is provided.

Enticing

Preschool art materials should be exciting and interesting to all of the senses. Offer a variety of materials with a range of exploration possibilities. Everyday items should be presented in a manner that suggests a new or interesting creative opportunity.

Well Presented

Present materials in a way that invites students to create and simplifies the making of the article. Separate items into brightly colored bowls; provide obvious places for pencils, scissors, paintbrushes and glue sticks to rest. Establish an easy flow from one stage of the craft to the next.

by Robynne Eagan

TLC10339 Copyright © Teaching & Learning Company, Carthage, IL 62321-0010

Simple Snowballs

Fun to make and fun to play with!
Assistance may be required.

Materials

- 1 ball of white yarn for every four students
- 3" (8 cm) cardboard square per student
- masking tape

Directions

1. Show how to tape one end of the yarn to one side of the square.
2. Have children wind the wool around the square from top to bottom, over and over until the entire square is covered. The more it's wrapped, the snowier the snowball will be.
3. Help students gently remove the cardboard from the center of the yarn and tie a length of yarn tightly around the middle of the snowball.
4. Once the center has been tied, have students cut the folded edges of the yarn at both the top and the bottom, fluff out the yarn, and hang the snowball from the ceiling by the long center thread or keep it to play with.

Sudsy Snowballs

Snowball Soap makes a lovely winter gift for Christmas, New Year's, or Valentine's Day.

Materials

- 1 bar of Ivory™ soap for each pair of students
- large plastic bowls
- clear cellophane gift wrap
- white ribbon
- white construction paper
- scissors
- crayons or markers
- single hole punch

Preparation

1. Soak the bars of soap in water overnight.
2. Cut each soft bar in half so there will be a half bar of soap for each child.

Directions

1. Provide each child with a wet, soft half bar of soap in a large plastic bowl.
2. Let children play with the bars and shape them into snowballs.
3. Once they have the shape they desire, let it dry. It will look like a fluffy snowball.
4. Have children wrap their snowballs in cellophane wrap. Help them tie a white ribbon around the top of the snowball.
5. Invite children to cut a snowball from white construction paper and punch a hole along an edge for a tag.
6. Children can print their names on their tags and attach them to the ribbon.

Sugar Cube Creations

Simple "snowy" exploration experience.

Materials
- white sugar cubes
- tray or box lid for each child

Directions
1. Provide a handful of sugar cubes on a tray for each child.
2. Have children explore the cubes, count them, make patterns, build structures, use their imaginations, and just play with the snow-like building blocks.

Icicle Making Center

Materials
- make icicle templates made of wood with a hole punched or drilled in the top
- white or silver glitter and "snow" paint (acrylics)
- paintbrushes
- white or silver ribbon or yarn
- covered work surface

Directions
1. Invite each child to choose an icicle and paint it his or her color of choice.
2. When the paint has dried, children can thread ribbon through the hole and attach a tag (or masking tape) with their name.
3. Hang the icicles to dry.

Simple Stick-On Snowflakes

Materials
- waxed paper
- squeeze-on glitter glue (white or silver)
- marker

Preparation
Draw a pointed star on each sheet of waxed paper.

Directions
1. Invite children to trace over the star using glitter glue.
2. Leave it to dry on a flat surface for three days.
3. Have students gently peel their snowflakes from the paper and transfer them to the classroom window.
4. Snowflakes can be peeled and placed back on waxed paper and inside a sealed bag or envelope to take home.

The Great American Bald Eagle

During the winter, many cities along American rivers celebrate Bald Eagle Days. One such city is Keokuk, Iowa. Eagles come to nest along the Mississippi River in the winter months. The river has places where ice does not cover the water. Eagles can hunt for fish to eat in the open waters. People stand by the river and watch the eagles fly down to catch fish in their talons and carry them away to eat.

Show your class pictures of eagles from bird books, encyclopedias, and nature magazines. Point out that young eagles are mostly brown and do not have white on their heads as adults do.

Eagle Puzzle

Enlarge one of the eagles on page 113 and color it. Paste it to cardboard. Then use a utility knife to cut it into several puzzle pieces. Lay out the puzzle pieces on a table in scrambled order. Let children see how quickly they can put the eagle puzzle together.

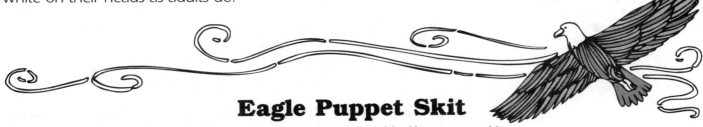

Eagle Puppet Skit

Choose two children to act out this skit as you read it.

Papa Eagle: "Fly!"

Baby Eagle: "No! It's too far down."

Papa Eagle: "Your wings will catch you. You will fly like the wind."

Baby Eagle: "No! Look down, Papa. It is a long way from our nest to the ground."

Papa Eagle: "Look up, not down, spread your wings, look at the sun, and GO!"

Baby Eagle: "No! I'm scared!"

Papa Eagle: "If you will try, I will give you a treat."

Baby Eagle: "A treat?"

Papa Eagle: "Yes, I will catch a big fish for you to eat."

Baby Eagle: "Can I eat the big fish all by myself?"

Papa Eagle: "Yes, if you will just try to fly."

Baby Eagle: "Okay, here goes. My wings are spread out really far. I am standing on my tip-toes. I am looking at the sun. I am ready to . . . WHEEEE!"

Papa Eagle: "Good job, you're doing fine. You are soaring as well as the finest eagle."

Baby Eagle: (Looked down at the river. He flapped his wings and said.) "Papa, hurry and catch my fish. This flying makes me hungry!"

by Mary J. Davis

Flying Eagle

Copy the patterns below onto heavy paper for each child to color and cut out. Show them how to cut two slits in the eagle pattern and insert the wing piece through. Let them pretend to fly their eagles around the room. Ask children to share ideas of where they might go if they could fly like an eagle. How would their lives be different?

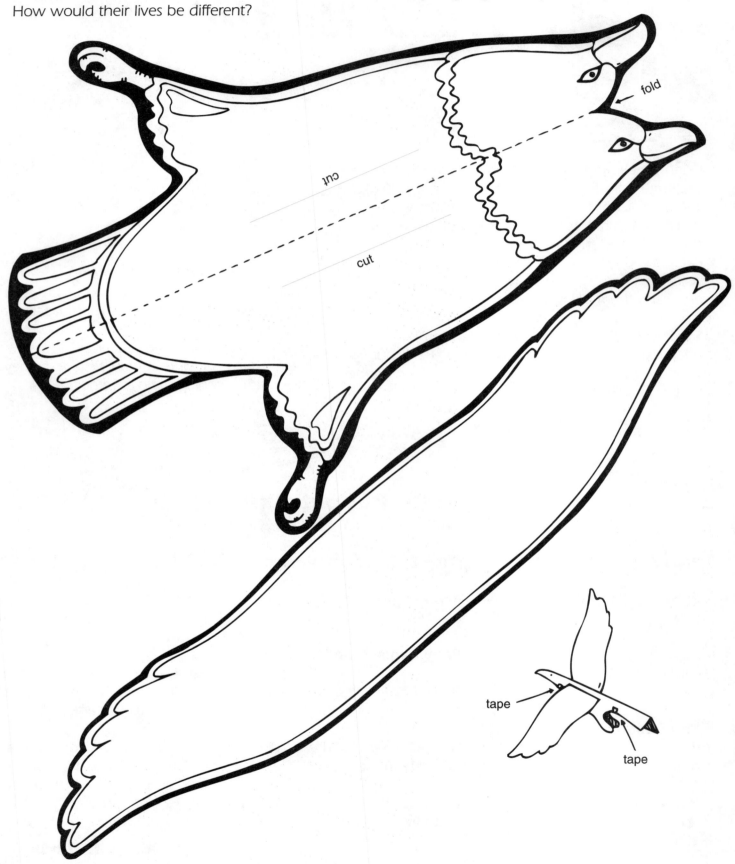

Eagle Mobile

Copy the patterns below on heavy paper. Give each child an eagle to color. Discuss each eagle pattern so the children will know how to color them. Then have the children cut out their eagles and attach string to them. Make three or four mobiles of the children's eagles, hanging them on sticks from different lengths of string. Hang the mobiles from the ceiling or lights so children can enjoy watching them "fly" every time a breeze stirs them.

Seal Life

Seals use their flippers
To move through Arctic snow,
To propel them underwater
Wherever they may go.

They navigate the water
In search of fish to eat,
To carry home so seal pups
Can have a tasty treat.

They swim down under ice floes,
And then pop up for air,
Always on the lookout
For roaming polar bears.

Pantomime

Talk about seals. Let children share what they know about them from having seen them in zoos and on TV. Then read the poem again and encourage the children to pretend they are seals, pantomiming the actions and, of course, making seal noises.

by Marie Cecchini

114

Name _____

Seals Love to Play!

Color the picture. Be sure the balls are all the right color.

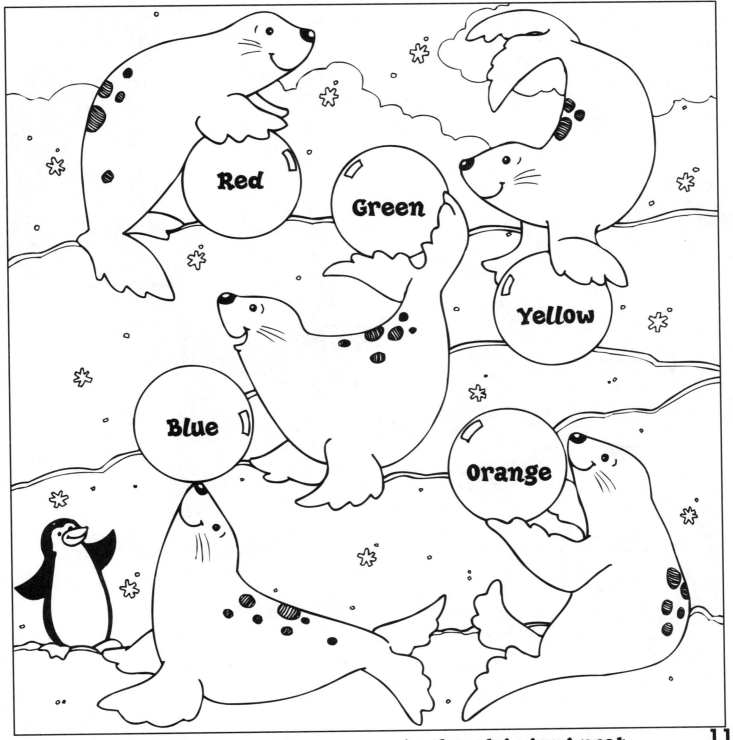

by Janet A. Armbrust

Snacktivities

Brighten dreary winter days with recipe projects to put smiles on small faces.

Warm-Up Punch

January—Winter Cold

Ingredients

2 qts. milk
1 c. maple syrup

cinnamon
cinnamon sticks (opt.)

Combine the milk and maple syrup in a saucepan. Warm over low heat, taking care not to scald. Float cinnamon stick "logs" in the liquid while warming. Pour into individual serving cups. Allow to cool slightly. Sprinkle with cinnamon and serve.

Mitten Munchies

January—Winter Clothing

Ingredients

bread slices
cream cheese, softened
bite-sized fruit pieces (fresh or canned)

Toast a bread slice for each child. Help the children cut their toast into large mitten shapes. Spread a cream cheese base over each mitten; then let the children decorate their mittens with fruit.

by Marie E. Cecchini

Igloo Treats

January—Winter Snow

Ingredients

vanilla ice cream   non-dairy whipped topping
angel food cake   maraschino cherries

Place a small mound of ice cream on a plate for each child. Cut the angel food cake into squares and let the children press the squares over the mound to make an igloo. Top each igloo with a dollop of whipped cream; then add a cherry with a stem for a smoke-stack.

Heart Tarts

February—Valentine's Day

Ingredients

English muffins   strawberry jam
strawberry cream cheese

Toast a muffin half for each child. Help the children use a cookie cutter to cut a heart shape from their toasted muffins. Spread each muffin heart with strawberry cream cheese; then top the center with a small amount of jam.

Cherry Mix-Up

February—Presidents' Day

Ingredients

oranges
cherries
honey
flaked coconut

Have children help prepare the oranges and cherries by peeling, pitting, and cutting them into bite-sized pieces. Place the fruit pieces in a bowl and toss to combine. Spoon into individual serving dishes, drizzle with honey, and sprinkle with coconut snow.

A Treat for Santa's Reindeer

December—Christmas

Ingredients

variety of cereals   pretzels
dried fruit   nuts

Put a variety of breakfast cereals, nuts, dried fruit and pretzels in individual bowls on a table. Give each child a zip-close plastic bag. Talk about what Santa's reindeer might like for a snack up on the housetop on Christmas Eve. Let each student go to the table and choose what treats to mix together in his or her bag. When all the treat bags are filled, let the children pretend to be reindeer and eat the snacks.

Decorating the Tree

December—Christmas

Ingredients

Christmas tree-shaped cookies   green icing
colored mini marshmallows   red licorice strips

For a creative and yummy project, give each child a Christmas tree-shaped cookie. Have the children ice the cookies with green icing. Provide colored mini marshmallows to use as ornaments and red licorice strips for garland. Let children decorate their trees by sticking marshmallow ornaments and licorice strip garland into the icing on the cookie.

Holly Treats

December—Christmas

Ingredients

bread slices   maraschino cherries
cream cheese   green food coloring

Toast a slice of bread for each child. Tint softened cream cheese with green food coloring. Help the children cut a holly shape from their slices of toast using a cookie cutter or a knife. Let them use craft sticks or blunt knives to spread green cream cheese over their holly-shaped toast. Cut each cherry into three or four pieces and place the pieces on the green toast to represent berries.

118

Bulletin Board

Supply the children with tagboard patterns of houses (patterns on page 19) to trace. Six to eight patterns for a class of 25 works well. The design of the house should fit on a sheet of 9" x 12" colored construction paper. Any color except black will work. The same design can be used by everyone, but three or four different architectural designs make the completed project more appealing. Children can trade patterns and decide which design they prefer.

After cutting out the houses, attach several windows made from yellow construction paper with glue or paste. A front door can be made from scraps of any color. Tiny curtains or drapes cut from wallpaper or construction paper can be glued on the sides of some of the windows.

Each child can draw, color, or cut out some symbols of the holiday celebrated in their home during the month of December (Christmas trees, wreaths, activity scenes, menorahs, candles, stockings, and so on). Glue these on the windows for display.

Tiny colored lights made from snippets of construction paper scraps make a nice addition to the outside of the house. Shutters can be added, as well as a chimney, or snow-covered shrubs and other details for those artistically inclined.

The completed houses are best displayed on a black background to make it look like a nighttime village scene. Finish the display by writing, *Happy Holidays from Our House to Yours* in the dark sky above the houses.

A photo of the child placed in a window of his or her house is a nice finishing touch.

by Karen Bjork

Happy Holidays from
Our House to Yours

Christmas Countdown

Have students hold up 10
fingers for the first two lines,
nine for the second two
lines, and so on.)

Ten days 'til Christmas;
I just can't stand to wait!

Nine days 'til Christmas.
I want to celebrate!

Eight days 'til Christmas;
Let's do a Christmas play.

Seven days 'til Christmas;
It's closer every day!

Six days 'til Christmas.
There are carols to be sung.

Five days 'til Christmas;
Our stockings are all hung.

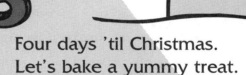

Four days 'til Christmas.
Let's bake a yummy treat.

Three days 'til Christmas;
We see lights on every street.

Two days 'til Christmas;
My shopping is all done.

One day 'til Christmas.
I'm ready for some fun!

Zero days 'til Christmas.
The day is finally here!
Let's all clap our hands
And let out a great big cheer:

Merry Christmas!

by Ann Richmond Fisher

Christmas Fun, Food, and Fingerplays

Candy Cane Snack

Ingredients
- white bread
- red jelly
- red food coloring

Directions
Melt a bowl of red jelly and add a few drops of red food coloring. Give each child a piece of white bread cut into the shape of a candy cane, and a small dish of the jelly. With clean paintbrushes, help the children paint stripes on the candy cane bread. Eat right away or save for a later snack.

Cookie Presents

Ingredients
- large square sugar cookies (6-8 inches)
- colored icing
- raisins, candy, colored marshmallows, etc.
- ribbon

Directions
Give each child a square cookie. Let him or her ice the cookie and decorate it with the candy. When the icing is set, tie a ribbon around each cookie like a gift and let each child take one home for someone special.

Present Match

Cut 20 squares out of Christmas wrapping paper—two each of 10 different prints. Glue each square onto a square of cardboard or heavy paper. Use the presents as a memory game for two children to play during a quiet time. Turn the squares over and let children take turns looking at the wrapping paper sides, two at a time, to find ones that match.

Variation: For a group activity to teach pattern recognition, give each child a chance to hold up a square. Whoever has the matching one holds it up, too. Collect the matching sets until all are found.

Stocking Guess and Pull

Fill a Christmas stocking with small toys that the children are familiar with. Give each child a turn to stick in a hand and guess what object he or she feels before pulling it out.

by Heather Tekavec

Stocking Mailbox

Cut large stocking shapes out of construction paper or felt. Staple two of them together for each child. Let children write their names on the stockings and decorate them with scraps of ribbon, yarn, wrapping paper, and glitter.

Christmas Puzzle Races

Collect several Christmas card pictures and cut each into four pieces (squares or strips). Mix them up, and give each child one piece. Play Christmas music while the children find the friends with the matching pieces and put their puzzles together.

Christmas Tree

Cut a green paper circle for every child. On each circle, cut a slit from an edge to the center. Overlap the sides to make a cone-shaped tree. Let children decorate their trees with sequins, yarn, small colored noodles or eggshell bits, beads, and so on.

Five Busy Elves

Choose five children to be the elves who stand and do the actions the song suggests.

Five busy elves making toys that we'll unwrap,
Five busy elves wearing funny shoes and hats,
But if one of those elves should stop and take a nap,
There'd be four busy elves making toys that we'll unwrap.

Four busy elves wearing funny shoes and hats,
But if one of those elves should stop and take a nap,
There'd be three elves making toys that we'll unwrap.

Three . . .
Two . . .
One . . .

No busy elves making toys that we'll unwrap.
Oh no! It's time to wake them up from their nap! (Children jump up and down, wave their arms and make noise!)

TLC10339 Copyright © Teaching & Learning Company, Carthage, IL 62321-0010

Calendar Gift

To make a New Year's calendar for children to give their parents, copy the pages of a calendar or make your own. Staple them together so each child has the full 12 months in order. As the calendar is opened, each month will have space above it for a big seasonal picture. Help the children decorate the months with drawings, magazine pictures, or photographs. Wrap up the calendars as Christmas gifts for parents.

Round the Circle

To the tune of "Jingle Bells"
Round the circle, round the circle
Goes the Christmas bell.
When the song is over
If you have it, ring it well.

Pass a bell around the circle as you sing this song. When the song stops, the person holding the bell gets to ring it as hard as he or she can.

Dear Old Santa

To the tune of "Old MacDonald"
Dear Old Santa has a sack,
S-A-N-T-A.
And in that sack he has a _____,
S-A-N-T-A.
He made it special just for me;
He'll put it underneath my tree.
Dear Old Santa has a sack,
S-A-N-T-A.

Give each child a chance to say what he or she would like for Christmas. Then sing the song, inserting their wishes.

Tree Ornaments

Have children dip Christmas cookie cutters in paint; then stamp them on contrasting colored paper. When the paint is dry, cut around the shapes, punch a hole for string and hang them on a tree.

If It's Christmas and You Know It

To the tune of "If You're Happy and You Know It"
If it's Christmas and you know it, hang a star,
(Pretend to hang a star on a tree.)
If it's Christmas and you know it, hang a star,
If it's Christmas and you know it and you really want to show it,
If it's Christmas and you know it, hang a star,

Continue with these verses:
. . . ring a bell *(shake an imaginary bell)*
. . . ride a sleigh *(shake and pull imaginary reins)*
. . . build some toys *(hammer)*
. . . cut the tree *(pretend to chop)*
. . . open gifts *(pretend to tear paper)*
. . . eat some sweets *(fill mouth with imaginary food)*

Christmas Mouse
Action Rhyme

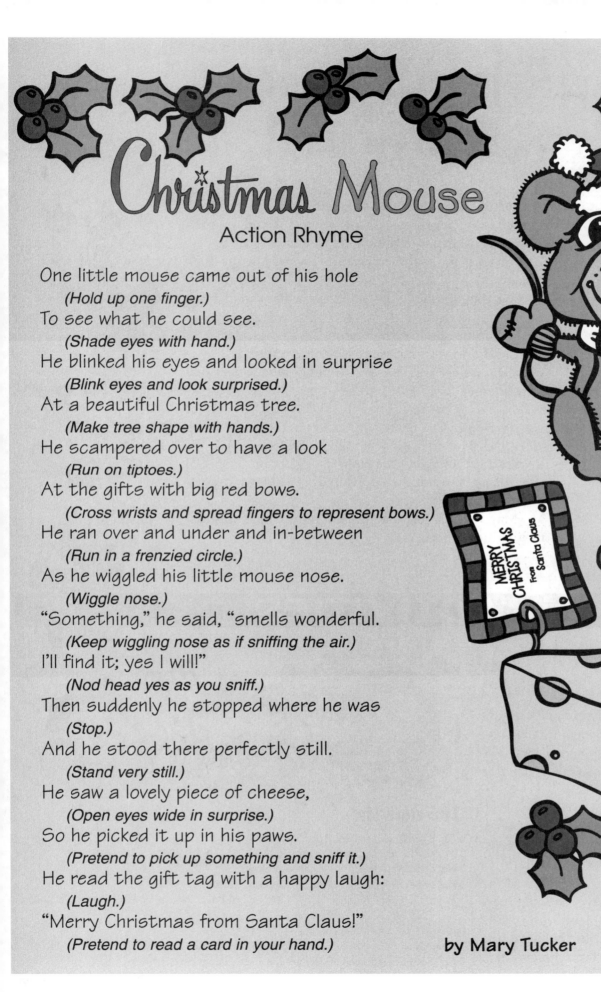

One little mouse came out of his hole
  (Hold up one finger.)
To see what he could see.
  (Shade eyes with hand.)
He blinked his eyes and looked in surprise
  (Blink eyes and look surprised.)
At a beautiful Christmas tree.
  (Make tree shape with hands.)
He scampered over to have a look
  (Run on tiptoes.)
At the gifts with big red bows.
  (Cross wrists and spread fingers to represent bows.)
He ran over and under and in-between
  (Run in a frenzied circle.)
As he wiggled his little mouse nose.
  (Wiggle nose.)
"Something," he said, "smells wonderful.
  (Keep wiggling nose as if sniffing the air.)
I'll find it; yes I will!"
  (Nod head yes as you sniff.)
Then suddenly he stopped where he was
  (Stop.)
And he stood there perfectly still.
  (Stand very still.)
He saw a lovely piece of cheese,
  (Open eyes wide in surprise.)
So he picked it up in his paws.
  (Pretend to pick up something and sniff it.)
He read the gift tag with a happy laugh:
  (Laugh.)
"Merry Christmas from Santa Claus!"
  (Pretend to read a card in your hand.)

by Mary Tucker

Reindeer, Reindeer Everywhere!

Every year at Christmastime, reindeer seem to multiply! How much do your students know about the real animal?

- Their scientific name is *Rangifer tarandus*.
- They spend the summer months grazing in the high Arctic.
- During the summer they eat grass, willow and birch leaves, and mushrooms.
- In the winter reindeer migrate to lowland forests.
- During the winter reindeer eat lichens and moss.
- Female reindeer are the only species of female deer that grow antlers.

Almost everyone has heard of Rudolph the Red-Nosed Reindeer, but do you know where he came from?

- Robert May created Rudolph in 1939 for a special advertising promotion sponsored by Macy's department store.
- Mr. May wrote a poem about Rudolph which was distributed to customers.

ACTIVITIES

Reindeer Chant

Reindeer, reindeer, will you come today?
Reindeer, reindeer, are you on your way?
Reindeer, reindeer, I can hardly wait,
Reindeer, reindeer, please hurry, don't be late!

Dramatization and Movement

Have the children pretend to be reindeer. Start by having them pretend to eat a breakfast of hay. Next, join in the "reindeer games." Have children paw the air, stomp their feet, run, walk, prance, and jump. Finally, have the tired reindeer curl up for a pretend nap.

Literature List

The Christmas Deer by April Wilson.
Inger's Promise by Jami Parkinson, Marsh Media, 1995.
The Little Reindeer by Michael Eoreman.
The Night Before Christmas by Clement Moore.
Olive, the Other Reindeer by J. Otto Seibold and Vivian Walsh, Chronicle Books, 1997.
Reindeer by Emile Lepthien.
Rudolph the Red-Nosed Reindeer by Robert L. May, Applewood Books, 1994.
The Wild Christmas Reindeer by Jan Brett, Paper Star, 1998.

by Pam Wattenbarger

What Am I?

I'm red and white and sometimes green;
My body's curled and long.
You might hang me upon your tree
Or lick me till I'm gone.
What am I? *(candy cane)*

I'm pretty on the outside
As I sit upon your floor.
But when you see what's in me,
You'll like me even more.
What am I? *(present)*

I'm tall and thin and colorful;
You use me most at night.
I flicker and I glow so nice,
And make your Christmas bright.
What am I? (candle)

I'm everywhere at Christmas,
Sometimes on your tree.
Or if you look into the sky
At night you might see me.
What am I? *(star)*

If you have a fireplace,
You'll see me hanging there.
And after Santa comes to me,
I'm so full I might tear.
What am I? *(stocking)*

When you pick me up,
I make a pretty noise.
I like to shake and jingle
In the hands of girls and boys.
What am I? *(bell)*

by Heather Tekavec

The CHRISTMAS Surprise

"Aw, this won't do!" Jimmy said, throwing down the card he had made. "I want to do something special for Grandma this Christmas."

"Your card is beautiful," said Mom as she picked up the card from the table. "It will be a wonderful surprise for Grandma."

"Mom, it's not good enough," Jimmy moaned.

Mom thought for a moment and said, "We could make her some cookies."

"That would be great!" Jimmy squealed with delight.

When the cookies came out of the oven, Jimmy laid 10 cookies on a large silver tray.

"Grandma will be surprised when I show up with a card and cookies on Christmas Eve!" Jimmy said.

He covered the cookies to keep them warm. Then out the door he flew.

Jimmy had not gone far when he ran into his neighbor Mrs. Allen.

"Hello, Jimmy. Where are you rushing off to on Christmas Eve?" she asked.

"I'm taking some cookies to my grandmother for a surprise," he said.

"Mmmm! They smell so good, and I'm so hungry. I haven't eaten a thing all day," Mrs. Allen said.

"Why don't you take a cookie? I have plenty," Jimmy said, holding out the tray.

Mrs. Allen reached under the towel and took two cookies. "Merry Christmas, Jimmy," she said and rushed along her way.

Jimmy continued on his way, but had not gone far when his friend Bob waved him down.

"Hey, Jimmy, where are you going?" he asked.

"I'm taking some cookies to my grandmother. It's a Christmas surprise," Jimmy said.

"Mmmm! They smell so good," said Bob. "I'm starving! I haven't eaten all day."

"Well . . . I guess I could spare a cookie," Jimmy said, holding out the tray.

Bob reached under the towel and grabbed three cookies. "Thanks Jimmy, you're a good friend," he said as he hurried off down the road.

by Linda Coleman

Jimmy continued along his way, but had not gone far when he ran into Mr. Miller, delivering Christmas baskets from his car.

"Hello, Jimmy. Where are you rushing off to on Christmas Eve?" he asked.

"I'm taking my grandmother some cookies. It's a Christmas surprise," Jimmy said.

"Mmmm, those cookies smell so good," said Mr. Miller, looking very hungry. "I've been so busy delivering baskets, I haven't had time to eat."

"Why don't you take a cookie? It's not much, but it's the best I can do," Jimmy said, holding out the tray.

Mr. Miller reached under the towel and took two cookies, then one more. "Merry Christmas, Jimmy," he said as he continued along his way.

Jimmy turned the corner to his grandmother's house. "Whoa!" Jimmy yelled, stopping just in time. "Sorry, Mrs. Hanson, I didn't see you standing there."

"Merry Christmas, Jimmy. Are you coming to see your grandmother?" she asked.

"Yes, I brought her some cookies. It's a Christmas surprise," he said with a beaming smile.

"Mmmm, they smell so good. My granddaughter promised to visit today. She always brings me freshly baked cookies," she said with a tear in her eye, "but I guess she forgot this year."

"Why don't you take a cookie. I'm sure they will be here soon," Jimmy said, holding out the tray.

Mrs. Hanson reached under the towel and took two cookies. "You're a good boy, Jimmy," she said, going back into her house.

Finally, Jimmy knocked on his grandmother's door. It was decorated with a big red bow she bought from a store.

"Oh, Jimmy, what a wonderful surprise!" she said, giving him a hug.

"I brought you a special Christmas gift." When Jimmy lifted the towel he yelled in surprise, "Oh, no!" He could not believe his eyes, there were . . . (Z E R O) cookies on the tray.

" T h e cookies are all gone!" Jimmy cried as he retold the story to his grandmother. A terrible feeling filled his insides. "I just wanted to give you a special surprise," Jimmy said, lowering his head.

"But, Jimmy," Grandma said with a warm smile, "you gave me a very special surprise." She placed her hand upon his head. "Having you here with me is the best surprise I could ask for."

With that, Jimmy didn't feel so bad anymore.

Discussion Questions
How many cookies were on the tray?
Who took the cookies?
How many cookies did each person take?
Why was Grandma happy even without any cookies?

Activity
Small reading groups can benefit from this story. Visual Aid: Place 10 cookies on a tray and play out the story. Then recall the story.

The Chickadees' Christmas

Merry Chickadee was the smallest member of the Chickadee family. She lived in the wood lot on a large farm with her mother and father and her two brothers. All the chickadees liked to visit the bird feeder on the windowsill of the farmhouse. It had been put there by the owners of the farm so that their little boy, Freddie, could watch the birds who came there, especially in wintertime.

Merry was not daring like her brothers, Cheerie and Chee-dee, who got into mischief quite often. But though she was timid, she was full of curiosity, and one morning, a few days after Christmas, something happened.

Freddie had received a lovely new sled for Christmas and soon had it outdoors to try. He tied a little silver bell on the front so he could listen to it jingle as he slid over the humps and bumps in the snow. Because he was just a little boy and couldn't tie very well, the tiny bell soon fell off. The wind blew it under some rosebushes, and there it lay and sparkled in the sunshine.

Next morning, two pairs of eyes saw the shiny bell. One pair belonged to Princess, Freddie's black cat, who had settled herself in her favorite spot by the back steps. The other pair belonged to Merry Chickadee, who had rested in the bushes for a minute while the rest of the family went on to the feeder.

The instant Merry spied the bright object below her on the ground, she had eyes for nothing else. She just had to get closer for a better look. Nearer and nearer she went, making her way carefully past the sharp thorns on the branches. At last she hopped down right beside it. How pretty it was! She gave it a little peck. *Tinkle*! went the bell. Merry was delighted. She pecked it again. Again the silvery tinkle.

"Dee-dee," sang Merry softly, "I must tell the others about this."

She looked up and there, only a short distance away, yellow eyes gleaming, black tail twitching, was Princess.

by Grace Lee

The big black cat gave a sudden leap. With a terrified chirp, Merry flew up into the bush. She felt a tearing in her wing and a sharp stinging pain. But she was safe! Princess would never try to follow her through the thorny branches; she was much too wise for that. There were much easier ways of getting a meal besides she wasn't very hungry anyway. She turned and walked slowly back to the house.

Mother Chickadee had heard her little one's cry of pain and hurried to her at once. Poor Merry; her wing was hurt badly. She just knew she couldn't fly with it.

Mother Chickadee spoke softly to her, "Don't worry, Merry, we'll all stay close by. You will be perfectly safe here. Your wing will soon heal."

A little later that morning, Freddie came out with his new sled. He too noticed the bell, and went to pick it up. Then he caught sight of Merry, sitting alone in the rosebush. When she did not fly away, he was puzzled and called his mother to come and see. Mother watched a minute or two, then reached out her hand. Merry hopped a little farther away, holding the sore wing close to her body.

"I believe she's been hurt, Freddie," his mother said. "I'm sure she can't fly."

"How will she get any food?" asked the little boy anxiously. "Could we put a feeder out here for her?"

"Well—" Mother looked around the yard.

"I have an idea, Freddie! I'm taking the Christmas tree down soon. We could set it up against the rosebushes, close to where the chickadee is, so that she can hop into it. We can hang some food on it; then she will have all she needs until her wing is strong enough to fly."

Freddie's face lit up with joy at the thought.

"It will be like having two Christmases, one for us and one for the birds."

He caught his mother by the hand and started for the house.

"Let's go in right now and start taking off the ornaments!" By noon the tree was back outdoors, and here and there on the branches were tied small balls of suet mixed with birdseed. It didn't take long for the chickadees to find it and to coax Merry over.

And Freddie, looking out of the back door, thought the tree looked prettier than ever. Looking up at his mother he whispered, "It's got real, live ornaments on it now, hasn't it?"

And Mother, giving him a little hug, agreed.

The Legend of the CHRISTMAS SPIDER

Chop. Chop. Chop. Hundreds of cedar trees were chosen and cut. Like ants marching one by one, the villagers of Hansburg dragged evergreens down Von's Mountain to their homes. Families were excited to decorate their special trees on Christmas Day.

Sun smothered the ground and circled the stumps of wood with rays of light. One towering oak shaded a blotchy patch of earth on the hill.

Oak Tree's branches sagged with shriveled foliage. Crackled brown leaves drifted to the ground.

Spider, Tree's dearest friend, danced from twig to twig on this unusually warm winter day. "Today is Christmas Eve. Why do you look sad, Tree?" he asked."

"I wish that I celebrated Christmas Day like the cut trees in the village. They enjoy gifts and decorated branches," Tree answered.

The tiptoeing spider tickled Tree's trunk and whispered, "I have a gift to share with you."

Spider twiddled his legs like knitting needles and fastened a loop.

"What are you doing?" Tree asked him.

"I'm making your gift," Spider answered, tugging at his flowing sticky thread.

"What will it be?" Tree pleaded excitedly.

"It's a surprise!" Spider maneuvered down the bumpy bark and flitted across a limb. He pranced back and forth, hooking here and tying there.

Moon switched places with Sun. Wind whistled frosty air and swirled leaves around the bare mountain. "Please climb under my bark and let me shelter you from the cold," Tree begged Spider.

Spider pricked his leg in the air and paused. "There will be time for that later. Now I want to make your present."

His crafty feet scurried high into the branches and he continued his tedious work.

Cotton clouds erased Moon and painted Von's Mountain and the village of Hansburg white. Wind snapped a branch off Tree and a twig swished past Spider onto the quilted ground of snow.

Specks of ice formed polka dots on Spider's black outfit while his shivering body continued weaving through the night.

by Kerry Morford Guinn in memory of Charlotte Morford

Tree's radiant glow spread across the land.

People from Hansburg paraded from their homes and stared with wonder. "Look at the sparkling tree on top of Von's Mountain," they gasped.
Tree swayed with delight and said to his friend, "Let's share the beauty of this gift on Christmas Day."

Tree and Spider joyfully lifted the web up into Wind.

Early Christmas morning, Tree had fallen asleep but Spider was too excited to close his eyes. He rested in a protected nook and proudly admired his completed delicate work of art.

Silver pieces of the web gently glided across the village. Showering thin strands floated down to the ground, and the people gathered bits of silver and placed them on their cut Christmas trees.

Snow stopped and the sleepy Spider gazed at the twinkling skies above him. Angels dancing, he thought and he drifted off to sleep.

Spider's love and devotion for Tree helped him find true happiness from the gift of giving.

Falling Star dropped down from heaven and kissed the top of Tree. Shimmering stardust blanketed Spider from the cold, and his web magically turned to brilliant silver.

Many years later the people in the village of Hansburg—and people all around the world—celebrate Spider and Tree's gift. And the legend and custom of hanging tinsel and a spider on the Christmas tree continues.

Sun's glistening rays of light awakened Tree and Spider. He dangled from the shining web and wished aloud, "May my gift to you bring happiness."

Tree marveled at the glittering threads draped through his branches. "Spider, you decorated my branches!" he exclaimed.

Author's Note: This legend was adapted from a story that was given to my mother by her friend many years ago—attached with a gift of tinsel and a spider ornament.

Crafts

Christmas Shape Fairy
Materials
- white construction paper cut-outs for each student:
  two small triangles, 4" x 5" x 5" (10 x 14 x 14 cm)
  1 large triangle, 8" x 8" x 8" (20 x 20 x 20 cm)
  1 round head, 2 inches (5 cm)
- miniature silver garland cut into 3" (7 cm) pieces
- craft glue and glue brush
- markers
- cotton

Directions
1. Have children use markers to draw a face on the fairy head and glue on a little cotton for hair.
2. Demonstrate how to wrap the garland around the head and glue it in place.
3. Have children glue the small triangles together at the back of the large triangle to form the fairy.
4. Glue the head on the top point of the large triangle as shown to complete the fairy.

front view

back view

Button Garland
Materials
- collection of buttons with large fastening holes
- thin, plastic-tipped shoelace

Directions
1. Tie a button, using a double knot to one end of each string.
2. Let children thread the buttons onto the shoelace until it is full of buttons.
3. Help each child tie a double knot on the outside of the last button, leaving a loop so the button string can be hung from a Christmas tree.

by Robynne Eagan

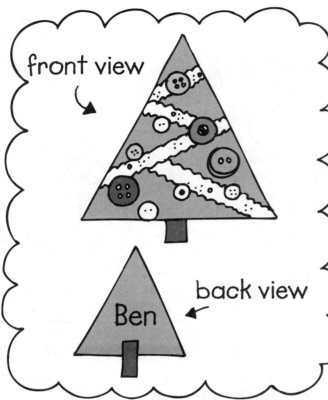

front view

back view

Ben

Button Trees

Craft Glue

Materials
- green tagboard
- brown construction paper
- craft glue
- collection of brightly colored flat buttons
- glitter

Directions
1. Pre-cut one tagboard Christmas tree "body" for each student. (You can cut this on a paper cutter.)
2. Pre-cut a brown tree trunk for each student.
3. Have each child print his or her name on the back of the tree, glue the trunk to the bottom, and then turn the tree over to decorate!
4. Have children paint generous amounts of glue on the tree, place their buttons on it, and sprinkle with glitter.
5. Help children wash glitter from their hands.
6. Leave the trees flat until they are dry.

Place Mat for Santa

Let students prepare the perfect place to leave Santa's snack.

Materials
- seasonal greeting cards
- scissors or pinking shears
- large poster board (rectangles)
- craft glue and glue brush
- hole punch (single or three-hole will work)
- colored yarn
- plastic darning needle

Directions
1. Let each child choose a piece of tagboard and a selection of cards to cut for a collage.
2. Have them paint the back of the cut-outs with glue and stick them to the poster board.
3. When the collage is complete, children should smooth the pieces gently in place.
4. Have each child write his or her name and the year on the back of the poster board.
5. Show children how to use the paper punch to punch holes along the edge of the board.
6. Help each child thread the yarn through a needle, sew around the outside of the mat, and tie the ends.

Try This
Laminate the place mat after step 4 and pre-punch the holes for students.

Kelli 2002

Snowscapes

You can adapt this snowy activity to fit any winter holiday. Add tiny evergreens for Christmas, tiny hearts for Valentine's Day, and so on.

Materials
- 2 cups (500 ml) Ivory Snow™ flakes
- 1 cup (250 ml) water
- found objects from nature or home
- sturdy white paper plates

Directions
1. Pour soap flakes and water into a large bowl and beat them until light and fluffy like snow.
2. Cover a table with newspaper or a vinyl tablecloth.
3. Give each child a white paper plate and a scoop of "snow."
4. Encourage children to cover their plates with snow to make snowscapes.
5. Have children arrange the found objects on the snow. Twigs, pinecones, pine needles, and so on will make a nice scene.
6. Send the snow scenes home as lovely centerpieces for winter celebrations.

Prancing Reindeer

Talk to your class about reindeer. Share stories of flying reindeer. Have they heard these tales?

Materials
- brown paper lunch bags (1 per student)
- 3-inch wide (1 m) wrapping paper tubes (1 per student)
- newspaper
- tape
- craft glue and glue stick
- stapler
- scissors
- markers

Directions
1. Pre-cut or draw the following on construction paper for students to cut out: antlers (brown tagboard), ears (brown construction paper), eyes (black construction paper), round nose (red construction paper).
2. Have students crumple enough newspaper to gently stuff the lunch bags.
3. Help each child fold the ends of a bag together; then staple the ends of the bag to the tube.
4. Have students cut or gather pre-cut antlers, ears, eyes, and a nose from the materials you prepared.
5. Let each child glue antlers to either side of a bag so they stick up.
6. Then have them glue an ear on either side of the head at the place where the antler joins the head.
7. Help each child use the black marker to draw a mouth around the end of the bag.
8. Students can add a little flair by decorating the tube with markers, sparkle glue, and so on.
9. Let students "ride" their reindeer.

Reindeer Habitats

Discuss the climate where reindeer live. Discuss how reindeer are specially adapted for this climate. (They have special fur which protects against cold and is water-proof; they migrate to a "warmer" area in the winter.) Give each child a sheet of blue construction paper and a copy of the reindeer pattern. Have each child color and cut out the reindeer and glue it to the blue construction paper. Have the students show the weather in the picture.

Reindeer Food for People

6 cups Cheerios™
6 cups Chex™ cereal
2 cups peanuts
1 (8 ounce) package m&m's®
1 (6 ounce) bag pretzels
2 (6 ounces) packages white chocolate chips
2 teaspoons vanilla

Melt white chocolate chips on high power in microwave for three minutes, stirring after each minute. Add vanilla and stir. Add the rest of the ingredients and stir until well coated.

My Little 10-Point

His antlers are my handprints.

My footprint is his head.

I added shiny glitter

Because Rudolph's nose is red.

I hope you'll hang this 10-point

Where everyone can see,

Because this reindeer was captured

By no one else but me!

This poem should be copied, cut out, and glued on a piece of construction paper. Brush each student's hands and the sole of one foot with washable tempera. Then place the footprint on the construction paper, making the heel the nose. Place the handprints above the toes as the antlers. After the paint dries, laminate, and glue red glitter on Rudolph's nose!

by Jennifer Crook

by Janet A. Armbrust

Name _____

The Kwanzaa Kinara

During Kwanzaa, candles are placed in a special candle holder called the kinara. There are seven candles used, each representing one of the seven principles of Kwanzaa.

Color your own kinara using the correct colors of candles.

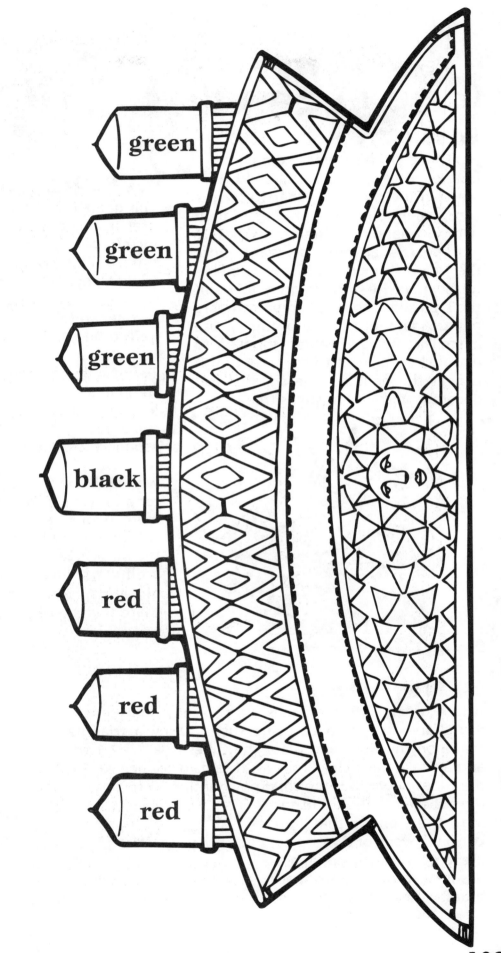

Holiday Games

Puzzle Tree

Here's a chance to recycle old jigsaw puzzle pieces. Give each child 15 pieces. Glue these together to form a tree (triangular shape). Experiment with overlapping different pieces to get the special look you want. Once the tree is formed, let it dry completely. Next, invite the children to paint their puzzle tree with green tempera paint. Again let it dry thoroughly. Use miscellaneous decorating supplies to add flowers or fruit to the tree, or if it is near the holidays, the children can decorate it like a Christmas tree.

A Holiday Gift Surprise

This game is based on the "cake walk" concept. To prepare for this game, you will need several boxes incremental in size (they fit inside each other). Fill the smallest box with candy or small trinket toys. Gift wrap this box and place it inside a bigger box. Wrap each box separately and place them inside each other.

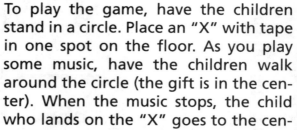

To play the game, have the children stand in a circle. Place an "X" with tape in one spot on the floor. As you play some music, have the children walk around the circle (the gift is in the center). When the music stops, the child who lands on the "X" goes to the center and starts unwrapping the first box. The excitement begins, as the children do not know there will be more gifts inside the first box. Then start the music again and repeat the process. Make sure a different child is chosen each time to unwrap a gift. When you get to the last box, have this child share the "goodies" inside with the group.

Holiday Bowling

Attach green Christmas trees, stars, or any related holiday shapes to 10 toilet tissue tubes. Draw a triangle shape on the floor and place the tubes in a 4-3-2-1 triangle. Have each child roll a soft ball to try and knock the tubes down. Get the children counting by setting up the tubes and also by counting the ones that are knocked over. For a variation, use empty plastic soda bottles instead of the cardboard tubes.

by Tania K. Cowling

140

Reindeer Movement

Discuss the way reindeer are hitched together when pulling Santa's sleigh. They must all move at one time. What would it be like to be attached to a partner and move together? Hold hands with a partner and follow these directions:

- Walk, run, hop, or skip.
- Instead of holding hands, hold a scarf or piece of rope with your partner.
- Move together to music.

Hunting for Gelt

Hide-and-seek is an all-time favorite game for children. This hiding game includes an added sense of holiday excitement when the hidden treasure is Hanukkah gelt (a monetary symbol). Before the game you will need to make numerous pieces of "gelt." Cut out 3" circles from cardboard. Cover these with aluminum foil.

When the students are out of the room, hide the "gelt" in the classroom. When the children return, have them search and collect the "gelt" pieces. Have each child count the gelt he or she found.

A Menorah Relay Race

For this game you will need eight toilet paper rolls and one paper towel roll painted in Hanukkah colors (blue, yellow, gold, white) for each team. Attach construction paper or tissue paper flames to each roll with tape or glue.

To play the game, divide your class into teams of eight. Run the relay two teams at a time. Set up two paper towel rolls several feet apart at the farthest point of your race. Explain to the children that they represent the shamash candle of the menorah. Give each child a toilet paper roll candle. When the race begins, have the children run one by one to place their candles on one side of the shamash; then run back and tag the next team mate for a turn. There should be four candles on either side of the shamash at the end. The first team to complete the menorah correctly wins.

Santa, Santa, Down the Chimney

To the tune of *"Bluebird, Bluebird, Through My Window"*

Santa, Santa, down the chimney,
Santa, Santa, down the chimney,
Santa, Santa, down the chimney,
To bring a special toy!

Have the students stand in a circle with their hands joined and raised in the air. One player is Santa. While the group is singing this verse, Santa weaves around the players in the circle. When the singing stops, Santa stands in front of the child nearest him or her and sings, "What kind of toy do you want?" The child answers, "I want a (kind of toy)." All players then sing "(child's name) wants a (kind of toy)." This child now becomes Santa and the game is repeated.

The Colors of Kwanzaa

The colors red, green, and black are an important part of Kwanzaa. *Red* stands for struggle. *Black* stands for the African American people. *Green* stands for three things, the hills of Africa, the future, and hope. Play this counting and sorting game in the classroom.

Cover and tape red, green, and black construction paper around three containers. Provide students with an assortment of objects in these colors and invite them to place the objects in the matching containers. Count the number of objects together. Sort the objects by size, too (teaching the skills of "big" and "little").

A Kwanzaa Game

During Kwanzaa, candles are place in a kinara (candle holder). Provide seven painted wooden clip clothespins, three red, three green, and one black. Make two sets so two students can play at once (on either side of the box). Use a shoe box to represent the kinara and invite your students to clip the Kwanzaa candles to the side of the box.

Christmas Crafts: A Holiday Craft Book

by Judith Hoffman Corwin
Franklin Watts, 1996

Ring in the holidays with this festive craft book! Activities will spice up the holiday season with such items as Simon Snowman, Gingerbread Bears, Brave Soldier Star, and Christmas Eve Stars. Also included is background information on many Christmas traditions. Other books in this holiday series are *Hanukkah Crafts* and *Kwanzaa Crafts*.

Hanukkah Fun: Crafts and Games

edited by Andrea R. Weiss
Boyds Mills Press, 1992

Welcome Hanukkah with this marvelous array of decorations, crafts, games, cards, and mobiles. Your youngsters will enjoy fun-filled games such as Flip the Latke and Pin the Candle on the Menorah. They can also make gifts such as dreidel note pads, Star-of-David picture frames, and Hanukkah jigsaw puzzles for their families and friends. Many of the craft materials are simple items that you can easily find around the house.

Madeleine's Christmas

by Ludwig Bemelmans
Viking, 1984

'Twas the night before Christmas and no one in the house was stirring except for Madeleine. Since everyone had colds, including Miss Clavel, Madeleine was busy cooking and taking care of the sick "patients." Everything ends well, though, when a rug-selling magician comes to Madeleine's rescue with a simple "Abracadabra." All of the sudden the kitchen is clean and the 12 girls in the house are sent flying home on magic carpets to spend the holidays with their families.

by Mary Ellen Switzer

143

If You Take a Mouse to the Movies
by Laura Numeroff
illustrated by Felicia Bond
Laura Geringer Book, 2000

Ever wonder what would happen if you took a mouse to the movies during the Christmas season? Well of course he would want some popcorn and then perhaps to string it together to decorate the family Christmas tree. But that's only the beginning! This humorous story continues on with a rollicking holiday "chain reaction" you'll never forget!

Disney's Winnie the Pooh's Christmas!
by Bruce Talkington
illustrated by Alvin White Studio
Disney Press, 1991

It's Christmas Eve at Hundred-Acre Wood and Winnie the Pooh has a big problem—seems he's forgotten to get presents for his friends this holiday season. When he turns to Christopher Robin for help, the boy gives the distressed bear some of his old mismatched socks for Christmas stockings. Pooh soon learns that the stockings make perfect holiday gifts for all his delighted friends. The grateful Tigger loves his new sleeping bag, Piglet adores his stocking cap, Rabbit likes his unique carrot cover and Owl really enjoys his new wind sock!

Sergeant Sniff's Christmas Surprise
by Valerie Garfield
HarperFestival, 2000

That super sleuth Sergeant Sniff is back, just in time for a holiday mystery! When Sergeant Sniff gets a Christmas present, she decides to put her detective skills to work to figure out just what's in the festive box by "sniffing" the clues. She compares the smell of items around her house to her mystery present. Follow along with Sergeant Sniff and see if you can help solve the mystery!

Hanukkah!
by Roni Schotter
illustrated by Marylin Hafer
Little, Brown and Co., 1990

Hanukkah! is the perfect read-aloud picture book to introduce youngsters to the customs of this important Jewish holiday. Discover the joy of Hanukkah as a happy family gathers in celebration, engaging in such activities as the lighting of the menorah, making the delicious latkes, and spinning the traditional dreidels. Also included is background information on the history of Hanukkah, as well as a vocabulary list.

144

Toby Belfer Never Had a Christmas Tree

by Gloria Teles Pushker
illustrated by Judith Hierstein
Pelican Publishing Co., 1991

A Jewish girl named Toby living in a small southern town decides to invite all her non-Jewish friends to a Hanukkah party at her house. Her friends enjoy the experience of learning the traditions and customs of this important Jewish holiday, such as the lighting of the menorah. They also feast on her grandmother's delicious potato latkes and play a game called dreidel. The book also provides directions for building a big menorah, rules of the game of dreidel, and Toby's grandmother's recipe for potato latkes.

Seven Candles for Kwanzaa

by Andrea Davis Pinkney
illustrated by Brian Pinkney
Dial Books for Young Readers, 1993

Learn all about the joyous celebration of Kwanzaa, the important African American festival that begins every year on December 26 and lasts until the first of January. The book's beautiful illustrations capture the spirit of this unique holiday as the family gathers every day to light one of the seven candles in the kinara. As each candle is lit, the family discusses the principle and meaning of that particular candle. Finally, on the seventh day of Kwanzaa, the family celebrates the holiday with a delicious feast. To find out more about this special holiday, read *Kwanzaa* by Dorothy Rhodes Freeman and Dianne M. MacMillan (Best Holiday Books, 1992).

Frozen Noses

by Jan Carr
illustrated by Dorothy Donohue
Holiday House, 1999

Brrr! It's the magical season of winter again and time for an "ice-citing" day in the snow. Discover the pleasures of the season as you join a group of children while they play in a snowy wonderland. Whizzing down a hill on sleds and gliding around an icy lake on skates add up to an unforgettable winter adventure for everyone. This charming winter story in rhyme with its bright appealing collage artwork should be at the top of your reading list this season!

145

January

January is the coldest month
Of the entire year!
(Hug self and shiver.)
So bundle up, stay warm, and think—
(Pretend to put on mittens, scarf, hat, etc.)
Spring will soon be here!
(Smile broadly.)

Icicles

Icicles hang from the trees
With a mighty grip.
(Hold hands with fingers spread and pointing down.)
Then the winter sun shines down—
(Form "sun" over your head.)
Drip! Drip! Drip!
(Flick fingers with each "drip.")

Brotherhood

When we love each other
And treat our friends real good,
(Hug a friend.)
When we're nice and helpful,
(Shake hands with a friend and smile.)
That is brotherhood!

Santa Is Coming

Santa will soon be here—I feel it in the air!
(Smile broadly.)
Although you can't see them, his elves are everywhere.
(Look around and point all over.)
They're looking for children who have been very nice.
(Shake index finger knowingly.)
So before you say or do things, you better think twice!
(Tap finger on head and think.)

My Shadow

I have a funny shadow
That does everything I do.
(Make different movements—wave, kick, jump, etc.)
I am only one, of course—
(Show one finger and nod knowingly.)
But it looks like I am two!
(Show two fingers.)

by Judy Wolfman

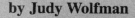

Valentines

Valentines, valentines—
Red, white, and blue.
(Pretend to hand out valentines.)
I'll find a nice one
(Pretend to look through them.)
And give it to you.
(Pretend to give it to a friend.)

Five Little Valentines

Five little valentines were having a race.
(Hold up five fingers.)
The first valentine was covered with lace.
(Wiggle one finger.)
The second valentine had a funny face.
(Wiggle second finger.)
The third valentine looked quite blue.
(Wiggle third finger.)
The fourth valentine said, "I love you."
(Wiggle fourth finger.)
The fifth valentine was sly as a fox—
(Wiggle fifth finger.)
He ran the fastest to the valentine box.

A Healthy Heart

When you run and play and jump,
(Run and jump in place.)
Your heart will really start to pump.
(Put hand over heart and beat chest.)
That makes the blood inside you flow
(Trace veins and arteries down arm with finger.)
So you can think and work and grow.
(Tap head with finger and rise up on tip-toe.)

Signs of a Cold Winter

I hear wind whistle in the chimney.
  (Cup hand to ear and listen.)
I feel snow in the air.
  (Shiver and hug self.)
I see frost on the windowpane.
  (Pretend to wipe frost from the window.)
There's cold everywhere!
  (Shiver, blow into hands, rub hands rapidly together.)

Slide Down the Hill

See this great big hill?
  (Extend arm out straight.)
It has snow all over the side.
  (Use other hand to indicate snow on the hill.)
Let's get on our sleds
  (Place hand at the top of the extended arm.)
And down the hill we'll slide.
  (Rapidly slide hand down the arm.)

My Dreidel

Mother and I went out to shop
  (Look around as if shopping.)
For a dreidel—a Hanukkah top.
  (Sit on floor.)
I'll make it spin and when it stops,
  (Spin around on your bottom.)
It will fall over, and then drop.
  (Lean to one side, then drop.)

Hanukkah

It's time to light the candles
  (Pretend to light candles.)
Now that Hanukkah is here.
Then we'll enjoy some latkes
  (Pretend to eat.)
At this special time of year.

Story Time

Your youngsters' hearts will pitter-patter with delight when they hear these sensational seasonal read-aloud favorites.

New Year Books

Welcome a brand-new year with these exciting holiday books.

New Year's Day (True Books)
by Dana Meachen Rau
Children's Press, 2000

Did you know that in Greece, children sometimes go door to door serenading people with songs to wish them a good year? Find out some fascinating facts about the customs and history of New Year celebrations all over the world. Award-winning author Dana Meachen Rau takes us on an interesting worldwide journey to discover the many different ways people ring in the New Year. The book's vibrant, colorful photographs bring each celebration to life. Also included is a vocabulary list of important words pertaining to the holiday, along with a list of books and web sites on the subject.

Friendship Stories You Can Share
Reading Rainbow Readers
SeaStar Books, 2001

Friendship Stories You Can Share features selections from popular children's books, such as *Days with Frog and Toad* and *Mr. Putter and Tabby*. Also included in this collection are selections from well-known books by James Marshall, Charlotte Zolotow, and Joanne Rocklin.

by Mary Ellen Switzer

The Dancing Dragon
by Marcia Vaughan
illustrated by Stanley Wong Hoo Foon
Mondo Publishing, 1996

Gung hay fat choy! The Chinese New Year is here! Celebrate the holiday with this delightful rhyming story. The bright colorful illustrations in this appealing accordion book capture the excitement of the customs of this important Chinese celebration.

Snow Shapes
A Read-and-Do Book
by Judith Moffatt
Scholastic, 2000

Winter is here! Join Minky and his friend Mouse as they enjoy a day playing in the snow. The two friends will also give instructions on how to make seasonal paper crafts which will bring a touch of winter to your classroom. Some of the crafts include a snowflake, a snowman, and a holiday flower.

This Next New Year
by Janet S. Wong
illustrated by Yangsook Choi
Frances Foster Books, 2000

A child recounts what the Chinese New Year means to him and his friends in this beautifully illustrated book. The boy tells about some of the special traditions of the holiday, as well as his hopes and dreams for a fresh start as the New Year approaches.

Teacher's Book Shelf

Abracadabra! Bring some magical moments to your classroom with the "enchanting" ideas in Better Homes and Gardens *Make Believe* (Meredith Corporation, 1989). Meet Max, a delightful dragon, who will introduce your youngsters to a variety of arts and crafts projects, all with a make-believe theme. Have your budding artists build their own shoe box castle fit for a king or make a cozy gingerbread house. Let your little kings and queens create their own royal crowns or jester hats. Playing "make-believe" has never been such fun!

Don't throw away those shopping bags! *Look What You Can Make with Paper Bags,* edited by Judy Burke (Boyds Mills Press, 1999) features over 90 crafts and other ideas for transforming ordinary bags into magnificent decorations, gifts, games, puppets, toys, masks, and costumes. The book's easy-to-follow directions and colorful illustrations make craft time lots of fun! Other books in the series include *Look What You Can Make with Boxes* and *Look What You Can Make with Paper Plates.*

150

A Tree Full of Friends
Read & Do Storybook Series

contributing writer Jane Stanley
Better Homes and Gardens, 1990

This charming story of friendship is a perfect book to share with your youngsters on Valentine's Day. When Max the Dragon and his sister Marci move to a new neighborhood, they soon find a "friendship tree" right in their own backyard. Much to their delight, the neighborhood children have made the willow tree into a clubhouse and the two newcomers soon join in the fun. Soon they discover that with a little imagination, the willow tree can be transformed into a magical playground.

Also included in the book are some fun projects to enhance the story. Easy-to follow directions show how to create a friendship chain and a picture frame house, topped off with a recipe for tasty cinnamon popcorn.

Biscuit's Valentine's Day

by Alyssa Satin Capucilli
illustrated by Pat Schories
HarperFestival, 2001

Join Biscuit and a little girl as they enjoy a lively walk one snowy Valentine's Day to deliver valentines to special friends. When the two arrive back home, they find a valentine surprise in their mailbox! This charming story will get everyone in the mood for Valentine's Day.

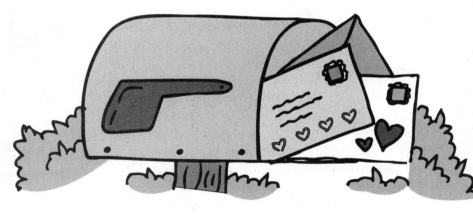

Sergeant Sniff's Secret Valentine Mystery

by Valerie Garfield
HarperFestival, 2001

Calling all detectives! Sergeant Sniff has a valentine mystery to solve. It seems that someone has been sending her some valentine presents—a bouquet of roses, a special sandwich, and a tasty box of candy. Can you help her find the secret admirer?

Arthur's First Kiss

by Marc Brown
Random House, 2001

Uh oh! Parties are supposed to be fun, but Arthur isn't so sure about this one! It seems that Francine plans to kiss Arthur at Muffy's party. As far as Arthur is concerned, he'd rather kiss a frog. He is certainly not looking forward to the party. Luckily, this story has a happy ending when Arthur's sister, D.W., and his dog, Pal, come to the rescue to "save" Arthur from Francine's kiss.

151

Countdown to Midnight

Count down to midnight.
Five, four, three, two, one . . .
So bang that drum.
Toot the horn.
Pop the popper.
The New Year has come.

Count down to midnight—five, four, three, two, one. Happy New Year! Toot your horn. Pop a popper. Beat the drum. Make all the noise you want. Why? Because it's a brand-new year and that's how we celebrate.

On New Year's Eve, December 31st, we wait for midnight. That's when the first day of the calendar year, January 1st begins—the new year.

Not all countries or cultures celebrate New Year's Day at the same time. People in different parts of the world use different calendars, and for them the New Year begins on different days.

The New Year is a special holiday for many people. It gives them a chance to say "good-bye" to the old year and "hello" to the New Year.

People all over the world celebrate the start of a New Year. But they celebrate it in many different ways.

In Japan, people start laughing when the New Year begins. They believe this will bring them luck in the year to come.

In China, people believe there are evil spirits around at New Year. They set off firecrackers to scare the spirits away.

Out with the old—in with the new. That's what people in Scotland believe. They light barrels of tar on fire and roll them through the streets to burn up the old year to make way for the New Year to arrive.

In Greece, children leave their shoes out by the fire on New Year's Day. They believe Saint Basil will come and fill the shoes with gifts.

by Nancy Vaughn

152

In Iran, Muslims celebrate by planting wheat or barley in a little dish a few weeks before New Year's. By the time the New Year begins, the plants have started to sprout. This reminds them of spring and the New Year of life ahead.

In Brazil, most people wear white clothes on New Year's Eve. They believe this will bring them good luck in the New Year. If they are near the beach, they jump seven waves and throw flowers in the ocean to bring them even more luck.

In Colombia, people make stuffed dolls and put things inside that have made them sad the past year. Then the "Mr. Old Year" dolls are burned along with the bad memories.

The New Year is a holy time called Rosh Hashanah for Jewish people. They think about what they have done wrong in the past and promise to do better in the future.

Just like each morning is the beginning of a brand-new day, the New Year is the beginning of a brand-new year. So on December 31st, fasten your seat belts. Start the countdown and get ready to blast off. There's a New Year just up ahead!

New Year Noisemaker

Materials
2 aluminum pie pans that are the same size
construction paper
2 pieces of thick yarn
transparent tape

Directions
1. Lay the pans on a table with the bottom sides facing up.
2. Have an adult poke two small holes in the center of each pan about 2" apart.
3. Cut out designs from construction paper and tape them on the bottom of each pan.
4. Push the ends of one piece of yarn through the holes in one pan to make a holder. Make sure to leave a big enough loop for your hand to fit through.
5. Turn the pan over and tie big knots at the ends of the yarn so it can't slip through the holes. (You may need an adult to help you.)
6. Then make a holder for the second pan in the same way.
7. Put your hands in the holders. Crash the edges of the pans together with a brushing motion. Now you're ready to welcome the New Year.

Martin Luther King, Jr. Day

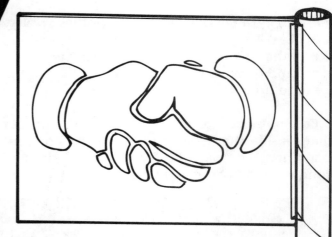

Materials
- pattern on page 155
- paper towel tube or cardboard handle
- tape or glue
- crayons, colored pencils, or watercolors

Directions
Color the pattern page, then tape or glue the paper towel tube (or cardboard handle) to the side to make a flag. Discuss what the two hands joined together symbolize.

Everyone Is Very Special
To the tune of "Jesus Loves the Little Children"

Everyone is very special, everybody in the world—
Red and yellow, black and white,
Everyone has equal rights.
Everyone is very special in this world.

Activity
Dr. Martin Luther King, Jr. was a great African American leader. Many Americans supported his idea that all people should be treated fairly. Dr. King preached that violence was wrong and that people needed to learn to live together peacefully.

Read any of the books listed to familiarize children with Dr. King. Most of the books mention Dr. King's famous "I have a dream" speech. Ask the children what dreams or hopes they might have for making people happy or for making the world a better place. Discuss these dreams and have children draw pictures of them.

Books
My Dream of Martin Luther King by Faith Ringgold, Dragonfly, 1998.
Martin Luther King by Rosemary Bray, Mulberry Books, 1987.

by Dyan Beller

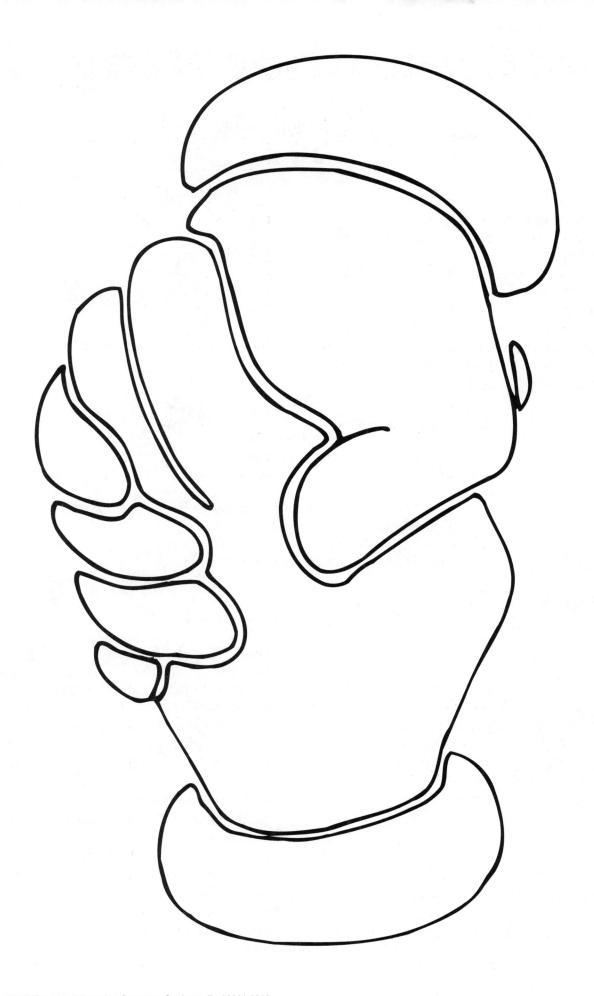

Groundhog Day

Color the picture. Draw a sun if you think the groundhog will see his shadow. Draw clouds if you think he will not see his shadow.

by Janet A. Armbrust

Groundhogs

Three groundhogs
come out to play,
(Hold up three fingers.)
See their shadows
and run away.
(Pretend to run.)

Two groundhogs
come out to play,
(Hold up two fingers.)
See it's raining
and do not stay.
(Put hands over head.)

One groundhog
comes out to play.
(Hold up one finger.)
"Winter's over!"
he shouts, Hooray!
(Raise fist above head.)

by Elizabeth Giles

Celebrating International
Chocolate Lovers' Month

February is International Chocolate Lovers' Month, a month that your students will enjoy celebrating. Use the following ideas to incorporate chocolate into your everyday curriculum.

As with any activity involving edibles, please consider the size of food items brought into the classroom and the risk of choking, as well as any food allergies or dietary restrictions your children may have.

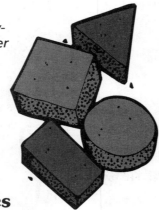

Chocolate Shapes

Bring chocolate to class in a variety of shapes: circles, squares, rectangles, and tri- angles. (Bake chocolate brownies, then cut them into the four shapes.) Ask children to identify the shapes. Then make the challenge a bit more difficult by changing some of the shapes as your students watch. Cut the square in half to form two rectangles, cut the rectangle in half to form two squares, and cut the triangle in half to form two triangles. Can children identify the new shapes? When the shape identification and discussion is done, ask each child his or her favorite shape. Let each child have one of those chocolate shapes for a little snack.

Where Chocolate Comes From

Explain to children that chocolate is made from the seeds of the cacao bean that grows on trees in South America. Show them on a world map where South America is. Then point out where they live and let them see the distance that has to be crossed for them to have chocolate to eat.

by Mary Tucker

Charting Chocolate

Mount a large sheet of poster board on the wall. Print across the top of it the caption, *Chocolate Makes It Better.* Ask children to share their favorite ways to eat chocolate (candy, cake, pie, pudding, milk, hot chocolate, and so on). As they mention ways to eat chocolate, print their ideas across the top of the poster board in columns. When the top line is filled, skip halfway down the chart and continue the listing. Then hand out old magazines for children to look through. Challenge them to find pictures of the different foods on the chart, cut them out, and glue them in the appropriate columns on the chart.

The Taste of Chocolate

Explain that the chocolate we are used to eating is not pure chocolate. Other ingredients are mixed with it to make it taste good. Provide a tiny taste of bitter, unsweetened chocolate for each child to taste. Ask them what it needs to make it taste good. Most will realize that it needs sugar. Then hold up a chocolate bar wrapper and read the list of ingredients aloud. Ask students why chocolate is not a food we should eat a lot of. If they need help, talk about the dangers of eating too much sugar.

Edible Artwork

Give each student a graham cracker and a plastic knife or a craft stick. Provide canned vanilla and chocolate frosting as well as mini chocolate chips, chocolate sprinkles, and broken-up pieces of chocolate. Let children frost the graham crackers and add whatever chocolate decorations they want. Explain that their chocolate creations will be given to school helpers (lunchroom cooks, janitor, principal, librarian, and so on) to show appreciation for their hard work. (Before this activity, arrange for the school helpers to come by for their treats at a certain time.) Encourage each child to do his or her best to make a beautiful, tasty treat. Then let children make smaller chocolate treats for themselves (perhaps half a graham cracker for each one).

Counting and Categorizing Chocolates

Give each child a small plastic bag with 15 m&m's™ in it for the following activities.

Have each child guess how many candies are in the bag. Then have them take the candies out and count them. Ask children to sort the candies and line them up by color. Which color does each child have the most of?

Have children divide the candies into three equal groups. Then five groups. Let each child eat three candies, guess how many are left, then count them to be sure.

Ask children to divide the remaining candies in half. Then let the children eat the candies.

A Rhyme About Chocolate

Read children this rhyme about chocolate throughout the year. Have them fill in the missing words.

In January when the weather's so cold,
A cup of hot chocolate is what I _____ (hold).
February is a wonderful time
To get a chocolate _____ (valentine).
In April it's my parents' habit
For Easter to give me a chocolate _____ (rabbit).
On the Fourth of July my mom likes to bake
A great big, yummy chocolate _____ (cake).
In October, Halloween is handy
For trick-or-treating for chocolate _____ (candy).
In December I know that there will be
Chocolates under my Christmas _____ (tree).

Keep on Smiling

Use these activities to emphasize good dental habits during Dental Health Month in February. To provide some background information, invite a dentist, dental hygienist, or oral surgeon to talk to your class about having healthy teeth and a beautiful smile.

This Is the Way We Brush and Floss
Activity Play

Place a Styrofoam™ egg carton on the table with the bumps up. Sprinkle the carton with baking soda and invite children to brush the "teeth" clean with a toothbrush. Also, let them use a length of yarn (or floss) like dental floss to get in between the teeth, making sure they get clean.

Cleaning Teeth
Activity Play

Cut a large tooth from white construction paper and laminate. Using dry-erase markers, mark the tooth with lines to represent stains on the tooth. Let children use toothbrushes to remove the stains.

Good Foods and Bad
Science

Cut pictures of different kinds of food from magazines. Show these pictures to the children. As you talk about each food, decide whether it is good or bad for your teeth. Have each student place (tape) a picture on a chart that is divided in half with *Good* on one side and *Bad* on the other.

Sing a Song of Healthy Teeth
Music

To the tune of "Here We Go 'Round the Mulberry Bush"

This is the way we brush our teeth, brush our teeth, brush our teeth.
This is the way we brush our teeth so early in the morning.
Brush 'em up and brush 'em down, in little circles 'round and 'round.
So brush your teeth every day and show your pretty smile!

by Tania K. Cowling

Playdough and Teeth
Art

Make a batch of homemade baker's clay and tint it pink with a drop or two of red food coloring. Have the children form a "U" shape with the dough. This is the gum line. Show them how to press white navy beans into the dough to represent teeth.

Baker's Clay Teeth

4 cups flour   1 cup salt   ½ cup water

Mix the flour, salt, and water. Knead until smooth, adding extra water if the mixture is too stiff. Shape the clay and add the beans. Place these figures on a piece of foil and then on a cookie sheet. Bake at 300°F for about one hour. (This can be done at home that evening.)

Dental Floss Painting
Art

Have the children dip a strip of dental floss into tempera paint and then lay it on a sheet of paper, leaving the end of the floss sticking out over the edge of the paper. Do this same procedure with several strips of various colors. Tell children to fold the paper in half and pull out the floss. When they open the paper, they'll see a unique picture.

Losing Teeth
Teacher Resource

This is the age when children lose their baby teeth. Make this poster to honor each child that loses a tooth (that day or the night before). Cut a large tooth shape from white poster board and laminate. Hang this in the classroom. When a child brings news of a lost tooth, write his or her name on the tooth with an erasable marker. This child should be recognized and given a special treat. A new child's toothbrush would make an excellent gift, or you can create a gift box filled with stickers, pencils, rings, and trinkets from which the child may choose. When the day is over, erase the child's name and keep the tooth poster ready for the next event.

A Smiling Snack
Snack

Give each child two apple wedges, peanut butter, and six mini marshmallows. Invite them to spread the peanut butter on each apple wedge; then put marshmallows in a row on one slice. After they place the other wedge on top, they'll have a "toothy smile" to eat and enjoy!

Tooth Holder

During Dental Health Month this February, let students make their own tooth holders to keep any teeth they lose. Maybe they'll want to put them under the pillow for the Tooth Fairy to find and leave them a reward!

Tooth
Holder

Materials
- white felt
- scissors
- glue
- crayons or markers
- clip art pattern and tooth pattern

Directions
1. Have children trace around the tooth pattern on white felt to make two teeth exactly alike.
2. Have them cut out the two felt teeth and glue them together along the edges, leaving the top open.
3. Copy the "tooth holder" clip art onto plain paper. Have children write their name in the banner, color, and cut out. Glue it to the front of the felt tooth holder.
4. Children may take their tooth holders home to use.

by Christine Fischer

162

Healthy Heart

Lub-dub, lub-dub.
Inside my chest
My heartbeat-beats without a rest.

Thump-thump, thump-thump.
I play outside.
I run, skip, jump, and exercise.

Lub-dub, lub-dub.
I eat good food;
My heartbeat-beats,
Thank you! Thank you!

by Heidi Roemer

163

Grandmom's Valentine

Jenny and Jesse sat happily at the kitchen table, addressing valentines.

"One more and I'll be done," said Jenny, picking out another card.

"I've got two more," said Jesse. "Then I'm going to recheck my list."

"Good idea." Jenny started looking over her list. "Oh, no!" she cried. "I don't have a card for Grandmom. I was going to use my allowance to buy her a really fancy one. How did I ever forget?" Jenny put her elbows on the table and ground her fists into her cheeks. Her happy look had vanished. "What am I going to do?" she asked despairingly.

"Make her one," suggested Jesse.

"Oh, sure," replied Janet. "What can I make before tomorrow morning?"

"You could print one out on your computer," said Jesse. "That would be cool."

"That would be boring," snapped Jenny. "Don't you know anything? Special valentines are supposed to have lacy paper, red ribbons, cupids, hearts, and pretty flowers. I don't have any of that stuff." Tears of frustration threatened to spill from her eyes.

"It's okay, Jen," said Jesse soberly. "Grandmom will understand. She won't feel bad if you just tell her you forgot."

"But I'll feel bad," declared Jenny.

"Why don't you just sign your name with mine on the card I got her? The card can be from both of us." Jesse was pleased with his solution to the problem.

"No," blurted Jenny. "That idea stinks."

Jesse rested his chin in his hand for a long minute. Finally he said thoughtfully, "Doesn't Mom have heart-shaped cake pans somewhere?"

"Yes, I think so."

"Well, you know how much Grandmom likes cake, and she never bakes one for herself. You could make her a heart-shaped cake, if we can find the pans."

"That's a great idea, Jesse!" exclaimed Jenny. "Sometimes you absolutely amaze me. Go ask Mom if it's okay. I'll hunt for the cake pans."

by Jean K. Hunger

TLC10339 Copyright © Teaching & Learning Company, Carthage, IL 62321-0010

Jesse rushed off to find Mom. By the time he got back, Jenny had found the pans and a box of cake mix.

"Mom said it's okay," reported Jesse, "as long as you're careful and don't leave a mess in the kitchen."

Jenny got out the mixer. "You can help, Jesse. The cake can be from both of us."

"Okay," he said, "but I get to lick the bowl."

Soon the kitchen was humming with activity. The mixer buzzed and spoons clattered. When the batter was ready to bake, Jenny slid the cake pans into the oven. Jesse was busy scraping the last bit of batter out of the mixing bowl and licking it off the spoon.

"Yummy," he said. "Why don't you just give Grandmom a jar of batter? It tastes great."

"You're crazy," said Jenny, smiling. "Come on, help me get this stuff cleaned up."

Jenny and Jesse washed and put away the mixer, bowls, spoons, and measuring cups. Mom came home from the neighbors' just as the timer on the oven buzzed. She tested the cake to make sure it was done, then took it out of the oven. "It smells delicious," she said.

Jenny turned the layers out of the pans, then left them upside down on the cake rack to cool. In the meantime, she made the fluffy white frosting Mom had taught her to make. When the cake layers had cooled, she put one on a cake plate and spread on the frosting. Then she set the second layer in place and spread the frosting over the top and sides. Jesse waited, spoon in hand, ready to scrape the sides.

"That looks perfect," Mom said. "Now, let's see what I can find to decorate it." She searched through the spice cabinet and found red sugar and a little bottle of red cinnamon candies. "Do you want to use these?"

"Oh, yes," cried Jenny. "They're perfect!" Carefully, she outlined the cake with the cinnamon candies

and finished it with a sprinkling of red sugar. She turned to Mom and said, "What do you think?"

"I think your Grandmom's going to be surprised and happy," said Mom. "We'll take it to her right after school tomorrow."

Jenny's eyes glowed with pride.

The next afternoon, Jenny and Jesse hurried home from school, eager to deliver Grandmom's surprise.

"Get the cake, Jenny," said Mom, "and you and Jesse wait in the car. I'll be right out. I've got to get my coat and keys."

Jenny picked up the cake carefully and headed for the car, moving as if she were on a balance beam. She hardly dared to breathe. Jesse was following close behind. As they got to the car, he reached across Jenny for the door handle, and his hand slipped. Then he lost his balance. Before Jenny realized what was happening, Jesse's hand had come down SPLAT, right in the middle of the cake!

Jenny stood frozen in horror. Jesse stared stupidly at his hand, which was coated with white frosting and red sugar. Suddenly, reality struck.

Tears swam in Jenny's eyes. "You wrecked it! It's ruined!" she screamed.

Jesse felt terrible. "I'm sorry, Jenny. I didn't mean to wreck it."

165

Mom came running out to the car. "What happened? What's the matter?"

"EVERYTHING," wailed Jenny. "My beautiful cake is ruined!"

"I didn't mean to wreck it," repeated Jesse miserably.

"Don't worry," said Mom. "We'll fix it."

"It won't be the same," wept Jenny. "It's hopeless."

"We'll see." Mom took the cake out of Jenny's hands. "Come back into the kitchen with me." Quickly she found a spreading knife, dipped it in hot water and handed it to Jenny. "Now, calm down and swirl the frosting into little peaks."

Jenny stopped crying and swirled the frosting.

"Doesn't that look pretty?" asked Mom when Jenny was finished.

"I think it looks better than it did before," said Jesse.

Grandmom certainly liked it when Jenny proudly presented it to her. "My word," she said. "This is the most beautiful valentine I have ever received. Thank you, Jenny. And thank you, too, Jesse. Did you give your sister a hand with the baking?"

"He sure did Grandmom," spoke up Jenny. "Jesse gave me a BIG hand with this cake."

Two spots of color flared in Jesse's cheeks as he licked a last grain of red sugar from his thumb.

Optional Follow-Up Activities

1. Provide students with a heart outline. Have them decorate their own valentine "cake." Then have students cut out the hearts for classroom display or as valentine gifts for someone special.

2. Give each student a heart-shaped cookie to frost and decorate. Provide two or three kinds of frosting, a variety of candies such as red hots, and decorative sprinkles. You'll also need dull knives or craft sticks for spreading the frosting and some washcloths or wet wipes for cleaning up.

3. Students may also create a gift of love for the birds. Provide a cardboard heart with a small hole cut in the top for hanging. Have students smear both sides of the heart with peanut butter, which they then press into a shallow pan of birdseed to create "cakes" for their feathered friends. They can take the treats home to hang from tree branches, or the treats can be used to decorate a tree in the school yard.

Blooming Hearts Craft

Materials (for each)
- four 6" green chenille stems
- green, pink, and red construction paper
- one 2¼" diameter paper cup
- 2" diameter plastic foam ball
- hole punch
- pinking shears
- serrated knife

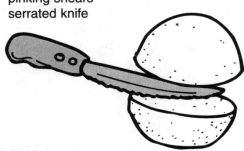

Directions

1. Using a serrated knife, cut a foam ball in half. Wedge one of the halves, rounded side up, into the bottom of the cup.

2. Using pinking shears, cut four small red hearts (each measuring about 1" across), four larger pink hearts (about 2" across), and four green leaves (about 2½" long) from construction paper.

3. Center one red heart on top of one pink heart. Using the hole punch, make two holes in both hearts at once. One hole should be directly above the other.

4. Repeat step 3 for the remaining three sets of hearts.

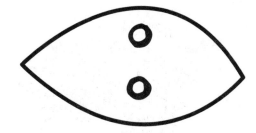

5. Using the hole punch, make two holes in each green leaf. One hole should be above the other.

6. Assemble each flower by threading a green chenille stem (from the back) through the bottom hole of each pair of hearts, then through the top hole. Fold about ½" of the chenille stem down in the back to hold the hearts together.

7. Thread the bloom of each chenille stem through a leaf and slide the leaf up into position on the stem.

8. Push each stem into the foam ball until it is secure, arranging the flowers in a pretty bouquet.

Optional: The cups may be decorated using markers, construction paper, ribbon, and so on.

by Karen S. Hopkins

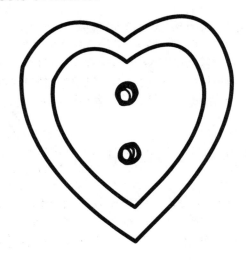

Valentines for Sarah C.

Sarah clutched her backpack. "This is going to be the worst day of my life," she thought. Sarah took a deep breath and entered the classroom.

"Hello, Sarah," said Mrs. Martin. "I've been waiting for you. Today is going to be a very special day." Mrs. Martin showed Sarah her seat at a round table with three other children. There was Jan, Sam, and Sarah K.

"Hi, Sarah C. I'm Sarah K. We have the same first name," said Sarah K.

The day was not much different from a day at her old school. But this was not just any day, it was Valentine's Day. There was sure to be a party with valentine cards given out. Everyone would have valentines except for Sarah C.

"OK, children, time to put your things away. We must get ready for the party," said Mrs. Martin.

Sarah decorated a heart-shaped cookie with red candies and sprinkles. She played a valentine game with her new friends. Sarah was having a wonderful time, until . . .

At the end of the party, Mrs. Martin started letting the children get their valentine boxes filled with cards and candy. "Please take your seats quietly and wait," she said.

"Everyone has a box but me," Sarah thought sadly. "This is the worst day of my life."

Mrs. Martin leaned over Sarah and placed a box decorated with red hearts in front of her. On the side of the box was written *Valentines for Sarah C.* "Happy Valentine's Day, Sarah," she said. "We made this box for you and filled it with valentines. We wanted you to know how glad we are to have you in our class."

"Thank you," Sarah said with a smile. She took a deep breath and opened her box of valentines. "This has to be the best day of my life," thought Sarah C.

by Linda Coleman

Name _____

Valentine's Day Consonant Match

Match the Valentine's Day present with the letter it begins with.

G

F

R

C

H

M

Numbered Valentines

Beginning with number 1, draw a line to connect the
hearts in numerical order. Color the hearts when you are done.

Name _____

Picture Me as President

In the box below, draw a
picture of something you would
do if you were President.

171

Name _____

Chinese New Year

Celebrate Chinese New Year by making your very own dragon. Color each piece and then glue together.

by Janet A. Armbrust

by Janet A. Armbrust

Holiday newsletter

A Family Take-Home

This holiday season, help your child learn the meaning of the words *gratitude* and *giving* by reaching out to those who are less fortunate. As a family, you can: 1. Volunteer your services at a local soup kitchen; 2. Work to collect food, warm clothing, and blankets for a homeless shelter; 3. Surprise home-bound neighbors with baked goods or simple services such as raking autumn leaves or shoveling winter snow; 4. Invite someone who lives alone to join your family celebration; 5. Collect and wrap new toys for a nearby children's home or other group in need. Reaching out to others during the holiday season reminds us of how grateful we should be for what we have and allows us to experience the joy of giving.

Simple Science

Many holiday celebrations during the winter months revolve around family gatherings and food preparation. Since preparing foods requires constant clean-up, a simple at-home science lesson for this season could be to investigate the absorbing powers of various types of kitchen materials. Help your child collect pieces of wax paper, plastic wrap, aluminum foil, and paper towel, along with a dishcloth, a coffee filter, a sponge, and a dish towel. Have your child name each item; then arrange them on a table or countertop. Provide small amounts of cooking oil and water in separate containers and teaspoons or medicine droppers. First observe what is similar/different about the oil and water. Let your child drip both oil and water onto each item in the kitchen collection and note what happens. Which material would best clean spills? Which materials would not work?

On the Move

Just how long is one minute? Help your child find out with this indoor basketball game. You will need a large basket, several socks in seasonal colors, and a watch or clock with a second hand. Set the basket on the floor, roll each sock into a ball, and determine a standing line for tossing. Now challenge your child to see how many sock balls he or she can toss into the basket in one minute. You might also make this a family game and keep score.

Creative Kitchen

Invite your child to help prepare a festive pudding dessert as a sweet treat to add to any holiday celebration. You will need 2 three-oz. packages instant banana pudding, 1 qt. milk, 1½ c. seedless green grapes, 1 six-oz. jar maraschino cherries, and yellow food coloring. Prepare the pudding as directed on the package, stir in a few drops of food coloring, and set aside. Next, cut the grapes and cherries into small pieces and add them to the pudding. Mix well and refrigerate until firm. Serve in individual pudding cups topped with whipped cream.

by Marie E. Cecchini

Communication Station

Turn the fronts of greeting cards into a language experience for your youngster. First, remove the front panels from several greeting cards. Leave each as one piece or cut out the parts you would like to use. Glue these at the top of a sheet of construction paper. Let your child make up a story about the chosen pictures for you to write below. Prompt him or her to use descriptive and action words to embellish the story. Encourage the use of complete sentences.

Poetry in Motion

Create a family songbook by challenging each family member to write new words to sing to a familiar tune. For example, sing these words to the tune of "Frere Jaques."

Happy Kwanzaa, Happy Kwanzaa,
Hear the call, hear the call.
Love and kindness to you, love and kindness to you,
One and all, one and all.

Compile your new songs into a book. Make singing these songs a part of your family holiday tradition.

From the Art Cart

Greeting cards can be recycled into art projects. Project 1: Remove the picture from the front of a card, glue it to a piece of cardboard, cover it with waxed paper and a heavy book, and allow the glue to dry. When it is dry, turn the picture over and draw puzzle piece lines on the cardboard. Cut along the lines to make the puzzle. Puzzle pieces can be stored in an envelope or a self-sealing plastic bag. Project 2: Cut people and animal shapes from appropriate card fronts. Tape each to the top of a craft stick to make a puppet. Create a storyline and have a puppet show.

Mathworks

Create a listening and counting game using small gift boxes and household odds and ends. Into each box place a specific number of small items, such as dry beans, buttons, holiday candies, paper clips, or beads. Close each box with a rubber band to secure it. Then shake each box while your child listens. Challenge your child to name what the box contains, and then to estimate how many of these items are in the box. Open the box to see what it holds; then count how many items there are to compare the guesses with the actual results. To avoid confusion, work with only one box at a time.

The Reading Room

Make time to relax and read with your child this holiday season. Check to see if your local library carries any of the following titles:

Gingerbread Baby by Jan Brett, G.P. Putnam's Sons, 1999.

Hedgie's Surprise by Jan Brett, G.P. Putnam's Sons, 2000.

Mother Hubbard's Christmas, retold and illustrated by John O'Brien, Boyds Mills Press, 1999.

Thanksgiving Treat by Catherine Stock, Bradbury Press, 1999.

Holiday newsletter

Welcome the new year by spending some time outdoors enjoying the fresh, crisp air. Take a walk around your neighborhood or a local park. Collect interesting bits of nature for making a collage or pinecones to turn into a wreath. Decorate an evergreen tree or bush with pieces of stale bread, bagel, or dough-nuts to feed the birds, or use birdseed to write a special new year message in the snow or on the grass. Pretend you are Punxsutawney Phil on Groundhog Day and settle into your own little "den" somewhere in your yard. Choose a person to be "it." On a special signal, all groundhogs must leave their dens to run around the yard. "It" will chase and try to step on someone's shadow. That person then becomes "It" and the game begins again. Use your imagination to enjoy together-time outdoors. Then come in for some hot cocoa, snuggle under a throw, and share a good book.

Simple Science

The pleasure of sharing a storybook with your child can be extended when you use the book as a starting point for additional activities. This winter, share the all-time favorite *The Snowy Day* by Ezra Jack Keats with your child. Talk about how the main character, Peter, dresses for his day in the snow and why. After you finish reading the book, review Peter's sequence of activities for the day. Now bring the story to life. Dress as Peter did, then go outside and try to duplicate his snowy day activities. Can you remember everything Peter did? Do you think you had as much fun as he did?

On the Move

Active play not only provides exercise, but also helps children develop control over their young, growing bodies. You can help by providing your child with time and opportunities to be physically active. This season, use materials you have on hand to create outdoor games for winter fun. For a snowball or pinecone toss, tie or staple evergreen branches to a plastic or cardboard ring to make a wreath. Suspend this wreath from a tree branch and take turns tossing the balls or cones through the center. If you have snow on the ground, divide family members into teams for a snowball rolling contest. Each team rolls a ball of snow until they can no longer push it. The team with the largest snowball wins. You can also use snow to create an outdoor maze or obstacle course to follow, or pile snow to make hurdles for jumping. Making use of what you have on hand challenges you to think creatively.

The Reading Room

Reading together is the perfect way to spend a quiet winter afternoon. Here are a few story ideas that may be of interest to you.

Animals in Winter by Henrietta Bancroft and Richard G. VanGelder, HarperCollins, 1997.

The Big Snow by Berta and Elmer Hader, Simon & Schuster, 1967.

Footprints in the Snow by Cynthia Benjamin, Cartwheel Books, 1994 .

It's Valentine's Day by Jack Prelutsky, Mulberry Books, 1996.

Love and Kisses by Sarah Wilson, Candlewick Press, 1999.

Shades of Black by Sandra L. Pinkney, Scholastic, 2000.

by Marie E. Cecchini

Creative Kitchen

Celebrate National Bird Feeding Month this February with a recipe for Birdie Brunch. Slice a bagel in half, making two rounds. Spread peanut butter over both bagel halves; then press birdseed into the peanut butter. Thread a piece of string through each bagel hole; then tie the bagel feeders to tree branches outdoors. Be sure to hang them where you can easily watch the feathered visitors from inside.

Communication Station

As you read through your shopping list to pick up your groceries or read a recipe to prepare a special dish, your child becomes aware of the fact that reading has a purpose. We get meaning from the printed word. Try this kitchen food game to help your child learn to recognize familiar words. Have your child draw a large bowl shape on a piece of paper. Ask your child what foods he or she would fill the bowl with. As the child names each food, write the word inside the bowl. Continue until the bowl is filled with "food."

Poetry in Motion

Young children enjoy the rhythm and rhyme of words in familiar nursery tales and song. This winter team up with your child to create a rhyming verse or two of your own—one that you can act out, outdoors or in. Warm up the creative flow with the following example:

Snowflake Fun
Catch them on your mitten,
Snow art in your hand!
Catch them on your tongue
And they melt where they land.

Slide your feet, then stomp them
To make tracks as you go,
Or pack the flakes to shape a man
Completely made of snow.

From the Art Cart

Stress the importance of taking care of your teeth during Dental Health Month in February with this unusual art project. Help your child draw and cut out a large tooth shape from yellow construction paper. Prepare a mixture of three parts corn syrup, one part white tempera paint, and one part liquid dish detergent. Let your child use an old toothbrush to paint the yellow paper tooth with the corn syrup mixture. As your child brushes the large tooth, it will become white. The paint will dry to a glossy white finish, resembling a real tooth.

Mathworks

On a day when it's just too cold to get outside, warm up your child's counting and numeral recognition skills with this grid game. Prepare a nine space grid card for each player. Fill the spaces on each card with the numerals one through six, randomly placed. You will need these grids, old buttons or a similar item to use as markers, and a die. To play, each player takes a turn to roll the die. The player counts the dots on the die for each roll, then covers the corresponding number on his or her card with a marker. The first player to fill a row, horizontally, vertically, or diagonally, wins the round.

Ho Ho Ho

_____
(child's name)

is doing a

Jolly

good job in

_____!
(subject or skill)

PEACE ON EARTH

HAPPY HOLIDAYS

Peanut Butter Lovers' Month

Did You Know...
It's Kwanzaa!

Let's Celebrate!

_____
(child's name)

has just learned to

_____ !
(skill)

_____   _____
(teacher's signature)   (date)

Fall in Love with Books!

cupid

♥ A

special reward

No Two Children Are Alike...

Clip Art for Winter

COOL

NEWS!

_____'s

skills in

_____
(student)

_____
(subject)

are going

UP, UP, UP!

_____
(teacher's signature)

Kid Space
Outdoor Learning Discoveries
for Little Ones

From the Stillness of Winter to the Celebration of Spring

The changing of seasons is a magical time.
In North America the months of March and April mark the end of winter and the beginning of spring.

Winter

Winter is a time of rest for the Earth and all her creatures. Encourage children to think about the changes that happened when the world readied for winter. The plants stopped growing, some trees lost their leaves, flowers went to seed, some plants died leaving bulbs and roots safely in the ground for next year, animals gathered their stash of winter food and stayed closer to their nests, some animals hibernated, and the sun didn't shine as long as usual. All of these events happened in preparation for the restful winter after a full cycle of activities throughout the spring, summer, and fall.

Spring

Spring is a time of excitement—the beginning of a whole new growth cycle for the Earth after a long quiet winter. Take your students outside to watch for signs of an awakening world.

- The days become longer as the sun is more visible in the sky each day.
- New green shoots of plants begin to poke their heads through the soil.
- Trees are growing new leaves and flowers.
- Animals become more active and venture farther out from their homes as the weather becomes warmer.
- Birds build their nests and hatch their eggs.
- When the conditions are just right, animals will come out of hibernation.

by Robynne Eagan

Animals in Spring

Animals love spring because new growth means new sources of food. It can be difficult for animals to find enough food in winter so they are often very hungry by spring. Spring provides a succulent feast. Herbivores (animals that eat plants) munch on the tasty new shoots of their favorite plants. Many new babies are born or hatched in the spring and also need to be fed. With all these animals out feeding, the predators have more food to hunt, also.

Animals use all their senses to find new sources of food and to protect themselves while they are eating. This is the biggest job any animal has for survival.

You Need
- open space to run, hop, or slither
- wall or rope line to mark a starting space

Get Ready
Talk about the changes that occur in nature in the spring, how new growth appears, how hungry animals enjoy the feasts of spring and how baby animals are born at this time of year.

Directions
1. After discussing many animals that might be seen in spring and what they might be doing, take your students outside for a little fun.
2. Have children stand in a line facing you—this could be against a school wall or along a rope line you have set up.
3. Ask children to return to you as rabbits, deer, foxes, hawks, geese, or whatever you choose.
4. When they find their way to you, you can talk about how that animal moved and what it might be doing in the springtime.
5. Send the children back to the line and invite them to be another animal. Discuss this animal when they join you again.

Do the Bunny Hop

Celebrate by pretending to be one of spring's symbols of new life.

You Need
- hoops of different colors
- open area
- tambourine

Get Ready
Place lots of different colored hoops around an open area.

Let the children warm up in an open area. Suggest ways of moving that will get all of their muscles working—walk, run, jump, hop, skip, move sideways and backwards, make yourself small or tall, roll, crawl, or slither.

Directions
1. Demonstrate to the children how to hop around the hoops without touching them.
2. Have children hop around the hoops while you beat on the tambourine. Can they hop to the beat?
3. When you stop beating the tambourine, children should listen carefully for an instruction, such as "Hop inside a red hoop," "Hop over to a blue hoop," or "Hop into any hoop with a friend."

Try This
You can reinforce many concepts using this simple game. Put items or flash cards with letters or numbers in the hoops and use these in your instructions. Encourage cooperation and number sense by instructing children to form groups of a specific number in each hoop.

Wet Chalk Art

Wet spring weather presents wonderful opportunities for wet chalk fun!

You Need
- bucket of sidewalk chalk
- wet pavement or something to collect meltwater to dip chalk into

Directions
1. Invite children to make spring drawings on damp pavement. Suggest rainbows, rain clouds, spring sunshine, flowers, bugs, shapes, numbers, or whatever their imaginations come up with.
2. Encourage children to combine colors, try to make different kinds of lines, draw on different textures of concrete, and use different parts of the chalk they are holding.

Try This
Take photos of the outdoor art creations. Display these on a Rainbow of Colors bulletin board.

Pussy Willow Prowl

You Need
- children in weather-appropriate walking gear
- small garden shears or pocket knife
- damp paper towel
- plastic bag
- bucket or large jar

Get Ready
Find pussy willows in a wet area near you.

Directions
1. Take children on a hike to help you find fuzzy pussy willows.
2. Once the pussy willows have been found, encourage children to make observations about them. How do they feel? What kind of area do they grow in? Is there a pattern of pussy willows on the branches?
3. Cut some branches and wrap them in wet paper towels until you get back to school. Place the cuttings in water and observe them over time. Change the water often. When the cuttings grow roots you can transplant them into a damp area in your school yard or nearby where children can observe their progress over their years at school.
4. Visit the pussy willow site again and observe the changes that have occurred. Observe as the furry fluff is replaced with green willowy sprigs and bushes.

Find the Meltwater

Have you ever wondered where all the ice and snow go when winter turns to spring? As the sun and warmth melt the snow and ice they become something scientists call meltwater.

Can you find any meltwater on a warm spring day? Where does it come from? Where is it going? Can you follow it?

Can you find any meltwater dripping from a roof? Watch what happens to this meltwater when the temperature drops again.

Caution
Talk to your students about the dangers of run-off. Streams can appear where there were none before. Rushing water can be dangerous. It can pull you in and under before you have time to call for help. Students must never venture near running water without an adult.

Hello, Spring!

Hello, robin!
Hello, flower!
Hello, sunshine!
Hello, shower!

Hello, bunny!
Hello, jay!
Hello, April!
Hello, spring day!

Spring Things
Read this poem to the children. What other spring things can they name? Invite the children to sing like a robin, spring up like a flower, pitter-patter like raindrops, hop like a bunny, and pop out of the clouds like the sun. On a sunny day, take the children outside for springtime activities like rope skipping, hand-clapping games, hopscotch, and tag.

by Jacqueline Schiff

WHAT IS WIND?

March is known as a windy month! Sometimes the wind is gentle, and sometimes it blows hard.

What is wind? We can't see it. We can't smell it. We can't taste it. But we can feel it, hear it and see what it does. Wind is air that moves. When the air moves gently, we call it a breeze. When the air moves hard and fast, we call that a storm. And when there is no wind at all, we say it is calm.

We get wind when the cool air around us tries to push the hot air that is on the ground out of the way. All that pushing makes wind.

Feel the Wind

Stand in front of a fan that is turned on. Can you feel the wind? Blow up a balloon and gradually let the air out and blow on your face. Can you feel it?

Make Your Own Wind

You have air inside you and can make your own wind. Try this: Hold a feather, tissue, light piece of paper, or cloth in front of your mouth and blow. Did you make it move? What happens when you blow gently? Harder?

Catch the Wind

Blow up a balloon. With your fingers, gently spread apart the mouthpiece to let the air out slowly. Stretch the mouthpiece in and out. Did your balloon "sing" for you? Now, blow up the balloon again and let it go. Watch the balloon "dance" all over the room as the air escapes faster. Blow it up one more time, and this time tie off the end. Hit the balloon gently with your hands. How long can you keep it in the air?

Air Goes to Work

Spray or splash water on the chalkboard. Watch it dry as the air in the room (that we can't see) dries it. You can help it along. Fan a piece of paper or cardboard in front of the board. Use your own air and blow on it. Or use a hair dryer on the board. Which way dries the board faster?

Fly a Kite

Take a square piece of construction paper and decorate it. Turn the square so it looks like a diamond. Cut a long strip of paper about one inch wide and staple it on the bottom point. Punch a hole in the top point of the diamond and insert a long piece of string through the hole. Tie it in place. Fly the kite either inside or out. Does it fly better when you stand, walk or run?

Learn a Poem

Did you see the blustery wind
As it came blowing by?
(Move as if being blown around.)
I surely didn't see it
(Shake head back and forth.)
But it blew something in my eye!
(Close one eye and point to it.)

Discover More About the Wind

Go outside on a windy day and watch the wind blow leaves, paper, seeds, and anything else. Put a hat on your head and see if the wind can blow it off. Watch the wind blow your clothes and make them wave. What else can the wind do?

by Judy Wolfman

March Wind

As you read this poem, have children
act it out as if the wind is blowing them.

March comes in like a lion
And gives a big roar!
Its wind blows me over
As it roars once more.

It whirls and twirls me
Around and around.
It spins me so fast
My feet leave the ground!

It blows at me
With one last shout,
And then like a lamb
It drifts gently out.

by Ann K. Smiley

CALLING ALL PIGS

Children who love pigs will be in "hog heaven" because March 1st is National Pig Day. This is the time to do a unit on pigs or incorporate them in a farm animals theme. Pigs are short, big animals with four legs, mostly living on farms. They provide us with ham, bacon, and pork. Pigs are also called hogs or swine. A male pig is called a boar; the female pig is a sow. Pigs are considered dirty because they roll in the mud. They do this to cool off because they have no sweat glands. Use this day to promote appreciation of pigs for being the intelligent, clean animals they truly are.

A PIGGY FINGERPLAY

Two mother pigs lived in a pen. *(Raise thumbs.)*
Each had four babies and that made 10. *(Raise all fingers of both hands.)*
These four babies were black and white. *(Wiggle 4 fingers of one hand.)*
These four babies were black as night. *(Wiggle 4 fingers of the other hand.)*
All eight babies loved to play. *(Wiggle fingers.)*
And they rolled and they rolled in the mud all day! *(Roll hands.)*

CALLING ALL PIGGIES (GAME)

Gather the children in a circle (this is the pigpen). Choose one child to be the "parent pig." Ask the parent pig to "fall asleep" (close eyes) and then signal another child (piglet) to run away from the pen and hide in the classroom. Now ask the parent pig to wake up and go looking for the piglet. As the parent pig walks around the room, have the other piglets (children) oink loudly if he or she is going in the right direction or oink softly if the parent pig is going in the wrong direction. When the missing piglet has been found and brought back to the pen (circle), choose new players and start the game again.

PIG THE TAIL ON PIGGY (GAME)

This is a variation of Pin the Tail on the Donkey. Draw a large pink pig and hang it on the wall. Use pieces of pink curling ribbons as tails. See who can tape the curly tail the closest to the pig's hindquarters.

BY TANIA COWLING

PiGS iN THe MUD (ART)

Invite children to glue a pig cut-out on green construction paper. With a marker, draw in a pigpen fence. Give each child a small amount of chocolate pudding in a paper cup. Allow students to fingerpaint the pig playing in the mud. What great new texture to tickle the senses. Allow the paper to dry before hanging it. Note: Make sure the kids' hands are clean before this project, as they will lick their fingers clean after they paint. Mmmm!

PiG SLOP (SNACK)

Prepare some chocolate pudding for a snack on Pig Day (instant pudding is the easiest). Discuss how farmers feed pigs with a mixture of leftover foods called "slop." Bring in a variety of food items like chopped nuts, cereals, raisins, chopped bananas, mini m & m's™, and so on. Let the kids take turns adding one of these ingredients to the "mud." Mix and serve in individual paper cups or bowls. As the children eat their slop, ask them to show their appreciation with loud grunts. Oink, oink, oink!

A LiTTLe LiTeRATURe
(LANGUAGe ARTS AND GAMe)

Read the story "The Three Little Pigs." Emphasize the differences in houses. Each is made from different materials and of different colors. Show the class a real brick, a stick, and some straw. Demonstrate, by blowing, the strengths or weaknesses of each item. Help students understand the story by asking, "Which house was the strongest?" "How did the wolf try to trick the pigs?" "What happened to the wolf in the end?"

Play a "huff and puff" game with the children. Apply some masking tape to the floor marking a start and finish line. Invite the children to blow a Ping-Pong™ ball between the two lines.

TORN PAPeR PiG (ART)

Kids love to tear paper, so why not make a cute art project with it. Give each child a pig-shape from construction paper. Provide different types of pink paper, construction paper, tissue paper, and facial tissue. Invite students to tear the paper into bits and glue them on the pigs, giving them a wonderful textured finish. Use a black marker to add features.

PAPeR PLATe PiG FACeS (ART)

This is a two-part project that can be done in two days or a morning and afternoon. First, have your students paint a paper plate with pink tempera paint. Let it dry thoroughly. Next, have them glue on eyes (wiggle craft eyes or cut-paper eyes). Glue a pink cupcake liner on for the nose. Cut and glue pink construction paper ears and draw a mouth with a crayon or marker.

Peter Pig

Oh no! Peter Pig is lost! Help him find his way home to the barn.

by Janet A. Armbrust

Pigs Are Everywhere!

Color the sad pig blue.
Color the happy pig pink.
Color the tired pig yellow.

Color the biggest pig red.
Color the smallest pig green.
Color the shy pig purple.

by Janet A. Armbrust

Purim Fun

Purim is a happy, noisy Jewish holiday. At temples and synagogues, Jewish children all over the world listen to the story of Esther, Queen of Persia. They shout, shake their noisemakers called gragers, and stamp their feet every time they hear wicked Haman's name.

Children dress in costumes when they go to the Purim service. After the service they parade, sing songs and enjoy refreshments. The favorite food is Hamantaschen. It is a special three-cornered cookie filled with jelly. It reminds children of the three-cornered hat Haman wore.

Purim is also a time to share. Children give baskets of food and toys to people who are poor, sick, or lonely.

You don't have to be Jewish to enjoy the happy holiday of Purim. Join in the fun!

Dramatize the Story

Read the play, *Queen Esther: A Brave Queen* as a theater presentation. Older children can read it for younger ones. Or, after hearing the story, let the children act it out. Narrate the story, pausing to allow the characters to speak. Ideas for easy costumes are bathrobes for King Ahasuerus, Mordecai, and Haman; Mom's old party dresses for Vashti and Esther. Puppets made from tongue depressors, paper plates, or socks can also be used to tell the story.

Masquerade Parade

Purim is a time when children dress up as one of the characters in the story, but other costumes are also worn. They can be brought from home or created in the classroom. Let the children parade throughout the school in their festive costumes.

Hear the Story

Read or tell the story of Queen Esther. The library, temple, or synagogue will have books or storytellers to help you. *Queen Esther* by Tomie de Paola (Harper & Row) or *Festival of Esther* by Maida Silverman (A Little Simon Book) are both good.

Make a Grager

As the story is told, help drown out Haman's name with your own noisemaker, or grager. First, find a container that closes tightly—a small box, screw top can or jar, or plastic soft drink bottle will work. Next, put dried beans, rice, or pebbles inside the container and seal the opening with tape. Finally, decorate the outside with colored paper, paint, ribbons, glitter, and so on in order to make your grager bright.

Fingerplay

Teach children the "Purim Fun" fingerplay on page 26. Have them use their "grager" noisemakers in the appropriate place in the rhyme.

by Judy Wolfman

Refreshments

Traditionally, a three-cornered filled pastry called Hamantaschen is eaten. This symbolizes the three-cornered hat worn by Haman. Hamanataschen are or maybe available in local stores, but maybe you'd like to make your own.

Directions

Cream together 1 cup sugar, ⅓ cup oil, and ⅓ cup shortening. Add 3 eggs and ½ cup orange juice and mix well. In a separate bowl, blend together 4 cups flour, 3 tsp. baking powder, and 1 tsp salt. Blend the dry ingredients with the previous mixture. Roll into a ball and divide into 4 parts. On a floured board, roll out each piece to about ⅛ inch thickness.

Using the rim of a cup or glass, cut circles from the dough. In the center of each circle drop different jellies as a filling. Lift up the right and left sides of the circle, leaving the bottom side down. Bring both sides to meet at the center, above the filling. Now lift the bottom side up to the center to meet the other two sides. Gently pinch the sides together to form a triangle.

Place the filled triangles on a greased cookie sheet, and brush the dough with a beaten egg. Bake in a preheated oven at 350°F for approximately 20 minutes. This recipe makes about 4 dozen Hamantaschen. Enjoy!

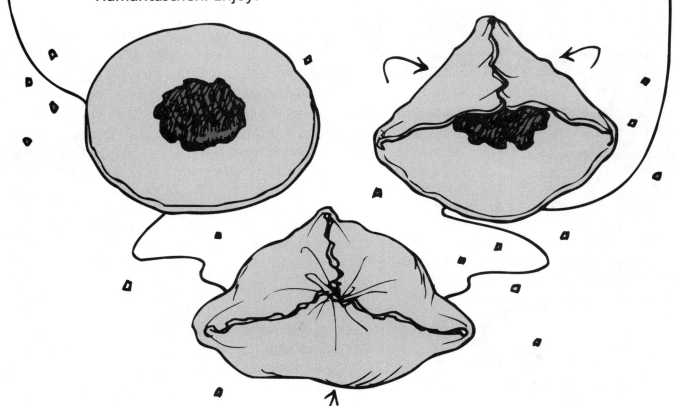

Shamrock Shenanigans

The ancient custom known as "the wearin' of the green" on St. Patrick's Day originated as a symbol of springtime and hope. Create your own springtime celebration with St. Patrick's Day-oriented learning experiences.

A Pot of Gold

Prepare for this activity by hiding 50-100 pennies throughout the classroom. Talk with the children about the Irish lore of mischievous leprechauns and the hidden pot of gold. Display a penny and explain that you are going to pretend it is a gold coin. Tell the children that these special "gold" coins are hidden throughout the room. Let the class treasure hunt for the coins. Place all of the collected coins into a container to create your own pot of gold. Count the coins to see how many were collected. Allow the children to take turns holding the pot of gold. Ask them to guess how much it weighs. Weigh the container of coins. How accurate were their guesses?

Shamrocks

Display a live shamrock plant or a picture of one and some common clover. Tell the children that the shamrock is the national symbol of Ireland. Find Ireland on a globe. Note how far the country of Ireland is from our own. Compare the similarities and differences of clovers and shamrocks.

Invite the children to make magic leprechaun wands using shamrock-shaped patterns, green construction paper, gold glitter, green crepe paper streamers, drinking straws, pencils, scissors, and glue. You will also need a stapler. Have the children trace and cut two green shamrock shapes. Outline one side of each cut out shape with glue and sprinkle gold glitter on the glue. Allow the glue to dry; then staple the two shamrocks back to back at the top of a drinking straw. Cut and staple two crepe paper streamers at the bottom of each shamrock. Invite individuals to tell what they will use their magic wands for.

Flags of Ireland

The flag that represents Ireland is made up of three equal vertical portions of the colors green, white, and red-orange. Have the children use paints and white paper to create their own Irish flags. When dry, staple each flag to a sturdy cardboard stick. Play a march or Irish step dancing music for your own St. Patrick's Day Parade.

by Marie E. Cecchini

Irish Jewelry

Show the children how to make beads from raw potatoes. Peel several potatoes (you may want to enlist the help of parent volunteers). Cut the peeled potatoes into cube shapes and push the cubes onto skewers. Allow the cubes to dry for about a week; then remove them from the skewers. Have the children thread these homemade beads, along with spinach macaroni or green craft beads on elastic thread to make bracelets or necklaces.

Rainbow Wash

Provide the children with white paper and several colors of crepe paper streamers. Have the children spray water from a spray bottle onto the white paper, then press lengths of colored streamer onto the wet paper. Place newspaper over the streamers and smooth over with both hands. Lift the newspaper and peel off the streamers. What happened? The color from the streamers transferred onto the white paper. Allow the papers to dry; then have the children cut them into rainbow shapes. Let the children draw and cut out black paper pot shapes to glue at one end of their rainbows. Place glue on the rainbow just above the pot and sprinkle gold glitter over the glue.

Potato Talk

Have the children draw and cut potato shapes from brown construction paper. Let them use scrap paper to create and cut out facial features. Glue these to the potato shapes. Glue on green yarn for hair. Staple each potato head to a cardboard stick to make a puppet. Have the children name their potato people; then invite individuals to make up short St. Patrick's Day stories about their puppets. Encourage the children to work together to create puppet shows during free time.

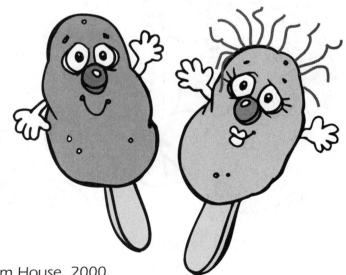

Reading the Green

Jack and the Leprechaun by Ivan Robertson, Random House, 2000.
Leprechaun Gold by Teresa Bateman and Rosanne Litzinger, Holiday House, 1998.
The Leprechaun in the Basement by Kathy Tucker, Albert Whitman & Co, 1999.
St. Patrick's Day by Gail Gibbons, Holiday House, 1995.
St. Patrick's Day in the Morning by Eve Bunting, Jan Brett (illustrator), Ticknor & Fields, 1983.

199

Name _____

To a Pot o' Gold

Write in the missing numbers on the path.

TLC10339 Copyright © Teaching & Learning Company, Carthage, IL 62321-0010

Pot-O-Gold Maze

Oh no! The leprechaun lost his gold!
Can you help him find it?

TLC10339 Copyright © Teaching & Learning Company, Carthage, IL 62321-0010

Name _____

Leprechaun Lesson

To celebrate St. Patrick's Day, some children have begun to draw a leprechaun. Finish each picture until it looks like the one in this frame!

by Becky Radtke

Name _____

The Rainbow's End

Leprechauns believe there's treasure at the end of rainbows! See how quickly you can match the halves together to make four pots of gold!

by
Becky
Radtke

Easter Snow

Hareld, a snowshoe hare, was looking forward to working with his cousin, the Easter Bunny. Sunshine streamed into their workshop hidden behind a clump of yellow daffodils. Hareld clutched a paintbrush in one big furry paw and painted stripes on the eggs.

Then the Easter Bunny looked at Hareld's eggs and said, "Stripes must be straight and even. We can't have Easter eggs with narrow squiggly stripes here and wide squiggly stripes there."

"Oh," Hareld said, biting the end of his paintbrush. So he happily mixed all the paints and splashed one color on each egg.

Then the Easter Bunny looked at his eggs and said, "Easter eggs are blue, green, yellow, and pink. Nobody wants black, brown, and gray Easter eggs.

"Oh," Hareld said. He thought the eggs he'd painted as black and

by Jeanne Field Olson

shiny as a raccoon's eyes, as brown as deer fur, and as gray as the color of the wild geese flying overhead, were beautiful. But maybe just a snow-bunny wouldn't know that.

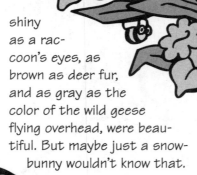

Hareld began making diorama eggs. He shaped one tiny figure after another. Hareld carefully arranged them inside the big hollow white sugar eggs.

Then the Easter Bunny looked inside one and exclaimed, "Easter eggs have pretty spring scenes, baby chicks, or flowers inside them. Whoever heard of an Easter egg full of airplanes?"

"Oh," said Hareld. He loved airplanes. But maybe it was just a silly snow-bunny's idea.

"Pack the eggs in baskets," the Easter Bunny said. "I'll finish the rest of the eggs."

Just beyond a thick hedge Hareld saw the Emerson twins playing catch in their yard.

"I can't wait for the Easter Bunny to come tomorrow," Andy said. He skimmed a yellow Frisbee™ at Amy.

"Me, too!" Amy exclaimed, her dark eyes shining as she leaped to catch the Frisbee™.

The Easter Bunny smiled. He painted ANDY on one of the largest Easter eggs, and AMY on another.

Hareld finished packing the Easter baskets. He packed all his rejected eggs in an extra basket. Surely someone would want them. He could hardly wait to help deliver Easter eggs.

But when Hareld poked his nose out of the Easter Bunny's burrow on Easter morning, there was snow everywhere. The daffodils were bent over with snow. There were snow-caps on fence posts, snow on telephone wires; heavy wet snow covered everything.

The Emerson twins saw the snow, too.

"Mom, can we build a snow Easter Bunny before church?" Amy asked.

204

"Good idea!"

The heavy, wet snow was perfect. Quickly the twins shaped a snow Easter Bunny with long ears and a tail.

"He looks cold," Andy said.

"We can fix that." Amy wrapped her long red scarf around the snowbunny's neck, and placed her red mittens on his feet for slippers. Andy lay his blue mittens on the snowbunny's paws. The twins giggled, and ran for the warm house.

The Easter Bunny and Hareld hopped through the snowdrifts delivering Easter eggs. The Easter Bunny stopped often to scrape the icy snow from between his toes.

"Brr" said the Easter Bunny. He couldn't stop shivering. "I'm freezing.

Hareld looked at him in surprise. He loved the snow. His big furry feet and heavy coat were made for cold snowy days. But he could see that the Easter Bunny's ears were blue and drooping with cold as they hopped into the Emerson yard.

"Here," Hareld said, hopping to the snowbunny. "These will help." He pulled Andy's red mittens down over the Easter Bunny's ears, and Amy's blue mittens over his feet.

"Now, hop on home and warm up."

"But," began the Easter Bunny.

"No buts," Hareld said. "I'm the perfect delivery bunny for today.

Hareld couldn't carry all the Easter baskets by himself. So he placed the basket with all his rejected eggs beside the snow bunny and stacked some of the Easter Bunny's eggs on top. He'd deliver them to the Emersons later.

Hareld hopped all over the neighborhood delivering Easter eggs here, Easter eggs there. Heading

back to the burrow, Hareld heard happy voices from the Emersons' yard.

"Look at these clever eggs with the swirly stripes! Oh, and there are beautiful brown, black, and gray eggs too," Amy exclaimed.

"Zowee! I can't believe it. There are tiny airplanes inside these two eggs. They are the BEST Easter eggs ever!"

Hareld turned somersaults in the snow until he was dizzy.

Maybe, just maybe, he wasn't just a snowbunny. He was "some"-bunny after all!

BUNNIES

Soft and white,
Fluffy and light,

Wiggly noses,
Bright eyes—

Bunnies hopping everywhere,
Even hopping out of sight!

Activities
1. **Paper Plate Bunnies:** Cut a large white paper plate in half to make ears. Staple both ears to another large white paper plate. Use construction paper to make facial details.
2. **Cotton Bunnies:** Draw a bunny and glue cotton on it for body and tail.
3. **Popcorn Bunnies:** Draw a bunny and glue popcorn on it for fur.
4. **Bunny Salad:** Mix carrot strips, raisins, nuts, sunflower seeds, and shredded lettuce with a little mayonnaise.

Recommended Books
Too Many Bunnies (Troll, 2000) by Tomie de Paola.
Bunny's Noisy Book (Hyperion Press, 1999) and *Runaway Bunny* (HarperFestival, 1991) by Margaret Wise Brown.
Mr. Rabbit and the Lovely Present (HarperTrophy, 1977) by Charlotte Zolotow.

by Mary Anne Quick

Easter Arrivals

These baby chicks hatched just in time to celebrate Easter!
Find and circle the two that look the same.

by Becky Radtke

Name _____

An Edible Easter Treat

Connect the dots in correct alphabetical order to find a big chocolate Easter goodie!

by Becky Radtke

208

Bunny's Basket

The Easter Bunny is getting ready to make his rounds. Count how many eggs are in his basket.
Then write that number in the center of the ribbon.

by Becky Radtke

Jeremy's Jelly Beans

Easter has come at last, and Jeremy loves the treats he gets!
Fill in each blank below with the letter "e" to spell the names of six colors.
Then use those colors to color Jeremy's pile of jelly beans!

purpl__   r__d   y__llow

blu__   gr__ __n   orang__

by Becky Radtke

Name _____

"Egg"citing Egg Hunt

The Easter Bunny has been decorating eggs! See if you can find the four in the box in the same order below. Look up, down, across, and diagonally.

by Becky Radtke

Story Time

Put your budding young artists to work this spring on the sensational activities in *The Giant Encyclopedia of Art and Craft Activities for Children 3 to 6* edited by Kathy Charner (Gryphon House, 2000). This fabulous book features easy-to-follow directions for over 500 art and craft projects. In addition, there are suggestions for extending each activity, as well as a related book list. Songs and poems are included with many of the activities to enhance the particular art or craft project.

Ready, set, it's party time! *Quick Classroom Party Ideas* by Mary Ann Duggan (Fearon Teacher Aids, 1998) is just what you need for that perfect holiday or seasonal party. This handy book provides over 200 classroom-tested party ideas. Some of the spring ideas include Confetti Eggs, Plastic-Egg Math, Colored Egg Twister, and Marshmallow Bunnies.

You don't need a "green thumb" to enjoy gardening! *Kids Garden! The Anytime, Anyplace Guide to Sowing & Growing Fun* by Avery Hart and Paul Mantell (Williamson Publishing Co., 1996) features wonderful ideas for simple gardening projects that will appeal to everyone. Turn your youngsters into junior botanists as they create a plant maze, a "popcorn pie," and begin a "jump-start" garden. Directions are also given for a Make a Wish in a Dish—a miniature garden with plants and action figures. Get out the potting soil and seeds and let the springtime gardening fun begin!

The Jelly Bean Fun Book
by Karen Capucilli
Little Simon, 2001

What's Easter without jelly beans? Challenge your youngsters to a "tasty" array of motivating activities, all with a jelly bean theme. This book features colorful photographs with counting games, puzzles, and other brainteasers. Everyone will love the book, but here's a warning—you will soon be hungry for some real jelly beans!

One More Bunny
Adding from One to Ten
by Rick Walton
Lothrop, Lee & Shepard Books, 2000

Who says learning math can't be lots of fun? Treat your children to this delightful story in rhyme that also introduces simple addition. Join in the counting fun as one lone bunny is soon joined by a host of rollicking bunnies at a playground.

by Mary Ellen Switzer

Sergeant Sniff's Easter Egg Mystery

by Valerie Garfield
HarperFestival, 2001

Ready, set, sniff? Sergeant Sniff has hidden all the Easter eggs for her friends to find. There are all sorts of sensational Easter treats—marshmallows, licorice, and gumdrops. The final mystery is the location of the coconut egg—can you "crack" the case?

Happy Easter, Emily! A Lift-the-Flap Book

by Claire Masurel
illustrated by Susan Calitri
Puffin, 2000

Join Emily and her friends on an "eggs"citing egg hunt as they try to fill their baskets with Easter treats. Lift the flaps for some holiday surprises! What surprise do you think is hidden in the biggest egg?

The Spring Rabbit

by Joyce Dunbar
illustrated by Susan Varley
Lothrop, Lee & Shepard, 1994

When a rabbit named Smudge asks his mother for a brother or sister, she replies, "Wait until the spring." There's only one problem for the impatient little rabbit—will springtime ever arrive? While he waits he makes a "pretend" leaf rabbit in the fall, a snow rabbit during winter, and a mud rabbit when the snow melts. Finally spring arrives and Smudge gets a triple surprise—two baby brothers and a sister. The elated Smudge makes the perfect gift to welcome them—a big moss rabbit!

Big Bad Bunny

by Alan Durant
illustrated by Guy Parker-Rees
Dutton, 2001

Watch out for laughs galore; the Big Bad Bunny is coming to town! Armed with a carrot, this mischievous rabbit visits a small western town taking food from some of the inhabitants. Soon, however, the bunny gets tired of being bad and bakes a special pie for everyone he has robbed.

Wake Me in Spring Hello Reader Series
by James Preller
illustrated by Jeffrey Scherer
Scholastic, 1994

A little mouse tries his best to convince his friend Bear not to hibernate as winter approaches. He reminds Bear of the pleasures of the winter season—sleigh rides, ice skating, hot chocolate, and making snowmen. Finally Bear convinces the mouse to wake him when spring arrives so the two best friends can have fun again.

It's Raining, It's Pouring
A Book for Rainy Days
compiled & illustrated by Sarah Pooley
Greenwillow Books, 1993

Don't let those spring showers get you down! Just open up this rainy-day favorite and let the fun begin! This unique book is a collection of poems and stories along with related activities, recipes, and crafts that will brighten everyone's day. After sharing "The Three Bears," treat your youngsters to tasty cheese bears—the recipe is included along with a pattern for a teddy bear mask. If you need some music to add to the merriment, there are easy-to-follow directions for simple instruments such as a kazoo, shakers, and glass bottle sets. You will also find directions for a nifty weather calendar so your children can keep track of all that spring rain!

Rhyme Time

April is National Poetry Month! Treat your youngsters to some delightful poetry during this special month.

Lizards, Frogs, and Polliwogs
by Douglas Florian
Harcourt, Inc., 2001

Little Dog Poems
by Kristine O'Connell George
Clarion, 1999

Animal Trunk
Silly Poems to Read Aloud
by Charles Ghigna
Harry N. Abrams, Inc., 1998

Teddy Bear's Mother Goose
by Michael Hague
Henry Holt and Company, 2001

Peanut Butter and Jelly: A Play Rhyme
by Nadine Bernard Westcott
Puffin, 1992

It's Here Again!

Now and then
A chilly blast,
A fickle sun
That doesn't last.

Tulips pelted
By the rain,
Pansies where
The snow had lain.

Now and then
A robin's song,
Winds that blow
A bit too strong,

Muddy tracks
When we come in—
Looks like April's
Here again!

Discussion
Talk about some other signs of spring that get mixed up with the end of winter such as wearing snow boots one day and regular shoes the next. Ask the children to share their favorite things about April as well as things they don't like about this month.

by Janice Kuharski

Make -in-a- Minute Crafts

Crafts should offer sensory stimulation and exploration of a variety of materials. These activities can reinforce concepts, while developing fine and large motor muscles, hand-eye coordination, listening skills, memory sequencing, and cooperation. Design activities to introduce and reinforce new vocabulary or concepts and to initiate reading and math readiness skills.

Leprechaun Footprints

Materials
- green tempera paint
- paint smocks
- pie plates
- white paper
- paper towels

Get Ready
- Pour some paint in the green pie plates.
- Set up a paper towel-blotting pad.
- If you do not have wash-up facilities close to this craft, supply a washing basin, soap, and towels for little green hands.

Directions
1. Have students form a fist. Help them find the soft fleshy side of the fist where the baby finger curls.
2. Invite students to gently place this curled side in the paint plate, then on a blotting pad before pressing it onto paper.
3. Dab a finger in the paint and then dot along the wide end of the print to form toes and turn the print into a leprechaun footprint.
4. Students can add more prints in a formation that will make it appear as though a leprechaun walked across the page.

Try . . .
Tempera paints can be used to make footprints across a window, chalkboard, or classroom floor. You will need a few pails of clean water and a sturdy sponge to help you clean up the mess, but the fun will be worth it!

by Robynne Eagan

St. Patrick's Day Potato Prints

Dress in green, put on some Irish music and make a St. Patty's day craft as you celebrate Irish heritage with your group.

Materials
- paper
- paint
- potatoes

Directions
1. Cut a potato in half. Cut a shamrock shape in one end and a simple coin in the other end.
2. Have students paint the shamrock shape green and press it on white paper.
3. Children can paint the coins yellow or gold and press them onto the white paper amongst the shamrocks.
4. Allow the children to make as many prints as they wish to fill their paper.

Spring Box Top Collage

Materials
- one shoe box lid or similar box top (for each child)
- an assortment of spring-themed objects with interesting shapes or textures (seeds, stones, flower shapes, **sand**, eggshells)
- glue
- scissors

Directions
1. Invite children to select items for their collages.
2. Have them put a generous dab of glue on their box top and then position an item in the glue. Have children continue in this manner until they are satisfied with their creations.
3. Allow them to dry thoroughly before moving them.

Spring Mini Book

Use a mini book to help your children better understand the concept of spring.

Materials
- magazines with spring pictures
- scissors
- paste
- construction paper
- stapler

Get Ready
- Fold construction paper in half and staple the center to make a simple booklet.
- Print the word *Spring* on the cover of each booklet.
- Set up a Spring Search Station with magazines, scissors, paste, and booklets.

Directions
1. Discuss spring with your students. What happens outside in the spring? In nature? In the school yard? In your backyard? What is the weather like? What do you wear in spring? What do you like to do in spring?
2. Invite children to make their own spring mini books. Encourage children to find pictures of spring in the magazines, cut these out, and paste them in the pages of their booklets.
3. When they are finished, help children print their names on the covers.

Get a Grip
on That Pencil!
Magical Musical Marks

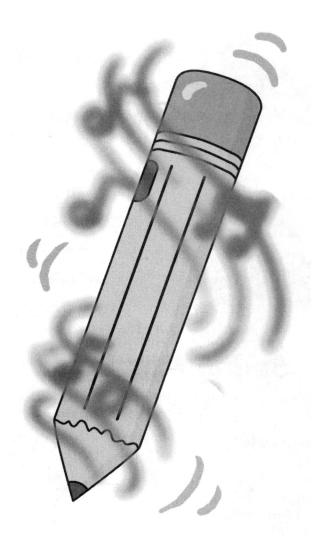

Little ones must develop the simple skill of holding and manipulating drawing and writing instruments before they can refine their drawing and printing skills. Provide opportunities that will entice children to have a little fun and make them want to work with drawing and writing tools. This exercise also encourages children to develop listening skills which are essential for sound recognition when they begin to learn to read and write.

Materials
- large sheet of newsprint
- crayons
- source of music (CD or cassette player with selected piece of music or live music)

Directions
Lead children through the following exercise:
1. We are going to do a little exercise making marks on our page.
2. When you get your paper, select a crayon, but keep your paper white without a mark until I explain what we are going to do.
3. I am going to play some music, and I want you to listen to the music very carefully. I am even going to ask you to close your eyes so you can hear the music better.
4. Grab your crayon, close your eyes, and wait for the music to begin. No peeking!
5. Once the music starts, listen carefully and then move your crayon around on your page to the music. Make marks to the music. Fill your page with marks that are guided by the sounds you hear. Listen carefully and let your hand and your crayon move freely.
6. When the music stops you can open your eyes and look at your amazing musical picture. The marks you made will tell something about how you felt listening to the music.

Making marks on a page can be fun. Sometimes we can just let our crayon go, sometimes we draw pictures, and sometimes we print letters. All of these marks can show something or tell something.

April Fools' Day
Upside Down Art

Introduce something new and have a little fun. Preschoolers will love exploring spatial relationships in this just-for-fun art activity.

Materials
- white bond paper (any size)
- masking tape
- classroom tables
- basket of markers or crayons

Get Ready
- Use masking tape to fasten papers to the underside of classroom tables.
- Place baskets with markers or crayons as needed under the table.

Directions
Invite children to lie on their backs under the tables and draw from an interesting new angle.

218

Barnyard Fun

Read the following poem aloud to your children. Encourage them to say the names of the animals to complete the verses.

On the farm you'll know it's spring;
The sun shines down on everything.
Farmer Brown is planting corn
And many little ones are born.
Babies wander all around;
Mothers search until they're found.

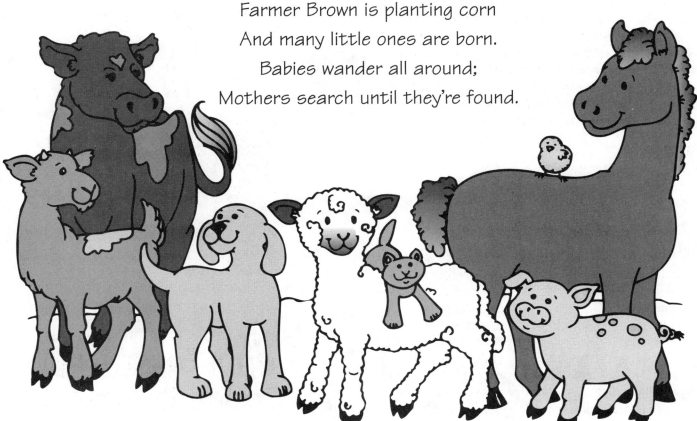

A little lamb is fast asleep.
Soon he's found by mother (sheep).

Baby goat thinks he's well hid,
But mother finds her little (kid).

Mother hen is very quick.
She'll never lose her baby (chick).

A little colt trots out of course.
He's not far from mother (horse).

A little calf is looking now.
Soon he'll find his mother (cow).

Mother dog looks down and up.
Looking for her baby (pup).

A little kitten's lying flat.
Hiding from her mother (cat).

You can join the babies' games,
Now you know the babies' names!

by M. Donnaleen Howitt

Use these patterns to create stick puppets. Let children act out the poem.

Name _____

Happy Birthday,
Mr. Andersen!

Hans Christian Andersen's birthday is April 2. Have you ever read any of his books? Here is a picture of one of his most famous book subjects. The book was called *The Little* _____. What is she? Use crayons to make a drawing to show the place she would live.

by Mary Tucker

A MONTH FOR MATH

April is Math Education Month, so spend some time emphasizing math in your classroom in some unique ways.

FLOWER POWER MATH

Cut daisy parts (circle centers and oval petals) from colored construction paper. Give each child a handful of centers and petals, enough to make several flowers. Print some numbers on the board, such as 7, 5, and 9. Ask your students to assemble daisies with corresponding numbers of petals and one circle center each. Have them carefully lay out the flower pieces on their desks. Go around the room and check the flowers to make sure children have added the correct number of petals, or let children exchange seats briefly to check one another's work. Complete the activity by asking children to count the total number of flower petals they have used, the ones they haven't used, and the total number of flower centers they have and haven't used. If possible, bring some real flowers to class and have students count their petals.

EASTER EGG ADDITION

Give each child a plastic, pull-apart egg and 10 jelly beans. Instruct each child to print a simple addition problem on a sticky note (such as 3 + 5 = 8); then put that many jelly beans in the egg and close it. Attach the sticky note problem on the outside of each egg. Pass the egg to the child on the right. That child solves the problem, then opens the egg and counts the jelly beans to check his or her answer. Continue until each child has solved several problems. Then have a jelly bean snack.

ADDING AND SUBTRACTING

April 30 is the 98th birthday of the hamburger in America. Draw a hamburger in a bun on the chalkboard. Ask children what they like on their hamburgers. List the ingredients on the board next to the hamburger (tomato, lettuce, mustard, ketchup, pickles, mayonnaise, peppers, cheese, and so on). Ask children to count the number of items to be put on the burger. Then present addition and subtraction problems, using the ingredients. (Examples: Ask how many ingredients would be left if you did not put lettuce or tomato on the hamburger. Ask how many hamburgers would be needed for everyone in the class to have one. Then ask how many would be needed if six children said they didn't like hamburgers.) Let students solve the problems, then count the items to check their answers.

BY MARY TUCKER

Name _____

Number Boxes

To celebrate Math Education Month in April, color the boxes where the number of dots matches the number word. Put an X on the other boxes.

four • • • •	two • •
six • • • • •	eight • • • • • • • •
five • • • • •	three • • •
one •	nine 
ten • • • • • • • • • •	seven 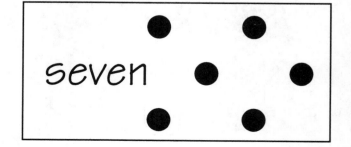

by Ann Fisher

Name _____

Spring Kite Fun

Look at the picture above.

How many kites are **above** the cloud? _____

How many kites are **below** the cloud? _____

How many kites are **on** the cloud? _____

Finish the Flowers

Read the description below each flower and follow the
directions adding what you need to finish the flower correctly.

This flower
has 5 petals.

This flower
has 4 leaves.

This flower
has 6 petals.

This flower
has 8 leaves.

This flower
has 3 leaves.

This flower
has 7 petals.

Yellow Daffodils

A Counting Rhyme

One yellow daffodil nods its little head.
(Hold up one finger and nod your head.)

Two yellow daffodils in my flower bed.
(Hold up two fingers and put hands together on one cheek.)

Three yellow daffodils brighten up the day.
(Hold up three fingers, then put hands by each side of your face and spread fingers apart.)

Four yellow daffodils bringing joy our way.
(Hold up four fingers, then put a finger on each side of your smile.)

Five yellow daffodils swaying in the breeze.
(Hold up five fingers and move back and forth.)

Six yellow daffodils underneath the trees.
(Hold up six fingers, then put arms out to your sides like branches.)

Seven yellow daffodils standing in the sun.
(Hold up seven fingers, then make arms into a circle around your head.)

Eight yellow daffodils having lots of fun.
(Hold up eight fingers, then put arms out to your sides, bend elbows up, and shake your hands.)

Nine yellow daffodils wonderful to see.
(Hold up nine fingers, then put hands around your eyes like glasses.)

Ten yellow daffodils growing just like me.
(Hold up 10 fingers, then point to self and smile.)

by Elizabeth Giles

School Yard Poetry

April is a time when nature begins a new growth cycle. Trees get new leaves, flowers start to bloom, small animals appear, and the sun feels warmer. It's a great season to focus on nature's gifts.

April is also National Poetry Month. What a combination—nature and poetry—sights and sounds children can discover right in their own school yard, playgrounds, or parks. To begin, read the following poem and discuss what treasures can be found outdoors:

> *When I go in my yard to play*
> *I have the nicest kind of day.*
> *There's a treasure to be found in every space.*
> *I think my yard's a magic place.*

Over the next weeks, choose one poem a day. An activity is suggested with each poem. Also, if weather permits, go outside to find examples.

> *The sun is rolling 'cross the sky*
> *Like a yellow ball someone threw up high.*
> *Its rays of shimmering, shining light*
> *Make my yard so warm and bright.*

Discussion: Where is the sun when you come to school in the morning? At lunch time? When you get home from school? Does it feel warmer now than it did in the winter? Are you wearing different clothes now than in winter? How are our activities different? (Remind children to never look directly at the sun!)

> *A butterfly with velvet wings,*
> *Trimmed with gold and scarlet rings,*
> *Flitted down briefly from the sky*
> *And fluttered its wings as if to say, "Hi!"*

Activity: Let children feel a piece of velvet and discuss its texture. Then have each child trace a butterfly and color its wings. Make mobiles with the paper butterflies and hang them around the room.

> *I dug into the damp, dark ground*
> *And, crawling in the dirt, I found*
> *A slippery, wiggly little worm.*
> *I picked him up and felt him squirm.*

Activity: Find the describing words—*slippery, wiggly*. Why are these good words to describe a worm? What word describes how a worm moves? (squirm) What other words could describe a worm?

by Elaine H. Cleary

228

Standing pertly in their places,
My pansies have such friendly faces;
They smile up at me, and so
I smile right back and say, "Hello!"

Activity: Read all but the last word. Ask children what word might be said back (try to elicit a rhyme). If necessary, give several words to choose from. Look at a pansy. See how its markings make a "face."

A puffy white cloud went sailing by.
I reached to touch it, but it was too high.
I'd like to have one for my bed,
A fluffy pillow for my head.

Activity: Pass out cotton balls and have children pull the fibers apart enough to make them look like clouds. Let children draw outdoor pictures, gluing on the cotton for clouds in the sky. Look at some clouds and imagine what their shapes look like—a face? An animal? A plane? What else?

I watched a rosebud as it grew,
Warmed by the sun and wet by the dew.
Until one day my beautiful rose
Shed her green cloak for pink petal clothes.

Activity: Find a rose with a bud that's ready to open and watch its progress. If a rose isn't available, make one with tissue paper, wrap it in green tape, then unwrap the tape a little at a time.

I have a big box filled with sand;
I like to feel sand in my hand.
It sifts through my fingers, and down it goes,
Until it covers up my toes.

Activity: It there's is not a sandbox available fill a plastic dishpan with sand for children to experiment with (preferably outdoors). Pour sand from one hand onto another instead of on feet.

A robin with a vest of red
Sat on the fence and cocked his head.
I asked him to please come and play,
But he chirped a song, then flew away.

Discussion: What is a vest? Animals don't wear clothes. Then why does it look like he's wearing a vest? What other animals have coloring that makes them look like they're wearing clothes? (mittens, boots on paws, hats on heads, glasses on eyes) Find pictures to display.

I heard a buzz and looked up high.
A yellow bee went streaking by.
It kissed the flowers one by one,
Then flew away when it was done.

Discussion: Discuss sound words—*buzz* for a bee; *drip, drop* for raindrop; *boom* for thunder; *squish* for water in boots, and others. Talk about why bees "touch" flowers for pollination.

Additional Activities

Poetry Booklets: Let each child choose three or four favorite poems. Print each on a separate sheet and have the children draw and color a picture to illustrate each one. Then make an appropriate cover. Preschoolers may want to use 8½" x 11" sheets, punching holes and tying the pages with yarn. Kindergartners can fold each sheet in half to make 5½" x 8½" sheets, writing the poem on one side and drawing the illustration on the other.

Memorizing Poems: Let each child choose a favorite poem to memorize. Have them draw a picture to illustrate it, then recite it for the class.

Making a Graph: Take a survey to find out which poem each child likes best. Then make a picture graph to show which poem is the most like the second favorite, and so on. Which poems do not show up on the graph at all? Why?

A Field Trip: Go to a nearby park or visit an area garden center looking for the "treasures" mentioned in the poems. Find other "treasures" of nature, too.

Field Trip!

Writing Poetry: Help the class write a collective poem about some other "treasure" that might be found in a yard or park in the spring. Following are some suggestions:

Add two more lines to these poem starters.
Tree
Reaching its leafy branches high,
My tree stretches way up to the sky.

Ant
A little black ant makes not a sound
As it quickly crawls across the ground.

Puddle
After the rain, guess what I found?
A great big puddle on the ground!

Add one more line to the following to make a couplet.
Grass
I sit on a carpet of grassy green—

Daisy
Daisies wear collars of petals white—

Chipmunk
A little brown chipmunk scurried by—

What might be said about these "treasures"?
stone, dandelion, raindrop, squirrel or rabbit

Have a Poetry Day and invite family members, friends, or older students to read poems of their choice. (Try to find poems about things in nature.)

Keep America Beautiful

Celebrate Keep America Beautiful Month in April with this bulletin board.

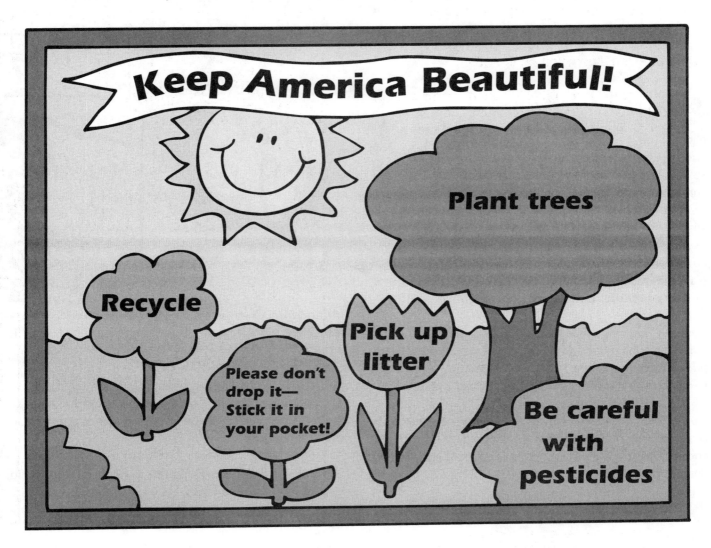

1. Cover the top of the bulletin board with blue wrapping paper and light green paper on the bottom half.
2. Cut out letters for the caption or print it on a colorful banner-shaped piece of wrapping paper.
3. Cut a large sun from yellow paper. Use a marker to draw a happy face on the sun.
4. Cut a tree shape from green paper and a trunk from brown paper. Using a black marker, print the words *Plant trees* on the tree.
5. Cut a bush from green paper. Print *Be careful with pesticides* on it.
6. Cut flowers from various colors of paper and make green stems and leaves. Print *Recycle* on one flower, *Pick up litter* on another, and the following rhyme on a third flower: *Please don't drop it—Stick it in your pocket!*
7. Mount all the pieces on the bulletin board.
8. Let children add natural items to the board such as leaves, pinecones, flowers, twigs, and so on.

by Mary Tucker

231

Abbey's Puddle

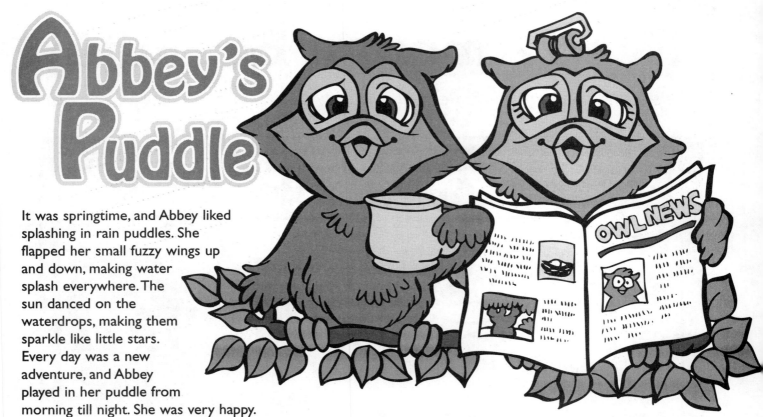

It was springtime, and Abbey liked splashing in rain puddles. She flapped her small fuzzy wings up and down, making water splash everywhere. The sun danced on the waterdrops, making them sparkle like little stars. Every day was a new adventure, and Abbey played in her puddle from morning till night. She was very happy.

But one morning Abbey woke up and her puddle was gone. It hadn't rained for a couple of days, and Abbey's puddle had disappeared. It was all dried up. "What happened to my puddle?" she cried. "Where did it go?"

Abbey didn't know what to do. She went over to a large oak tree and sat down in its shade. She thought and thought but could not figure out what happened to her puddle.

Mr. and Mrs. Owl were sitting in the tree having breakfast. They were talking about the weather. "I wish it would rain," Mrs. Owl said. "Everything is so dry. The trees and flowers need water."

Mr. Owl fluffed his silky brown feathers. "Well," he said, looking up at the sky, "when the rain clouds come back, then we will have rain."

"Rain clouds?" Abbey whispered to herself. "Where did they go? When I see them, I will ask them to send rain. Then maybe my puddle will come back, and everything will grow.

Every day Abbey sat by her dried-up puddle and waited for the rain clouds to come. But they did not appear. "Maybe they can't see me," thought Abbey. "Maybe I have to get closer to them and then ask them for rain." So Abbey climbed up the highest hill and called to the clouds.

"Hello, clouds," she shouted. "My name is Abbey. I was wondering, can you make it rain today? I want to play in my puddle." Abbey waited and waited but the white fluffy clouds did not answer. They just floated away, leaving Abbey standing there all alone. Abbey went back down the hill, feeling very sad. She would try again tomorrow.

by Lola De Julio De Maci

TLC10339 Copyright © Teaching & Learning Company, Carthage, IL 62321-0010

The next morning Abbey woke up bright and early and hurried up the hill again. "Hello, clouds," she called. "My name is Abbey. I was wondering, can you make it rain today? I want to play in my puddle." But the white fluffy clouds did not answer. They just floated away, leaving Abbey all alone again. Abbey was very unhappy. She was sure that the clouds did not like her. They did not talk to her or send her any rain. So Abbey went back down the hill. She slowly strolled over to the large oak tree and sat down.

Mr. and Mrs. Owl were discussing the weather again. "I think it might rain tomorrow," Mr. Owl said. "Look at the clouds. They're starting to get dark and gray."

"Well, we certainly can use the rain," Mrs. Owl said, looking up at the clouds that were no longer white and fluffy.

Abbey looked up at the sky. She did not know what a rain cloud looked like, but the clouds did look different today.

The next morning Abbey went back up the hill and called to the dark, gray clouds. "Hello, clouds," she shouted. "My name is Abbey. I was wondering, can you make it rain today? I want to play in my puddle."

Just then a loud crack of thunder echoed across the sky, and it started to rain. "Oh thank you. Thank you," Abbey called out, running down the hill. She was so happy. The clouds had heard her after all.

Abbey hurried over to her puddle and jumped in. "I like dark clouds best of all," she exclaimed happily. "White fluffy clouds are pretty, but they don't talk or send rain."

Abbey flapped her small fuzzy wings up and down, making water splash everywhere. The sun sparkled through the raindrops, making them glow like little stars. Springtime was certainly her favorite time of year. Even if it was her very first one.

233

Fun with Finger

Dance a Jig

(Sing this to the tune of "The Bear Went over the Mountain." Put hands on hips, right heel in front of you. As you sing the next three lines, alternate right and left heel, and you'll be dancing a jig.)

We'll dance a jig for the Irish,
We'll dance a jig for the Irish,
We'll dance a jig for the Irish,
Hooray! Hooray! Hooray!

(Thrust right arm above head; then left arm; then lower both arms back to hip position on the final "hooray.")

March Wind

March wind gives a mighty blow.
  (Blow hard.)
March wind makes the trees bend low.
  (Extend arms like tree branches and bend from side to side.)
March wind gives another blow.
  (Blow hard.)
March wind makes the leaves all go.
  (Flutter fingers downward, then hide them behind your back.)

Flying Kites

(Throughout this entire poem, walk around pretending to fly a kite.)

I like to fly my kite,
And fly it very high.
I like to fly my kite
Way up into the sky.

But while I fly my kite,
I think of just one thing.
I must always make sure
To hold on to the string.

Purim Fun

Purim is here. Come, everyone.
  (Beckon to everyone.)
Come with me; we'll have lots of fun.
We'll hear the great Megillah read.
  (Pretend to hold a book and read.)
And each time Haman's name is said,
We'll yell and scream as gragers spin,
  (Twirl real or pretend gragers overhead.)
Then settle down, settle down with a wide grin.
  (Give a wide grin.)
After that, there's a special treat—
Hamantaschen we get to eat!
  (Pretend to hold a cake and eat it.)

It's Spring!

It's spring! It's spring!
  (Be excited.)
Our skates we bring.
  (Skate around.)
We push the swing.
  (Swing back and forth.)
The sun is out.
  (Point overhead.)
Seeds grow and sprout.
  (Use fingers to show growth.)
It's spring! I shout.
  (Jump for joy and shout "spring.")

by Judy Wolfman

234

plays

Yellow Daffodil

I'm a yellow daffodil
(Stand straight and tall.)
That nods from left to right.
(Lean to left, then right.)
Here are my leaves so soft and green,
(Extend hands.)
That guard me through the night.
(Stand still.)

Beautiful Butterfly

I'm a beautiful butterfly
That's looking for some dew.
(Gently flap arms and "fly" around.)
I'll spread my wings and fly away
And wave "good-bye" to you!
(Flap arms stronger and fly away.)

Spring Rain

Listen to that thunder!
(Clap loudly on "thunder.")
Now the rain is pouring down!
(Wiggle fingers like rain.)
I wonder if it's better
(Put finger on chin, wondering.)
On the other side of town?
(Point to other side.)

Red Tulips

One red tulip in my garden grew,
(Show one finger.)
Up popped another; then I had two.
(Show two fingers.)
Two red tulips now I could see.
Look, there's another! That makes three.
(Point to "tulip" and show three fingers.)
Three red tulips—are there any more?
(Show three fingers and look around for more.)
Yes, there is one—and that makes four.
(Point to "tulip" and show four fingers.)
Four red tulips, sure as I'm alive!
(Show four fingers.)
Here is another! Now I have five.
(Pretend to pick "tulip" and show five fingers.)

Hungry Birdies

Here I have a pretty nest.
(Interlock fingers, palms upwards.)
Take a look inside.
(Look into hands.)
See hungry birdies with their beaks
Opening so wide.
*(Put index finger and thumb of each
hand together and open and close them.)*
Now my little birdies grow
A little every day.
*(Gradually spread hands apart to show
growth.)*
One day they'll spread their little wings
And fly far away.
(Flap arms and hands.)

Snacktivities

*Invite your children to try new tastes and food combinations
with tongue-tempting snack recipes.*

Temptation Towers

March—National Nutrition Month

Ingredients

mini rice cakes
peanut butter
fresh fruits and vegetables that will slice easily,
such as bananas, cucumbers, carrots, apples,
kiwi, and so on

Have the children help to wash, peel, and slice the fruits and vegetables. Let them spread peanut butter on a rice cake, then stack fruit and vegetable slices as they wish. Variations: 1) Have the children stack fruits and vegetables in a specific patterns, such as 1 banana, 2 apples, 1 kiwi, 2 carrots. 2) Have the children count how many slices they can stack before their tower tumbles.

Peanut Butter Cookie Roll

March—Peanut Month

Ingredients

⅓ c. peanut butter
⅓ c. light corn syrup
⅓ c. powdered sugar
½ c. powdered milk
finely chopped peanuts

Measure the peanut butter and corn syrup into a bowl. Cream together with an electric mixer. Use a mixing spoon to continue mixing as you gradually add the powdered sugar and powdered milk to the combined peanut butter and corn syrup. Roll the dough into a cylinder about 1" thick, then roll it in finely chopped peanuts. Wrap in waxed paper and refrigerate for at least two hours. Slice into 1" pieces to serve.

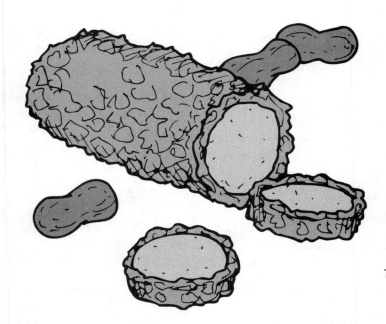

by Marie E. Cecchini

Fruit Sips

March—St. Patrick's Day

Ingredients

kiwi fruit
2-3 Tbsp. honey or sugar
1 c. skim milk
4 large scoops lime sherbet
fresh mint leaves (optional)
2 Tbsp. lime juice

Peel and cut kiwi into small pieces. Place 2 c. of the kiwi fruit, the milk, lime juice, and honey or sugar into a blender. Cover and blend until thoroughly combined. Add the sherbet, one scoop at a time, and continue to blend until thick and smooth. Serve in individual serving cups. Top with a sprig of mint leaves, if you like.

Pizza Eggs

April—Easter

Ingredients

Italian or French bread slices
tomato sauce at room temperature
cheese slices
assorted toppings, (olives, peppers, mushrooms, broccoli, etc., sliced or cut into small pieces)

Toast the egg-shaped bread slices. Place sauce over the toast and let the children decorate their snack with cheese and other toppings. Place finished designs in a toaster oven or under a broiler until the cheese begins to melt. Cool before serving.

Rainbow Pudding

April—Spring Rains

Ingredients

instant vanilla pudding
milk
food coloring
small baby food jars (one for each child)

Help each child measure 1 tablespoon of instant pudding and ¼ c. of milk into a jar. Add a few drops of one or more food colorings at this time. Some children may wish to try color blending. Tightly secure the lids on the jars and have the children shake, shake, shake their jars about 50 times. Allow the jars to sit in a cool place for 5-10 minutes, observe the children's color creations (like a rainbow?), then open the jars and enjoy.

Applesauce Raisin Pudding

April—Applesauce Week

1½ c. applesauce
¾ c. raisins
4 ripe bananas
nutmeg
4 Tbsp. peanut butter

Peel the bananas, cut them into chunks, then mash them in a mixing bowl. Add the applesauce and peanut butter and stir until thoroughly combined. Stir in the raisins, then spoon into individual serving bowls. Sprinkle each serving with nutmeg, then chill for about one hour before serving.

Spring Weather
to Sing About

Spring weather can be very changeable. You never know when you wake up in the morning if the day will bring rain, wind, snow, sunshine, a tornado, a hurricane, or calm, beautiful weather. But whatever the weather, we can enjoy it and even sing about it.

Teach these catchy songs to your students to help them appreciate the weather changes in springtime.

Rain Clouds Cry

To the tune of
"Happy Birthday to You"

The clouds in the sky
Grow as they pass by.
They fill up with water
And have a good cry!

Raindrops on My Umbrella

To the tune of "My Darling
Clementine"

I open my umbrella
To keep the rain off me.
I open my umbrella
And jump around with glee!
Raindrops fall in puddles,
Land on flowers and trees.
Raindrops on my umbrella
And my shoes, but not on me!

Pitter-Patter

To the tune of
"Old MacDonald Had a Farm"

Pitter-patter went the rain,
Falling to the ground.
Pitter-patter went the rain,
Landing on the ground.
Dripping here, dripping there,
Dripping, dripping everywhere.
Pitter-patter went the rain;
What a special sound!

238   **by Jennifer Crook**

Rain's a Symphony

To the tune of
"Row, Row, Row Your Boat"

Splish, splash, splish, kerplop!
Hear the rain fall down.
That's the music raindrops make
Falling to the ground.

Plink, plop, drippity-drop!
See the raindrops dance.
Twisting, turning through the leaves,
Waltzing on the plants!

Sniff, sniff, take a whiff!
Earth smells fresh and clean.
Hear it, see it, smell it, feel it;
Rain's a symphony!

Hurricane Harry

To the tune of "Twinkle, Twinkle, Little Star"

Hurricane Harry was a storm
That started when the air got warm.
The waves grew taller than before
And crashed into the sandy shore!
The wind got tired of being so scary,
And that was the end of Hurricane Harry.

The Sound of Snow

To the tune of "Happy Birthday to You"

A snowstorm can howl!
A blizzard can roar!
A snowflake can whisper,
"Listen for more."

Windy!

To the tune of "Frere Jacques"

March winds blow,
March winds blow,
Soft and strong, soft and strong!
I try with all my might
To hold on to my kite.
Watch it go! Watch it go!

Snowflakes

To the tune of "My Darling Clementine"

I can see the white snowflakes
Falling down from the sky.
When the winter wind blows
I like to watch them fly.
Oh the snowballs, oh the angels,
Oh the snowmen I will make!
And a million little reasons—
Frozen water, a snowflake!

RAIN DANCING

I'm looking out the window;
And everything is gray.
My mom says, "See? It's raining!
Too wet outside to play."

I can't see any raindrops.
I look and look and frown.
Oh there! They're in the puddle!
They're dancing up and down!

I'll go and get my crayons,
To maybe cheer my brain.
I'll make a rosy rainbow,
'Cause rainbows end the rain!

BY IRENE LIVINGSTON

240

Creative
Seasonal Tips

Finger Cymbals
by Georgeann Proett

Celebrate Music in Our Schools Month in March by making finger cymbals for each child in your class. All you need are some plastic poker chips, a glue gun, and elastic.

Hot glue a small piece of elastic (big enough to fit on a child's fingertip) to the back of each poker chip. Play music and have children use their finger cymbals to play along.

What Grows There?
by Tricia Wagner

In the spring it seems as if everything is growing! Here's an experiment your children will love. Before going outside for a class walk, have children pull old adult socks over their shoes (one for each child). Take them for a walk around the yard. After a few minutes, remove the socks and put them in labeled zip-up plastic bags. Place the bags in the window where they'll have a lot of light. Use a spray bottle of water to spritz the socks each day or so. Check them every day and after a while you'll discover the socks are growing! Help students identify what's growing on the socks if possible and enjoy them!

Jelly Bean Colors
by Christine Fischer

When children get jelly beans in their Easter baskets, do they notice the colors? Make several cardboard jelly bean templates for children using the pattern above. Have them trace the jelly beans on white construction paper, making several. Then have children color each jelly bean a different color. Help them print on each jelly bean the name of its color; then cut them out. Give each student a small paper lunch bag in which the paper jelly beans may be kept. Later, have them shake the bags; then pull out the jelly beans and say what color each one is.

Mime Week

*Celebrate Mime Week, the first week of April,
by involving children in these fun learning activities.*

Literature

Incorporate books about silence, quiet, and body movements into the classroom. Add picture books without words to the reading selection. Place books in the classroom library or reading space and read them at story time. Don't forget other areas of the classroom when introducing books. Add books to a dramatic play area, cooking activity, building center, or anywhere they have a theme connection. Try some of these books:

Picture books without words:
Trucks by Donald Crews, Tupelo Books, 1997.
Changes, Changes by Pat Hutchins, Aladdin Paperback, 1987.

Game: Mime Charades

Cut out pictures of people in a variety of occupations. Mount each picture on an index card or piece of construction paper. Choose one child to be the Mime. The Mime chooses a picture, looks at it and places it facedown on the floor. The group tries to guess the occupation as the Mime acts it out without words. Play the game again, acting out types of sports or animals.

Language: Make "Quiet Lists"

Brainstorm with children to make lists of things that are quiet. Compile lists such as: Quiet Animals, Quiet Jobs, Quiet Games, Quiet Toys, Quiet Places.

Math: Silent Numbers

Play a number guessing game without words. Give each child a set of number cards from 0-9. Begin the game by showing a question mark. Then present a number by clapping, beating a drum, or tapping two sticks together. Children count along silently, then hold up the appropriate number. Turn the game around: Show the question mark and then show a number. Children clap their hands or slap their knees the appropriate number of times.

by Carol Ann Bloom

Art: Mime Masks

Many mimes perform with white faces. Cut out an oval from white paper that will cover your face. Cut eyeholes in the paper mask. Use markers to decorate around the eyes and add a nose and a mouth. Place a hole on both sides of the mask. Tie a piece of yarn in each hole so that the mask can be tied behind the head. Wear Mime Masks for game and language activities.

Language: Say It Without Words

"Let's tell things about ourselves without words." Demonstrate by telling children "I'm happy" with gestures: "I'm (point to yourself) happy" (point to your smile). Ask children to tell something about themselves with gestures. Encourage other children to guess what is being said. Try phrases such as: I'm tired; I'm hungry; I'm thirsty; I'm hot; I'm cold; I'm strong; I'm sick; I'm reading; I'm painting.

Language: *The Story of Bip*

by Marcel Marceau (Stewart Tabori & Chang, 2001)

Marcel Marceau was a famous mime. Read the book he wrote about himself and talk about it. Ask some of the following questions:
What did Bip dream of being?
What did Bip become?
What happened to Bip's wings?
Where did Bip land before he went back to Earth?
What did he want to give Earth?
What was the black dot Bip saw on the horizon?
How did Bip speak to the world when he was speechless?
What was he trying to say?
(Note: *The Story of Bip* is out of print. However, a new version titled *Bip in a Book* was published in October 2001.)

Motor Skills: Wordless Jobs

Brainstorm with children to think of jobs or occupations in which people communicate without the use of words. When the list is completed, invite children to imagine they are performing the jobs by miming. Include jobs such as a police officer directing traffic, a flagman at a racetrack, a dog (or animal) trainer, and a magician.

243

Celebrate Earth Day

On April 22, 1970, over 20 million North Americans participated in the first Earth Day. Rallies and educational events were held, rivers and beaches were cleaned, the dumping of pollutants into the air was protested, and many people cooperated to make Earth a better place to live. Here are some creative ways to help your students think about the importance of taking care of the Earth and appreciating all we get from our planet.

Happy Birthday, Earth, Party

Cover a work surface, preferably outside, with newspaper. Place a tub of each of the following on a table or the ground: sand, dirt, gravel, salt. Have small pitchers of water available as well as old spoons and bowls. Let each child concoct his or her own earth-cake, using the materials in the tubs and water. Some will want to mix the materials using a spoon and bowl while others will want to mix and mold their cakes by hand. You may want to have each child wear an apron or an old shirt to keep good clothes from getting mud-splattered.

Let the earth-cakes dry; then have children use natural items to decorate their cakes: grass, stones, twigs, flowers, pinecones, and so on.

Take the earth-cakes to a park or to an area near a tree. Seat children in a circle around the tree. Sing "Happy Birthday" to Earth as you hold hands and sway back and forth. Then talk about all the good things trees do for us: (provide paper, lumber, and food; give us medicine; help prevent erosion and reduce flooding; produce oxygen for us to breathe, and so on). Then ask children to suggest some ways we can take good care of the trees around us (don't cut them down, water them, keep pollutants out of the water and ground so they can stay healthy, and so on).

Nature Collections

Have students work with you to collect a variety of nature items such as seashells, dried wheat and grasses, flowers, sand, rocks, bark, branches, and so on. Provide children with foam trays from meat or produce and glue. Let them create nature collages and plaques with these materials.

by Gail Lennon

244

Earth Tones

Help children make natural dyes from items such as red cabbage, beets, celery tops, carrot tops, and vinegar. Simmer each vegetable in water, drain it, and save the liquids. Mix a tablespoon of vinegar into each liquid and let it cool. Provide paintbrushes and let children use the natural colors to paint a large piece of muslin or cotton fabric. After it dries, hang it in the hall for everyone to see.

Earth Painting

Let students fingerpaint with mud outdoors. Show them how to mix dirt with water until it reaches the desired consistency. Then encourage them to paint on the sidewalk or on mural or fingerpaint paper. (If they paint the sidewalk, be sure to wash it off later.)

Earth's Wonders

Display natural Earth wonders on a table: seashells, rocks, crystals, geodes, pinecones, seeds, twigs, etc. Encourage all the children to add to the collection. Provide magnifying glasses so students can study the wonders carefully. Place books nearby that picture Earth's natural resources.

It Pays to Recycle

Explain to children how we can save energy as well as natural products when we recycle newsprint, tin cans, and glass bottles.

Celebrate Trees

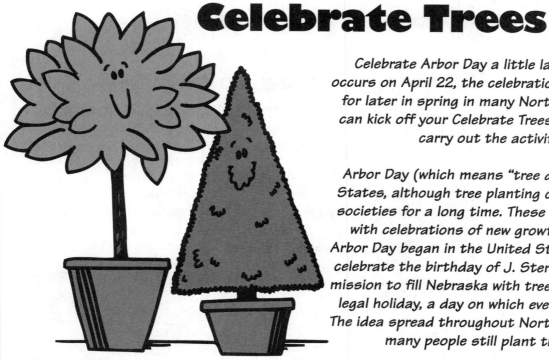

Celebrate Arbor Day a little late. Although Arbor Day occurs on April 22, the celebration of trees is better suited for later in spring in many North American climates. You can kick off your Celebrate Trees theme on Arbor Day and carry out the activities into May.

Arbor Day (which means "tree day") began in the United States, although tree planting ceremonies have been with societies for a long time. These were generally associated with celebrations of new growth in the spring season. Arbor Day began in the United States on April 22, 1885, to celebrate the birthday of J. Sterling Morton, a man with a mission to fill Nebraska with trees. This day was declared a legal holiday, a day on which everyone was to plant trees. The idea spread throughout North America and to this day many people still plant trees on Arbor Day.

The Wonder of Trees

- Trees are the largest and most majestic green plants on the Earth. They grow in gatherings we call forests.
- Some people call forests the lungs of the Earth because trees help clean the air we breathe. A tree's leaves produce oxygen, which is used by all living creatures to survive.

Tree Watching

Tree watching is a fun thing to do on a warm summer day. Take your group to your Kid Space to sit or lie under a tree and observe. There are so many kinds of trees to observe and so many exciting things happening in those branches.

Make Friends with a Tree

Have each child choose a special tree. Take a photo of the child beside his or her special tree.

Encourage children to describe their trees. How does the tree smell, feel, and look? Identifying the types of trees is not important. How does its bark feel? What do the leaves look like? How do they feel and smell?

by Robynne Eagan

246

The Truffula Tree

Read *The Truffula Tree* by Dr. Seuss, Random House, 1971.

Discuss the wonders of trees, the uses of trees by humans and creatures in nature, the importance of trees, and the sad fact that many of our forests are disappearing.

Tree Planting

Collect a few acorns, maple keys, pinecones, or chestnuts in the autumn. Have students plant these seeds in their gardens, at school, in a vacant lot, or on community property (with permission). Visit these sites in the spring and monitor the progress of these plantings throughout the school year.

Have students plant a tree on a special day—the first day of summer, Earth Day, Arbor Day, a school anniversary, etc. Take a photograph of the children beside their special tree each year on the same date.

Encourage students to mark special events in their lives with tree plantings. A birthday makes a perfect occasion. Suggest they have their photo taken each birthday beside their growing tree.

How to Plant a Tree

1. Choose a tree that is well suited to your location and climate. Read about different trees in garden catalogs. Look at pictures to see how the trees will look when they're fully grown.
2. Select the best spot in your yard to plant the tree. It should not be too close to a building, under a power line, or in the shadow of another tree.
3. Dig a hole at least twice as wide as the tree's root ball and twice as deep.
4. Position the tree in the center of the hole. Make sure you stand it up straight.
5. Crumble the soil back into the hole, adding compost as you do.
6. Fill the soil in around the tree and pack it gently.
7. Sprinkle a little water around the tree to help the earth settle. Top up with soil as needed.
8. Cover the soil with a layer of mulch to retain moisture and inhibit weed growth. Keep the tree well watered and monitor it for any signs of bug infestation or disease.

Imagine Living in the Forest

Take children to your Kid Space. Invite them to imagine and role-play the following situations.

Imagine how it would feel to be . . .

- a bird in the branches of a tree
- a bear in a cave
- a creeping inchworm
- a graceful butterfly
- a slithering snake
- an eagle soaring in the sky

Forest Creatures Listening Games

Provide opportunities for students to develop listening skills as they move and play as woodland creatures.

You Need
- hoops of different colors
- open area
- drum or tambourine to keep the beat

Get Ready
Place lots of different colored hoops around the open place. Demonstrate various ways that forest animals can move. Allow children to share their demonstrations and suggestions.

Directions
1. Signal to children that a new instruction is coming by sounding a drum, whistle, or tambourine. When children hear the instrument, they should stop and listen carefully for the next instruction.
2. Invite children to walk like a raccoon, scurry like a mouse, or hop like a bunny without touching the hoops.
3. Intersperse these instructions with more complicated requests for students to swoop like an owl into a white hoop, or gather in groups of bunnies in the blue hoops, and so on.

Forest Creatures on the Move

Children will learn about the ways creatures of the forest move in this living game of movement and fun.

You Need
- open space to run, hop, and slither
- boundary markers about 15 feet (5 m) apart

Directions
1. Take children outside and talk about the ways different forest creatures move.
2. Have children stand in a line facing the direction they will travel.
3. Invite children to join you as you travel from one line to the next as a hopping rabbit, scurrying mouse, graceful deer or other creature.
4. Once children reach that location, announce another animal and have students travel in that way back to the line they began on.
5. Invite children to suggest animals and demonstrate the various movements for their classmates.

Sing a Rainbow

Do you see a rainbow in the summer sky? Encourage preschool children's visual perception and social interaction with this color recognition activity.

You Need
- six or more children
- colored discs or other objects that can be used for color reference

Directions
1. Have children sit in a circle on the ground.
2. The game leader (teacher or other adult volunteer) holds up the corresponding color sample and sings a question such as "Who is wearing a hat that is blue? Hat that is blue? Hat that is blue? Oh, who is wearing a hat that is blue, this lovely summer day?" to the tune of "Here We Go 'Round the Mulberry Bush."
3. Children should be invited to sing their response to the same tune. "Oh, Jenny is wearing a hat that is blue, . . ."
4. The leader or a selected child may sing the next question and the search is on again.

Four Green Leaves

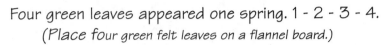

For this fun learning activity you'll need to use the patterns on page 251 to make four green leaves, four colored leaves (yellow, orange, red, and brown), four ladybugs, four raindrops, four snowflakes, and four small new leaves.

Four green leaves appeared one spring. 1 - 2 - 3 - 4.
(Place four green felt leaves on a flannel board.)

Each leaf had a green tip. 1 - 2 - 3 - 4.
(Point to and count each tip.)

Each leaf had a green stem. 1 - 2 - 3 - 4.
(Point to and count each stem.)

The leaves moved softly in the warm breeze. 1 - 2 - 3 - 4.
(Gently blow through lips and flutter hands.)

Four green leaves grew bigger all summer long. 1 - 2 - 3 - 4.
(Spread hands slightly apart.)

Each leaf had a bug crawl on it. 1 - 2 - 3 - 4.
(Point to ladybugs on leaves.)

Each leaf was splashed by raindrops. 1 - 2 - 3 - 4.
(Place four raindrops on flannel board.)

The leaves did not move in the hot sun. 1 - 2 - 3 - 4.
(Place finger on lips to indicate no movement.)

Four green leaves did not stay green in the autumn. 1 - 2 - 3 - 4.
(Shake head side to side.)

One leaf turned yellow.
(Place yellow leaf over green one.)

Its tip turned yellow.
(Point to tip.)

Its stem turned yellow.
(Point to stem.)

The leaves jumped in the cool air. 1 - 2 - 3 - 4.
(Bounce hand in the air.)

One yellow leaf fell to the ground.
(Place yellow/green leaf on floor.)

Three green leaves were left. 1 - 2 - 3.
(Count remaining leaves.)

Three green leaves did not stay green in the autumn. 1 - 2 - 3.
(Shake head side to side.)

One leaf turned orange.
(Place orange leaf over a green leaf.)

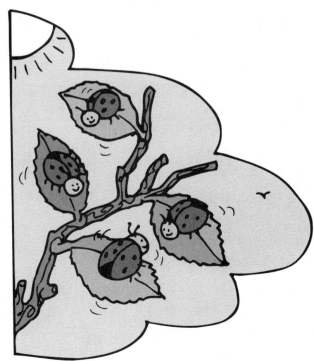

by Chris Chilcote

Its tip turned orange.
(Point to tip.)

Its stem turned orange.
(Point to stem.)

The leaves twirled in a chilly gust. 1 - 2 - 3.
(Twirl hand in air.)

One orange leaf fell to the ground.
(Remove orange/green leaf to floor.)

Two green leaves were left. 1 - 2.
(Count remaining leaves.)

Two green leaves did not stay green in the autumn. 1 - 2.
(Shake head side to side.)

One leaf turned red.
(Place red leaf over a green leaf.)

Its tip turned red.
(Point to tip.)

Its stem turned red.
(Point to stem.)

The leaves bounced in the cold, hard wind. 1 - 2.
(Bounce one hand on the other.)

One red leaf fell to the ground.
(Remove red/green leaf to floor.)

One green leaf was left. 1.
(Count remaining leaf.)

One green leaf did not stay green in the winter.
(Shake head side to side.)

It turned brown.
(Place brown leaf over last green leaf.)

Its tip turned brown.
(Point to tip.)

Its stem turned brown.
(Point to stem.)

Quietly a few snowflakes fell. 1 - 2 - 3 - 4.
(Cover raindrops with snowflakes.)

One brown leaf fell to the ground.
(Remove brown/green leaf to floor.)

Four leaves—yellow, orange, red, and brown—
were covered with snow. 1 - 2 - 3 -4.
(Place one hand over the other.)

But then spring came.
(Show four small, new, green leaves on flannel board.)

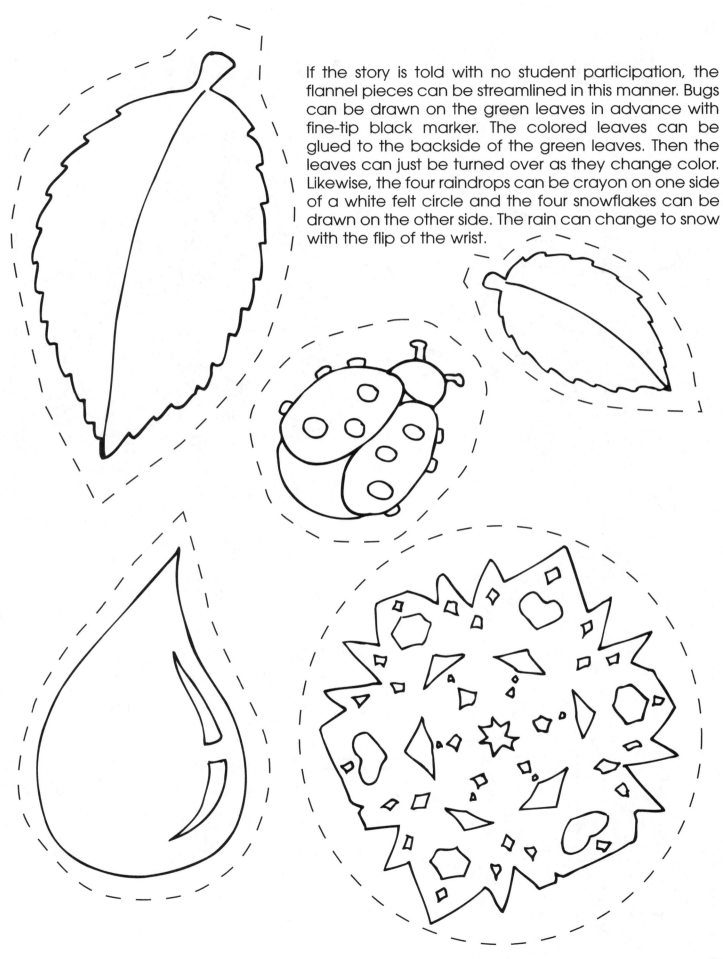

If the story is told with no student participation, the flannel pieces can be streamlined in this manner. Bugs can be drawn on the green leaves in advance with fine-tip black marker. The colored leaves can be glued to the backside of the green leaves. Then the leaves can just be turned over as they change color. Likewise, the four raindrops can be crayon on one side of a white felt circle and the four snowflakes can be drawn on the other side. The rain can change to snow with the flip of the wrist.

Name _____

May Day Tradition

On May Day people often fill baskets with beautiful flowers and then hang them on someone's doorknob. There are five different kinds of flowers in this basket. Count how many there are of each type and write the numbers at the bottom.

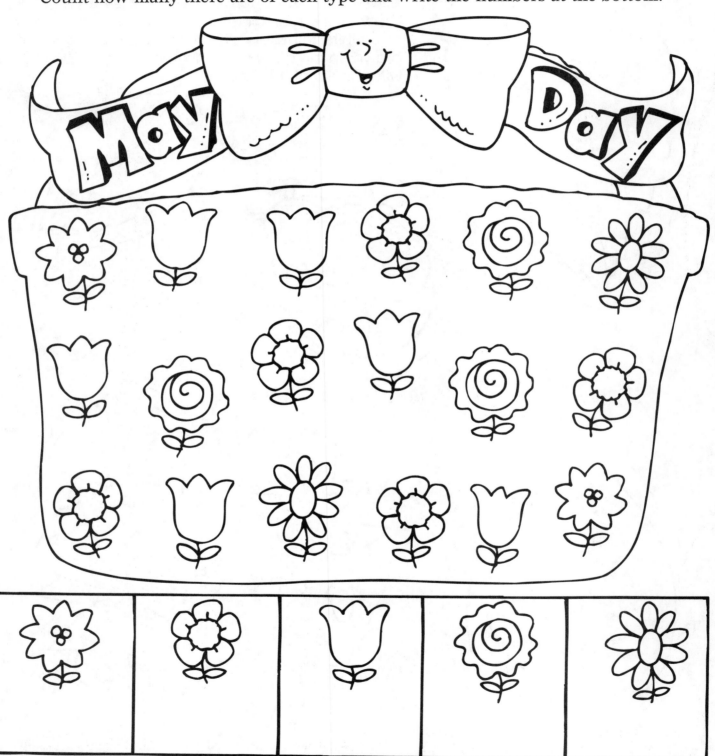

by Becky Radtke

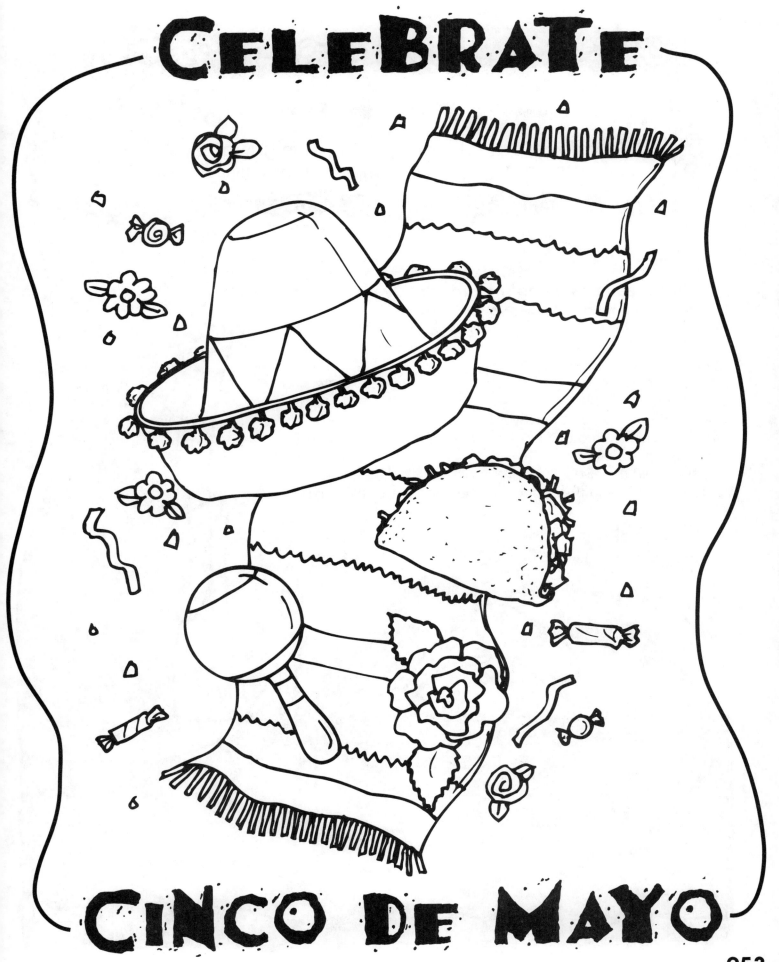

CeleBRaTe

CiNCO De MaYO

HAPPY LEi DAY!

Celebrate Lei Day, observed on May 1 in Hawaii, by singing this song and having children complete the activities that follow.

LiViNG iN HAWAii

To be read or sung to the tune of "Over in the Meadow"

Living in Hawaii where the deep waters run,
Was a mother humpback whale and her clever calf one.
"Breach!" said the mother.
"I breach!" said the one.
And they breached and they splashed where the deep waters run.

Living in Hawaii where the waves break blue,
Was a mother spotted dolphin and her dancing dolphins two.
"Surf!" said the mother.
"We surf!" said the two.
And they surfed and they boogied where the waves break blue.

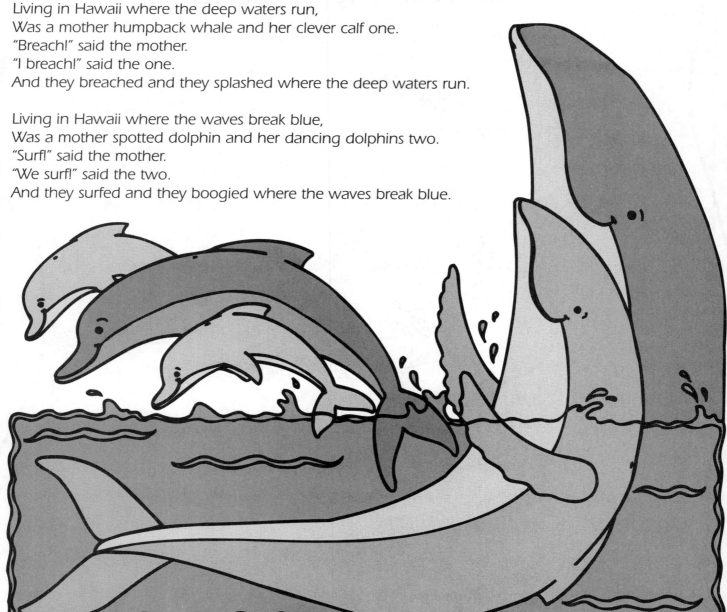

BY TERRY PiERCE

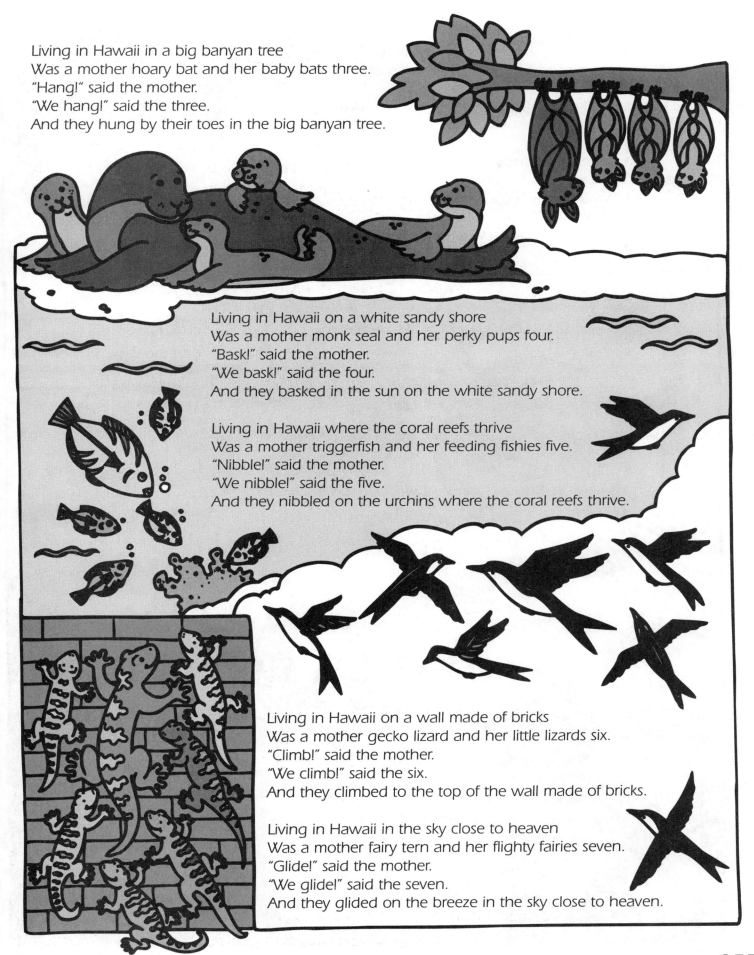

Living in Hawaii in a big banyan tree
Was a mother hoary bat and her baby bats three.
"Hang!" said the mother.
"We hang!" said the three.
And they hung by their toes in the big banyan tree.

Living in Hawaii on a white sandy shore
Was a mother monk seal and her perky pups four.
"Bask!" said the mother.
"We bask!" said the four.
And they basked in the sun on the white sandy shore.

Living in Hawaii where the coral reefs thrive
Was a mother triggerfish and her feeding fishies five.
"Nibble!" said the mother.
"We nibble!" said the five.
And they nibbled on the urchins where the coral reefs thrive.

Living in Hawaii on a wall made of bricks
Was a mother gecko lizard and her little lizards six.
"Climb!" said the mother.
"We climb!" said the six.
And they climbed to the top of the wall made of bricks.

Living in Hawaii in the sky close to heaven
Was a mother fairy tern and her flighty fairies seven.
"Glide!" said the mother.
"We glide!" said the seven.
And they glided on the breeze in the sky close to heaven.

Living in Hawaii where the lava flows are great
Was a mother nene bird and her gangly goslings eight.
"Waddle!" said the mother.
"We waddle!" said the eight.
And they waddled to their nest where the lava flows are great.

Living in Hawaii where the crystal waters shine
Was a mother sea turtle and her tiny turtles nine.
"Paddle!" said the mother.
"We paddle!" said the nine.
And they paddled and they glided where the crystal waters shine.

Living in Hawaii near a rocky coral den
Was a mother octopus and her octopi ten.
"Squirt!" said the mother.
"We squirt!" said the ten.
And they squirted off safely to their rocky coral den.

Sailing near Hawaii was a whale watching crew
With a group of happy children and their happy teachers, too.
"Care!" said the teacher.
"We care!" said the group.
And they cared for Hawaii and the Mother Earth, too.

256

HOW MANY ANIMALS?

Count the animals in each row. Write the number in the box.

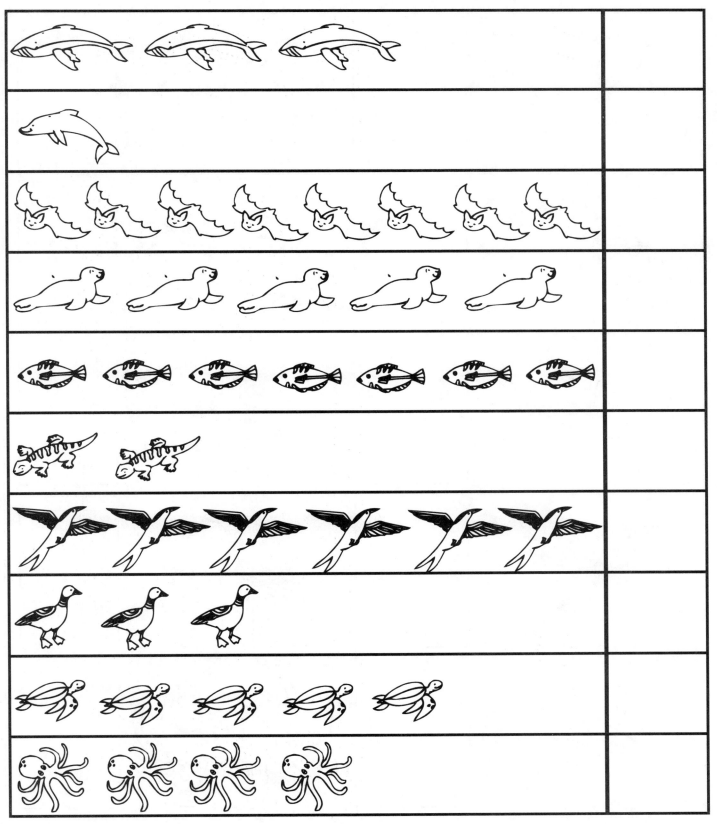

Name _____

WHAT LETTERS?

In the box, write the letter that each animal name begins with.

Cutting Project

1. Fold a sheet of paper (8.5 x 11) into three equal sections.

2. Trace the dolphin pattern onto the paper.

3. Cut out the dolphin, leaving the folds uncut.

4. Open the paper and see the dancing dolphin.

Additional Activities

1. Use a larger piece of paper and fold it multiple times for more dancing dolphins.

2. Cut out more than one set of dolphins and tape them together across the wall.

Handmade Gifts for Mom and Dad

Mother's Day Flower Magnet

Materials
    craft sticks
    construction paper of various colors
    magnetic tape
    green markers or crayons
    fine-tip markers
    glue

Directions
1. Use a green marker or crayon to color both sides of a craft stick to a flower stem.
2. Cut two leaf shapes from green construction paper.
3. On one leaf print *Happy*. On the other leaf, print *Mother's Day*.
4. Glue the leaves to the craft stick stem.
5. Cut flower petals from various colors of paper and glue them on the craft stick stem in a flower shape as shown.

by Christine Fischer

A PoeTree

Some dads are tall;
Some dads are round.
But you're the best dad
To be found!

Everyone loves a sing-song rhyme. So why not give a poem as a gift for Father's Day? Write your own or copy this one. Then create this "PoeTree."

Directions
1. Snip or break a small branch (about 15" long) from a bush or tree.
2. Place the branch in a clear glass jar.
3. Fill the jar with colorful marbles or clean pebbles.
4. Copy your favorite poems on small pieces of paper and illustrate or decorate each one with marking pens.
5. Punch a hole in a corner of each poem and attach it to the branch with yarn or ribbon.
6. Tie a bow around the neck of the jar and give your "PoeTree" to Dad along with a great big hug!

by Carol McAdoo Rehme

Clothespin Container

Materials
wooden clothespins
plastic margarine dishes (about 2" deep)
colored markers
white glue

Directions
1. Wash and dry the margarine dish thoroughly.
2. Decorate the wooden clothespins with colored markers. Draw small pictures, or make stripes, dots, and zigzags. You can also write your name or other words on the clothespins.
3. Spread white glue on the outside of the margarine dish.
4. Slide the decorated clothespins over the rim of the dish. Line up the ends of the clothespins with the bottom of the dish. Place the clothespins side by side and as close together as possible.
5. Give the finished Clothespin Container to your dad to hold his pens and pencils.

by Carol Ann Bloom

Mother's Day Fold-Up Card

Materials
11" x 17" colored construction paper
crayons

Directions
1. Holding the paper vertically, draw a large flower with a tall stem on it as shown.
2. Print at the top of the paper next to the flower *and grows!* Print at the bottom of the flower *Love,* and sign your name.
3. Fold the paper down from the top one quarter of its length.
4. Draw another flower blossom like the first but slightly smaller at the top of the stem on the folded-over section.
5. Print on this folded-over section next to the flower . . . *grows. . . .*
6. Fold the paper over again the same length.
7. Draw another flower blossom like the first and second at the top of the stem on the folded-over section.
8. Print on the folded-over section next to the flower *My love for you. . . .*
9. Fold the paper over one last time.
10. Print on this folded over section *For Mom.* Draw some small flowers or butterflies around the words.

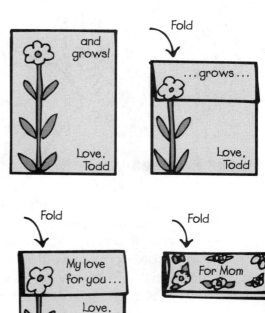

Your mom will love your Mother's Day message as she unfolds her card.

by Christine Fischer

Pet Parade

Pets are an excellent topic for language study especially during National Pet Week in May. The purpose of this unit is to provide students with opportunities to use a variety of language experiences in the development of knowledge and skills about pets. Activities provided will increase students' skills in comprehension, visualization, creative thinking, critical thinking, and evaluation. The unit may be used as a whole class pursuit, an enrichment theme for gifted students in the regular classroom, an individual activity, or as a parent/child home study theme.

Cat Handprint

Have each child trace and cut out a handprint with fingers together and thumb outstretched a little to make a tail. Let the child cut out a rug shape from a wallpaper sample book for the cat to sit on. Then put the handprint upright on the "rug." Use the top of a liquid detergent cap to make a circle at the top of the handprint to become the cat's head. Have the child use a marker to add facial features and whiskers. Have the children name their cats.

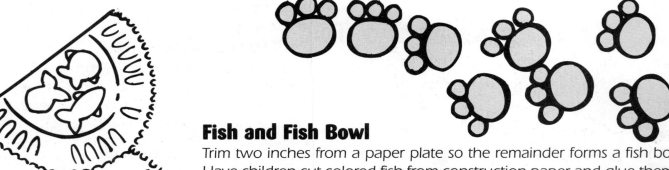

Fish and Fish Bowl

Trim two inches from a paper plate so the remainder forms a fish bowl. Have children cut colored fish from construction paper and glue them to the paper plate. Attach string and hang the fish bowls from the ceiling.

Paper Puppies

Have children make puppies from brown lunch bags. Stuff each bag with crumpled newspaper. Tie a ribbon around the bag about one-third of the way from the top to make the head and a ribbon one-third of the way to make the body. Have children glue on facial features made from scrap paper and felt. Add ears and a tail.

by Gail Lennon

My Five Pets

Teach your students the following rhyme. Have them do the actions as they repeat the rhyme. Work together to write rhymes about other pets.

I have five pets I'd like you to meet.
They live with me on Mulberry Street.
    (Hold up hand.)
This is my chick, smallest of all.
He comes a-running whenever I call.
    (Point to little finger.)
This is my duckling. He says, "Quack, quack, quack"
As he shakes the water from off his back.
    (Point to third finger.)
Here is my rabbit. He runs from his pen.
Then I must put him back in it again.
    (Point to middle finger.)
This is my kitten. Her coat's black and white.
She loves to sleep on a pillow at night.
    (Point to first finger.)
Here is my puppy who has lots of fun!
He chases the others and makes them run.
    (Hold up thumb. Move thumb slowly and fingers rapidly.)

Pet Day

Plan a Pet Day with your children. Invite them to bring in their pets or photos of their pets for others to see. Give each child a chance to talk about his or her pet and tell how it is cared for.

Pets and Owners Game

Have half your children pretend to be pet owners and let the other half pretend to be their pets. Have the owners pretend to do activities such as feeding, walking, petting, and playing with their "pets." Then let the children reverse roles.

Pet Painting

Cut out different animal shapes for easel art or sponge painting.

Humane Society

Invite a speaker from your local Humane Society to visit your classroom. Find out about educational services, tours, and classes for children.

Pets in the Classroom

Unfortunately, due to allergies and diseases, the number of pets allowed in the classroom is dwindling. However, there are still a few possibilities. One of these is walking sticks! These interesting creatures are available at pet stores. They require little maintenance beyond water and blackberry branches. Put them out before the kids arrive and let them discover them on their own. Later take one out and let students hold it. If you touch it, it will move its leg like it is waving at you. Put the walking sticks in a container with blackberry branches and spray them with a water bottle. Keep the leaves moist but not drenched. You don't want puddles on the bottom of the container or the walking sticks will drown.

Puppet Play

Using stuffed animals or puppets as props, have students demonstrate the proper way to hold, pet, bathe, feed, and play with pets.

Animal Guessing Game

Cut pictures of animal pets (two of each animal) from magazines or coloring books. Give each child a picture of the animal he or she is supposed to be. Have children make sounds, movements, and behavior like those of the animals they are acting out. Have all the children move around the room behaving like the pictures of their animals. The object is for each child to locate his or her matching animal without using the pictures, until they have named the other's animal. If they are incorrect in their match, they keep moving until they have found the correct match.

Animal Cracker Sorting

Animal crackers can provide excellent sorting and matching experiences for children. And the best part is once you have finished the task, everyone gets to eat the assignment!

Animal Shape Cookies

Roll out a favorite sugar cookie recipe. Have children use cookie cutter shapes of various animals to cut out the cookies. Cookies may be frosted, then decorated with nuts, raisins, coconut, sprinkles, etc.

Animal Hospital Play Center

Set up an area of the classroom to be a pet hospital. Have students brainstorm ways to make the area look like an animal hospital. Let them make a sign and decorate the area themselves. Use cotton swabs, empty milk bone boxes, cloth bandages, Band-Aids™, rubber gloves, white shirts for lab coats, stethoscope, scale, clipboards, paper, pencils, basket with pillow and blankets for overnight guests, dog food dish, water dish, stuffed animals from home, telephone, thermometer, and so on.

Pet Snacks

Use cookie cutters to cut toast into bone shapes for doggy snacks and fish shapes for kitty snacks. Then children can eat the snacks themselves.

"This Kitty" Fingerplay

(Start by holding up all five fingers on one hand. At the end of each line, take one away. On the last line, have the final finger run through a hole made by the left hand.)

This kitty said, "I smell a mouse."
This kitty said, "Let's hunt through the house."
This kitty said, "Let's go creepy creep."
This kitty said, "Is the mouse asleep?"
This kitty said, "Meow, meow, I saw him go through this
    hole just now."

Pet Songs

Collect pet songs and put them on an audio tape. Have children sing along. Here are the lyrics for one to include for sure!

How much is that doggie in the window? (Bark! Bark!)
The one with the waggly tail?
How much is that doggie in the window? (Bark! Bark!)
I do hope that doggie's for sale.

Three Little Kittens

Read or recite the poem "The Three Little Kittens." Have the children illustrate their favorite parts in paintings.

Three little kittens lost their mittens and they began to cry: Meow, meow, meow. What? Lost your mittens? You naughty kittens! Then you shall have no pie. Meow, meow, meow.

Three little kittens found their mittens and they began to cry: Meow, meow, meow. What? Found your mittens? You good little kittens! Then you shall have some pie: Meow, meow, meow.

"The Cat of Many Colors"
Stick Puppet Play

Cut cat shapes from white, purple, red, orange, blue, green, yellow, and black construction paper, using the pattern below. Cut out a cat shape for each child. Attach each cat shape to a craft stick to make a stick puppet. Give a stick puppet to each child. Before you read the poem, ask children to listen carefully for the color of their cat puppet. When a child hears the color, he or she should wave the puppet in the air.

Once there was a cat all *white* who wished that he were *black* as night.
He was as thirsty as could be, and in the cupboard, what did he see?
Grape juice right before his eyes. He drank it, then to his surprise,
He turned from white to something new: deep, dark *purple* was his hue.
He peered into his little cup, saw tomato juice, and lapped it up.
He soon became the brightest *red*. He thought, "Maybe I should go to bed."
But he wasn't tired and so he looked for somewhere else to go.
He spied an orange on the floor. He pounced on it, and played some more.
As he played this little game, *orange* was what he became.
He played with some blueberries, too, and suddenly the cat turned *blue*.
A sour lime sat on the ground. The kitty licked it, and he found
That he felt strange and not so keen, for he had turned the color *green*.
Now he was a sad little fellow, so he ate a banana and turned bright *yellow*.
Just then he saw a tasty treat, another food he had to eat.
A long black piece of licorice gave the little cat his wish.
He ate it all, and soon he was *black* from his head down to his paws!

BUGS

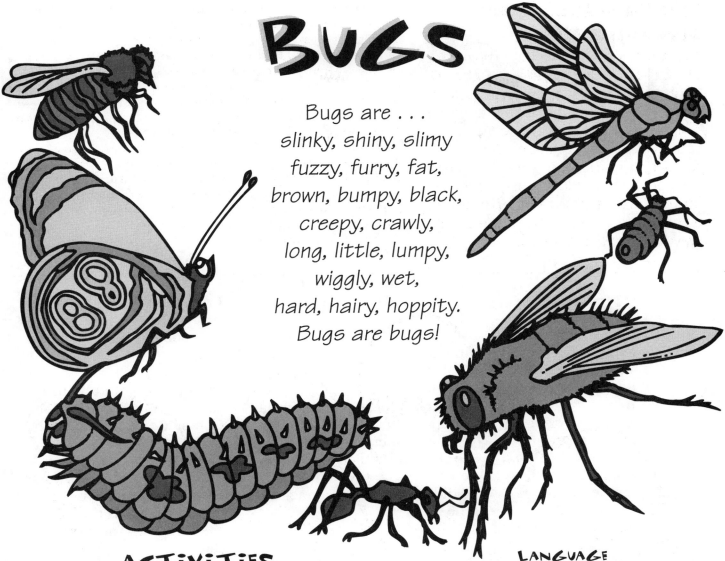

Bugs are . . .
slinky, shiny, slimy
fuzzy, furry, fat,
brown, bumpy, black,
creepy, crawly,
long, little, lumpy,
wiggly, wet,
hard, hairy, hoppity.
Bugs are bugs!

ACTIVITIES
FINE MOTOR

Paper Plate Bugs
Have children paint small paper plates brown, black, or green. When the plates are dry, children may glue paper strips to them for legs and buttons for eyes.

Egg Cup Bugs
Cut out egg cup sections from cardboard egg containers. Have children paint them. When they are dry, help children poke pipe cleaners through them to make legs; then glue on buttons for eyes.

Egg Carton Caterpillars
Read *The Very Hungry Caterpillar* by Eric Carle. Cut a cardboard egg carton in half (cup section) lengthwise. Children can paint the half cartons green, use pipe cleaners for legs and paint on eyes.

Fingerprint Bugs
Have children make fingerprints on paper using a black stamp pad; then use markers to add legs, antennae, eyes, and so forth.

LANGUAGE

Observe bugs in a jar (then set them free) or take a walk and observe bugs on the ground, bushes, and plants. Study them with a magnifying glass. Have the children discuss their observations.

Find spiderwebs early in the morning when the dew is still on them. Have children look at them carefully. Then have students suggest words to describe the webs.

AUDITORY
Ant Cities by Arthur Dorros, HarperTrophy, 1988.
Anteater Named Arthur by Bernard Waber, Houghton Mifflin, 1977.
The Grouchy Ladybug by Eric Carle, Scott Foresman, 1996.
Two Bad Ants by Chris Van Allsburg, Houghton Mifflin, 1988.

BY MARY ANNE QUICK

267

Freda's Lucky Day

Freda hopped by the gray trunk of a dead tree. A large gray bird with long legs, a heron, stood there. The heron stood so still that the little frog didn't see it at all.

Suddenly the heron struck at Freda with his long sharp beak. She leaped. The hungry heron missed the little green frog.

PLOP. Freda landed on a big, green lily pad.

PLOP, PLOP, PLOP. The little green frog hopped from one lily pad to another. She hopped far out into the lake. She made the lily pads shake.

A fly buzzed around her head. Freda closed one eye. She opened her mouth wide and caught that fly as he flew by. One fly.

Freda peered into a yellow water lily flower. She ate two ants trapped inside the flower. One fly, two ants.

Sticking out her tongue, she caught three bugs. One fly, two ants, three bugs.

Something moved in the water. Freda leaned out over the edge of the lily pad to see if it was something good to eat.

SPLASH! A large fish leaped at her from the water. Freda jumped back to the middle of the rubbery lily pad. She could feel the fish under her, bumping the lily pad. Freda didn't want to be a snack for the fish.

PLOP, PLOP, PLOP. Freda hopped from one lily pad to the next. She hopped all the way back to shore, as fast as she could.

Freda sat on the shore, breathing hard. All at once, everything looked dark as night.

"Hey, Sis, come see the little frog that I caught under my cap," Bob called.

"Let's take it home," Jessie said as she came running.

Freda slipped out from under the cap. She hopped into some tall grass. She hid.

"A pet frog would be fun. But this is where it belongs," Bob said. He picked up his cap.

"Looks like the frog thought so too," Jessie said. She laughed as Bob looked for the little frog that wasn't there.

by Jeanne F. Olson

Summer Clouds

When the sky is all blue,
And it stretches for miles,
And the sun is so warm
It just sits there and smiles,

Or I see little clouds
Looking fluffy up there,
Then I feel kind of happy,
Like walking on air.

But what I love best
Is the wind blowing high
When it's looking like paint
Has been streaked through the sky!

Big swishes and swashes
And swooshes of cloud,
And I'm feeling so good
I could holler out loud,

"Oh, what a great day!
I could fly! I could sing!
On a day like today.
I can do anything!"

by Irene Livingston

Summertime

Summertime
is the right time
for playing in the sun.

Summertime
is a good time
for having lots of fun.

Summertime
is a great time
for swinging on a swing.

Summertime
is the best time
for doing everything.

by Elizabeth Giles

Activity
Have children suggest other activities
that are fun to do in the summertime.

270

Sunflower Booklet

Copy these pictures and the ones on the next page for each student. Have students cut the pictures apart and color them. Help them assemble the pages in correct order into a booklet. Show them how to use colored construction paper to make a cover for the booklet. Help them print the title, *Sunflower Friends* on the cover and sign their names. Staple the cover and pages together on the left side.

Ask students to tell the story of their wordless sunflower booklets as they page through them.

by M. Donnaleen Howitt

272

A Yummy Basket

Fill the picnic basket with good things to eat. Draw them or cut pictures from magazines.

by Kim Rankin

273

Octopus

Four-year-old Emily held onto the side of the pool and looked at her mother, who was standing close by in the water. Other children splashed around the pool, too busy to notice Emily and how scared she was.

"Okay, let go and swim to me," her mother said as she backed up and held her hands out toward Emily.

"I can't! I'll sink!" Emily cried.

"I'm right here. I won't let you go under. Just remember to kick hard, keep your bottom up, and move your arms around in big circles. Come on, you can do it," her mom said.

"Okay, but don't move!" After a moment, Emily pushed away from the side. She kicked her legs and moved her arms around in big cir- cles. But no matter how hard she tried, she just couldn't do it. She started to sink.

Her mother caught her and helped her back to the edge of the pool. "Let's try it again," she said.

Emily tried and tried. She was getting tired. "I just can't do it. I'll never learn how to swim!" she cried. She smacked the water with her hand, accidentally splashing her mother.

"Sorry," Emily mumbled. "It's just that I'm so mad!"

"I tell you what, let's take a break. Why don't we check out that aquarium we saw from the highway," her mother said.

"Yeah!" Back in the hotel room, Emily quickly changed into dry clothes and smoothed her long, wet hair back into a ponytail. "I'm ready, Mom!"

by Robin M. Adams

274

On the way to the aquarium, Emily thought about swimming. As her mother parked the car and bought the tickets, Emily thought about swimming. And especially when they were walking by the tanks amidst all of the fish, she just couldn't stop thinking about swimming!

She watched as the stingrays waved their fins up and down and their tail from side to side. The sharks moved through the water with a swish of their tails. Small fish wiggled their tail fins, while the larger fish moved their bodies to and fro in a slow, graceful way. Then she came to the octopus tank.

The octopus moved everything at the same time and slid through the water with ease. Up, out, down; up, out, down went the octopus' arms. Emily moved her arms up, out, down. She stood on one foot and moved her leg up, out, down. I can do that, she thought.

"Mom, when we get back to the hotel, I want to go swimming again!" And that's just what she did.

As soon as they returned to the hotel, she put on her suit, grabbed her towel and raced her mom back to the pool.

Emily jumped in and waded to the edge. First, she moved her arms through the water just as the octopus did up, out, down. Then she held onto the side of the pool and moved her legs up, out, down. After that, she held her breath and let go. Up, out, down moving her arms and legs at the same time. And when she came up she saw that she was no longer near the edge. She was in the middle of the pool!

"I did it!" she cried.

"Yea, Emily!" Her mother was sitting on the steps, clapping. She had been watching the whole time! "You swam all by yourself!"

Emily grinned and for the rest of that afternoon, she practiced swimming just like the octopus.

How many children in your class know how to swim? Have children share learning-to-swim experiences.

Celebrating
Moon Day

Moon Day on July 20 marks the anniversary of the first moon landing in 1969. The mission was made in the spaceship *Columbia* by three American astronauts—Neil Armstrong, Edwin Aldrin, Jr.; and Michael Collins (who served as the pilot). Neil Armstrong was the first to set foot on the moon, saying, "That's one small step for a man: one giant leap for mankind." Then he and Aldrin walked on the moon and planted an American flag, gathered rock samples, and took photographs. This is the week to tell your students about this historic story. For them, it's a story from another lifetime, but kids love outer space and after this story when they look up at he moon, it will have new meaning.

Moonscape Art

Provide students with different sizes and shapes of Styrofoam™ packing pieces. Have them glue these onto a sheet of cardboard in any random order. When the glue has dried, invite students to lay a sheet of aluminum foil over the top of the cardboard square. Instruct them to gently press the foil down around the packing pieces to create a textured, silver "moonscape." Give each child a tiny American flag toothpick (sold at most craft and party stores). They can poke the flag into one of the Styrofoam™ pieces to commemorate the first moon landing.

The Night Sky Globe

Bring the night sky inside with a homemade snow globe.

1. Wash a baby food jar and remove any labels.
2. Let the child crumple a sheet of aluminum foil into the shape of a small moon. Place this in the jar along with foil stars (sold at craft stores), or place enough glitter in the jar to cover the bottom.
3. Fill the jar with water all the way to the top and add one small drop of dish soap to the water.
4. Run a bead of permanent glue along the edge of the lid and screw the lid on tightly.
5. To make a night sky shower, just turn the globe upside down and gently shake it. Recite this poem together as your children play with their globes.

Star light, star bright,
First star I see tonight.
I wish I may, I wish I might
Have the wish I wish tonight!

by Tania Cowling

A Parent Newsletter

Write a letter to parents to get them involved in observing the "night sky" with their children at home. Here are a few suggestions to keep it simple (especially for the younger set):

- Look for landmarks in the sky. Where's the moon? Can you see the face of the "man in the moon"? Why does the moon change shape? What shapes do you see? (crescent, full moon, half moon)
- Have a "moon rock" hunt in your yard with rocks that were painted at school. Expose them to a strong light for a few minutes and then hide them. Have the kids race to see who can collect the most moon rocks. Provide flashlights—it's much safer when you can see where you are going!
- Bring the night sky indoors. Read nursery rhymes, poems, and other stories to your children that talk about the stars and the moon. How about *Good Night, Moon; Good Night, Owl;* and *Hildilid's Night?*

Walking in Space

The concept of weightlessness and loss of gravity are very difficult for a preschooler to understand. A fun way to help them see this concept is to give each student an inflated balloon. Have them draw astronauts on their balloons. Let the students enjoy batting the balloons in the air. The weightless space people they created are floating in space.

Glowing Moon Rocks

Collect them; paint them! These glow-in-the-dark rocks are as much fun to make as they are to play with.

1. Take your class for a walk outside and gather several smooth rocks of various sizes for each child. (You could also buy a large bag of river rock at a hardware store.)
2. Go back inside and wash and dry the rocks.
3. Spread newspaper on some tables. Get out fluorescent tempera paints and some glow-in-the-dark stickers. Let your students go wild decorating the rocks.
4. Let the rocks dry.
5. Have a glow-in-the-dark scavenger hunt. Hide the rocks around the room, turn off the lights, then let the kids go on an indoor moon rock hunt.
6. Send children home with several rocks each to have outdoor moon rock hunts with their families.

Space Helmets

Astronauts need to wear space helmets in outer space. Cut a large face-hole out of the front side of a brown, paper grocery bag. Let each child decorate a bag with crayons to make a helmet. Invite children to wear their helmets and prepare to take an imaginary journey. After they blast off, have them pretend to float around the room weightlessly. When they land on the moon, have them leap and float in slow motion as they pretend to plant a flag, collect moon rocks and take pictures of their newfound surroundings. When the fun is over, instruct them to return to their ship and prepare for the journey back home to Earth.

Going on a Space Ship

Play this fun, open-ended game. Start by saying, "I'm going on a space ship. I have my space bag here. What do you think I should pack to take on my journey?" Have each child think up something that you might need on your voyage.

Moon Song

To the tune of "The Farmer in the Dell"

We're going to the moon,
We're going to the moon.
Put on your helmet, climb on board;
We're blasting off real soon.

We're walking on the moon,
We're walking on the moon.
We'll plant a flag and find some rocks.
We're walking on the moon.

Challenge students to come up with additional verses for this song.

278

Summer Celebration

We line the curbs of Main Street
To cheer a proud parade
Of reds, whites, and blues,
So brilliantly displayed.

Brass buttoned bands
March through sun and shade,
While we trick the heat
With snowcones, lemonade.

Afterwards we gather
To picnic in the park,
Play croquet and softball,
Until we're chased by dark.

At last comes the time
We've all been waiting for:
Sparklers, whistling pinwheels,
Volcanoes, and much more.

Then, Boom! Crackle! Bang!
Colors burst the sky!
What fun it is to celebrate
The Fourth of July!

by Paige Taylor

Activity
Give each student a sheet of black construction paper, glue, and glitter. Show them how to spread lines of glue on the paper in the shapes of exploding fireworks; then sprinkle glitter over the glue for a bright explosion!

Seasonal Science

Experiments help us answer questions about the world around us. We learn things we did not know before by testing and observing the results we achieve. Every experiment teaches us something. Invite your children to learn about summer with the following ideas.

Flowers

Activity

Take children on a wildflower hunt around the playground or a neighborhood park. Be alert for spots of color. Collect samples of any wildflowers you find such as violets, buttercups, and columbine. Pick the stem along with each flower, as well as a leaf sample of each so you can match leaves with flowers. Carry your samples back to the classroom in a plastic bag. In the classroom, match the leaves with the correct flowers. Examine the blossoms. Talk about the color and shape of each. Gently feel the texture of each flower, leaf, and stem. Note that the flowers will not live long now that they have been picked; however, you can preserve (save) them to enjoy for a long time by pressing them. To press flowers, place blossoms and leaves between the pages of an old phone book. Arrange the items carefully on a page of the open book, then close the phone book and weight the top down with other books. In a few days check the flowers. Allow them to remain pressed in the book if they are not quite flat and dry.

Project

Collect and press flowers for each summer month. Use a small amount of glue to stick matching leaves and blossoms to individual pieces of construction paper. Divide a bulletin board into a section for each month and label them accordingly. Place each pressed flower picture under the name of the month in which it was collected.

by Marie E. Cecchini

Colors

Activity

One way to keep cool during the summer is by drinking ice-filled, cold beverages. Use this keeping-cool idea to experiment with color change. First, use red and blue food coloring to prepare red and blue ice cubes. Prepare a pitcher of lemonade and add a few drops of yellow food coloring to brighten the color. Pour the lemonade into three clear glasses. In the first glass, add a red ice cube and stir. What happens? Add a blue ice cube to the second glass and stir. What happens? Add red and blue to the third glass and stir. What happens? Try the same experiment with milk. Talk about why the lemonade colors are different from the milk colors.

Project

Provide the children with white construction paper, white glue, large paintbrushes, and colorful pieces of tissue paper. Have the children brush white glue over the center of their paper; then lay tissue paper pieces in the glue. Some pieces will overlap and change into a new color. When these dry, cut each into the shape of a drinking glass. Staple a drinking straw to the top. Punch a hole at the top of each paper. Suspend your colorful summer beverages from the classroom ceiling.

Frogs

Activity

Let children observe firsthand the sequence of egg-to-tadpole-to-frog by hatching a few frog eggs right in the classroom. Collect a few frog eggs from the edge of a pond or swampy area along with some water. Place these in a classroom aquarium with an air pump or even a simple fish container. Have the children observe and describe the eggs. Note that you are keeping them in pond water because it is their natural habitat. Observe the eggs daily and before long, tadpoles will hatch. Sprinkle fish food into the water so they can eat and continue to grow. As the children continue to watch, they will note the development of back, then front legs. That is the time to release the little frogs back to nature.

Project

Let the children get a little exercise by dramatizing the sequence they have just observed. Lay a blue blanket on the floor to simulate a pond. Begin with the children circled into balls as frog eggs. As you tell the story of frog development, the children will hatch into tadpoles with their arms tucked into their sides and their legs extended for tails. Next they will grow one hind leg then the other, one front leg then the other. When they become frogs, they can hop around the pond in search of food.

Water

Activity

Tell the children you are going to do an experiment with water. Have each child collect one item from the classroom that will not be damaged by water. Talk about the meaning of the words *float* and *sink*. Separate the items the children have collected into two piles—one of things that children think will float and one of the things they think will not. Fill a large basin or your water table with water. Add peppermint extract to the water to make this a more sensory experiment. Have the children test the items in the water, then separate them again according to which ones floated and which ones did not. Were they surprised by some of the things that were able to float? Ask the children if they think people can float. How many children know how to swim? Discuss summer water safety rules such as never swimming alone.

Project

Make float-sink pictures. Have the children use blue markers to draw wavy water lines across the lower half of a sheet of paper. Provide them with a selection of small items you may have tried in your water experiment such as feathers, craft sticks, fabric and paper scraps, bits of waxed paper and foil, paper clips, buttons, pieces of foam, cardboard, sponges, etc. Have the children glue objects that float above the water line and objects that sink below it.

Seasonal Science

Invite youngsters to discover the wonders and workings of nature with these hands-on activities and projects.

Green Activity

Display a live potted plant and a plastic or silk one. Let the children contribute ideas on their similarities and differences. Help the children understand that one is living, while one is not. Discuss the differences between living and non-living things, namely that living organisms are able to process food and waste, grow, react to stimuli, and reproduce. Note that the non-living plant does not absorb water or need sunlight to flourish and it will not get any larger. Set up a table to display living and non-living things. Label each side of the table as such. Have the children help to contribute only items that are green to both sides of the display, in honor of St. Patrick's Day.

Project

Take a nature hike to look for small pieces of fallen tree limbs and trunks to collect for each child. You might also want to collect one larger one for the whole class. Have the children help to decide whether or not these pieces of wood are still living. Place each piece in a shallow baking dish (larger one in a plastic tub) or aluminum pie tin. Water each well, allowing some water to remain in the bottom of the pan or tin. Sprinkle each wooden piece with grass seed. Keep the wood moist and out of direct sunlight until the grass sprouts. The children may be surprised to discover that the grass will grow without soil.

Water Activity

Discover what plants do with water they cannot use. For this experiment you will need a clear plastic food storage bag, a potted plant, string or yarn, and a measuring cup. First note that the plant leaves are healthy, as determined in the previous experiment, because you have been watering the classroom plant. Next, cover the plant with the bag and secure the bag with string around the main stem of the plant. Place the plant in a sunny window. Note what happens after several hours. Droplets of water will form inside the bag. Plants do not use all of the water they take up. Plants release water vapor through tiny holes in their leaves. This process is called transpiration. Carefully remove the bag from the plant. If possible, use the measuring cup to see how much water was collected.

Project

Some plants produce leaves we eat. Display a few varieties, such as cabbage, lettuce, and spinach. Have the children name and describe each. Cut the cabbage in half and observe the arrangement of the leaves. Let the children pull off one sample leaf from each selection, wash, and taste their leaves.

by Marie E. Cecchini

Leaves

Activity

Talk with the children about leaves and their part in helping plants grow. What do leaves need in order to remain healthy and do their job? Choose a leafy celery stalk to display and name. Point out the leaves, then allow it to sit out overnight. The following day have the class comment on what has happened to the celery stalk and leaves (they have gone limp). How can we help? Prompt the children to deduce that the stalk needs water. Use colored water so you can observe how the plant carries water. Allow the celery stalk to sit in the colored water overnight. The following day conclude your experiment by noting any changes in the celery stalk, and cutting a cross-section to observe the tubes through which the water was carried. Now carefully scrape off the outside layer of celery to reveal stripes of color. Talk about the meaning of the saying, "April showers bring May flowers."

Project

Grow plant leaves from the leafy tops of radishes, turnips, parsnips, and pineapples. Sliced tops from radishes, turnips, and parsnips can be placed in a shallow pan with water. Pineapple tops can be placed in soil and kept moist. Let the children observe these cuttings over several weeks.

Wind

Activity

March comes in like a lion and goes out like a lamb. Have your children noticed how windy the month of March is? Ask them to tell you what wind is. Help them to understand that wind is moving air. Demonstrate this by having them fan themselves with pieces of cardboard. Talk about the different velocities of wind from a gentle breeze to a fierce hurricane or tornado. Demonstrate the effect of different wind speeds using a hair dryer or table fan with cotton balls. Place several cotton balls on a tabletop. Use the dryer or fan on high, medium, and low speeds to move the cotton balls. Invite the children to comment on what takes place. Invite volunteers to use their cardboard "fans" and a cotton ball for a race across an area of the room. If they move the cardboard more rapidly (as if on "high"), does the cotton ball move faster?

Project

For this project you will need a few feathers of different sizes, a measuring tape, and a day with a gentle breeze. Have the children take turns standing at a starting point and releasing a feather into the breeze. Watch where the breeze takes each feather. Measure the distance from the starting point to where the feather landed. How far does each feather float in the wind? Do smaller feathers float farther than larger ones?

Make -in-a- Minute Crafts

Balloon Tree

Materials
- paper towel roll
- green balloon
- string/wool
- brown paint and paintbrush
- masking tape

Directions
1. Have students paint the tree trunk (paper towel roll) brown.
2. Help each student blow up a green balloon.
3. Tie a string to the bottom of the balloon. Thread the string through the tree trunk.
4. Tape the string to the bottom of the tree so the tree's green "foliage" stands straight.

Caution: Balloons may be a choking hazard. Warn children not to put balloons or balloon pieces in their mouths.

Summer Mini Books

Each child creates a make-and-take mini book to reinforce concepts related to the season.

Materials
- spring magazines
- scissors
- paste and paste sticks
- scrapbooks
- paper cutter
- crayons, pencils, and markers

Preparation
1. Cut standard-sized scrapbooks into thirds using a paper cutter.
2. Collect spring magazines, flyers, and other materials that can be cut up.

Directions
1. Invite students to print their names and print the word *spring* on the outside cover of the mini book.
2. Provide students with the materials listed above. Invite them to search for pictures of items they see in the spring. Do this activity together and encourage everyone to find a spring picture in the magazines and flyers provided. Comment on their finds: "Look at the garden hoe; we use it in the spring to prepare our gardens! Oh, look what Peter found—a spring flower and a bird. We saw some spring flowers in our yard."
3. Have students cut out the pictures they find and paste them into their spring mini books. Comment on their findings and assist those who wish to print the name of the item they have found.
4. Children can work on these simple books throughout the season.

by Robynne Eagan

Bulletin Board Summer Tree

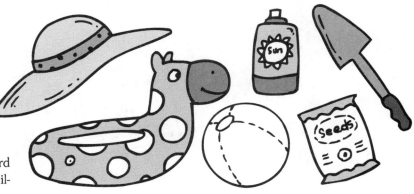

Materials

- brown and green construction paper
- masking tape or paste
- scissors
- templates for leaves, squirrels, birds, bird nests, flowers, apples, cherries, pears, children climbing, etc.

Preparation

Use brown and green construction paper to make a large tree to fill a classroom bulletin board or wall.

Directions

1. Invite children to fill the tree with things they might see there in the summer.
2. Provide materials that allow children to trace, cut, and paste their creations to the tree.
3. Discuss the items each child adds to the classroom tree.

Summer Sorting and Collage Activity

Encourage sorting, classifying, and creativity with summer materials.

Materials

- sand
- beach toys
- summer sporting equipment
- sun hat
- sandals
- sunscreen lotion
- pebbles
- flower petals
- grasses
- seeds
- gardening tools

Summer Sorting

Allow students to experiment with various summer materials. Encourage them to explore the shape, weight, texture, color, and smell of the materials.

Invite students to sort and classify on their own. Discuss the reasons for their organization of materials. Did they sort by color? Size? Type of materials? Place of origin of material?

Encourage students to think about how they might create with these materials. What can they make with this group of materials? What can they make by combining various groups of materials?

Create a Scene

Encourage children to create with materials at hand even if their creations will be non-permanent works of art. Invite children to make a summer scene in a sandbox using the materials they used for sorting. Invite others to observe the scene. Capture the creation on film to send home for parents to view.

Tiny Thumbody Greeting Cards

Materials
- colored, letter-sized paper cut in quarters
- ink pad and blotting pad
- fine-tip markers

Directions
1. Have children fold their paper in half, then quarters (which can be a lesson itself).
2. Provide a simple cut-and-paste message ("Thumbody Loves You") for children to paste to the front of the card. More advanced students can copy the phrase in their own printing.
3. Have each child make a thumbprint inside the card by pressing a thumb on an ink pad, then a blotting pad, and finally on the card.
4. Children can use fine-tip markers to turn their thumbprints into "thumbody" by adding eyes, ears, nose, hair, legs and arms, antennae, etc.
5. Have children carry the greeting from the front of the card to the inside by printing *Me!* beneath the thumbprint character and then signing their names.

Funky Flowers

You can make a bouquet for Mother's Day or fill a clay pot with these floral creations.

Materials
- floral/spring-theme cupcake papers
- pipe cleaners
- green tissue paper
- small clay flowerpots
- acrylic paints
- modeling clay

Directions
1. Pinch the bottom center of a cupcake paper.
2. Wrap a pipe cleaner around the pinched area.
3. Cut some leaves from green tissue paper and attach them to the flower using the pipe cleaner.
4. Paint the outside of the flowerpot.
5. Put some play dough in the flowerpots and have the children poke their flowers into the dough to hold them in place. When the play-dough dries, the flowers will stand up nicely. You can also decorate some tissue paper to cover the outside of the flowerpot.

286

Holiday newsletter

National Garden Month is celebrated during the month of April. Recognized in conjunction with Earth Day, it helps us remember to keep our planet healthy by cleaning up litter and planting trees, flowers, and vegetables. Timely activities you may enjoy doing with your family include planting flower seedlings to share with extended family members and neighbors, organizing a group of people from your child's school to help plant small flower gardens to beautify the grounds, and planning and planting a garden or two of your own. Try growing some vegetables your child enjoys eating. He or she will be amazed to watch vegetable seeds sprout, flower, and produce food. Gardening is not only a learning experience; it also allows us to exercise outdoors in the fresh air. When the work is done, be sure to relax in the shade with a tall, cool lemonade.

Simple Science

Invite your child to plant an indoor letter garden to commemorate the National Garden Month of April. Cut one or more letter shapes from household sponges. Letter-shaped sponges can also be purchased at educational and craft stores. Moisten the sponge letters and set them into a tray or pie plate about half full of water. Sprinkle the letters with grass seed. Cover the tray with plastic wrap and place it in direct sunlight until the seeds sprout. After the seeds have begun to sprout, remove the plastic wrap and place the tray in full sunlight. Water as necessary and watch it grow.

On the Move

Help your child develop coordination skills using berry baskets and a collection of milk jug lids. Begin by helping him or her weave colorful ribbons through the spaces in a berry basket.

Place the basket on the floor and challenge your child and a few friends to count how many lids they can toss into the basket from a few feet away. Adapt this game for Easter by using an empty Easter basket with foam or plastic eggs.

Creative Kitchen

Your child will be delighted to make this St. Patrick's Day dessert to share with the family. You will need one 3 oz. package lime gelatin, 1 c. boiling water, 2 ripe bananas, ½ c. honey, the juice of one lime, and one chilled can of evaporated milk. First, dissolve the gelatin in the hot water and set it aside to cool. Next, peel the bananas, cut them into chunks, and place them in a bowl. Mash the bananas with a fork or electric mixer. Stir the honey and lime juice into the mashed bananas. Now pour the cooled gelatin over the banana mixture and beat. Finally, add the chilled evaporated milk and beat until well mixed. Place in the refrigerator until jelled, then serve. For an extra special treat, tint whipped cream with green food coloring and use it to top each gelatin serving.

The Reading Room

Turn a dreary rainy day into something special by sharing a colorful, fun storybook with your child. Check to see if your local library has a few of the following:

The Egg Tree by Katherine Milhous, Simon & Schuster, 1971.

Guess How Much I Love You by Sam McBratney, Candlewick, 1996.

Planting a Rainbow by Lois Ehlert, Harcourt Brace, 1992.

The Tiny Seed by Eric Carle, Simon & Schuster, 1987.

The Very Little Leprechaun Tale by Yvonne Carroll, Pelican, 2000.

by Marie E. Cecchini

Communication Station

Have fun building bookworms in honor of Dr. Seuss' birthday this March. Use circles of poster board or construction paper to build these bookworms and help your child learn to build words in the process. Decorate one circle as the bookworm's head; then write letters on additional circles. Work with your child to build specific words such as his or her name by placing letter circles to the right of the head. Glue the circles in place and use the bookworm to mark your place in your favorite Dr. Seuss adventure.

Poetry in Motion

How many words can your child think of or invent that rhyme with *noodle*? That's the challenge during the National Noodle Month of March. Help your child create a list of real or invented rhyming words; then work together to use the words from the list to write an original noodle poem such as: *In a soup, or in a salad, I like oodles of noodles. But on a plate with red tomato sauce, Noodles are my FAVORITE foodle.* Help your child to write the poem in the center of a sheet of construction paper. Create a frame by doodling around the edges of the paper with marker. Post your creation for the whole family to enjoy.

From the Art Cart

Create baby bunny shakers to make music to welcome spring. You will need a small paper plate, cotton balls, pink pom-poms, black scrap paper, black yarn, pink construction paper, dried rice or beans, a stapler, glue, scissors, a paper punch, and markers or crayons. Fold the plate in half and staple closed around the outer edge, leaving a small opening at one end. Pour a small amount of rice or beans into the opening, then staple shut. Glue cotton balls to both sides for the fur, and add extra cotton to one end for a tail. Now at the opposite end, glue on a pink pom-pom nose, black yarn whiskers, black paper punch circle eyes, and pink paper ears. Allow the glue to dry; then shake to make your own special rhythms.

Mathworks

Use jelly beans to learn about estimation and measurement. Challenge your child to guess how many jelly beans will be needed to fill a teaspoon, a tablespoon, half a cup, and one cup. Count and fill to check your answers. Next, how many jelly beans will you need to place end to end to measure 6"? 12"? Check and find out. Now, arrange several jelly beans in a line, using a specific color pattern such as red, red, green, blue, yellow. Challenge your child to use additional beans to copy the pattern. Finally, eat and enjoy at least some of the "fruits of your labor."

Holiday newsletter

A Family Take-Home

Summer is right around the corner. School will be out and your daily routine will change, at least for a while. Throughout the summer you can help your child continue to learn new skills as well as practice those previously acquired at school. For instance, after you grocery shop, have your child put the groceries away in the correct places at home. Having company? Let your child help prepare the salad, dip, or dessert. Cooking helps children learn to estimate, sort, measure, count, and read picture recipes. Too hot to move? Pull out the board games. Playing board games helps children learn to cooperate, take turns, and play fair. They help children learn to have patience, and they teach the hard lesson of winning and losing. Summer offers us the time to relax a little and enjoy sharing activities, such as reading and telling stories. The season is short, make the most of it!

Simple Science

Use this simple science experiment to demonstrate the heating power of the sun in honor of the Summer Solstice. On a sunny day, fill two aluminum pie plates with water. Place one in bright sunlight and one under a shady tree. Later in the day let your child place a hand into each plate of water. Which is warmer? Can your child tell why? Use this power to make sun tea. Place water and tea bags in a clear, covered container. Set it in bright sunlight and observe the changes that take place. Sun power can also be used to provide birds with a warm bath. Set up a bird bath in a sunny spot outside. Talk with your child about the kinds of birds that visit the bath. Most importantly, remember to wear sunscreen when playing or working outdoors. The sun's rays can be harmful as well as helpful.

On the Move

Happy Birthday, U.S.A.! Celebrate Independence Day with eye-hand coordination fun. You will need empty soda bottles, construction paper, tape, a squirt gun, and water. Cover each soda bottle with a cylinder of paper. Cut large flame shapes from yellow paper. Tape a flame at the top of each soda bottle cylinder to make candles. Set the soda bottle candles in a row on top of a picnic table. Challenge your child to "put out" the flames by squirting them with the water gun from a distance of a few feet. This is a game your whole family will enjoy.

Creative Kitchen

Cool off your summer with nutritious watermelon pops you and your child can mix up in your blender. Place 1 cup watermelon chunks (no seeds), 1 cup orange juice, and 1 cup water in the blender container. Mix until smooth. Pour the mixture into small paper cups and place them in the freezer. When the pops are partially frozen, insert the bowl of a plastic spoon into each. Continue to freeze them until solid. Then peel off the paper cup to eat the pops.

by Marie E. Cecchini

The Reading Room

Explore nature with summer reading fun. Check your local library or bookstore for a few of the following:

Baby Bird by Joyce Dunbar, Candlewick, 1998.

Come Along, Daisy! by Jane Simmons, Little Brown, 1998.

For Pete's Sake by Ellen Stoll Walsh, Harcourt Brace, 1998.

Guess What I'll Be by Anni Axworthy, Candlewick, 1998.

In the Sand by Dawn Apperly, Little Brown, 1996.

Star of the Circus by Michael and Mary Beth Sampson, Henry Holt, 1997.

What Moms Can't Do by Douglas Wood, Simon & Schuster, 2001.

Communication Station

Try these easy parent-child activities to continue language learning this summer: 1. Read to your child each day. Talk about what you've read. 2. Check and sort the mail together. Notice the stamps on the envelopes. Match the ones that are the same. 3. Help your child write a short letter to a family member who will write back. Receiving a reply will be exciting and your child will begin to understand how people communicate through writing. 4. Work together to cut coupons from magazines and newspapers. How many products can your child identify? Have your child help cut out coupons for products you will purchase. At the store, let your child match the coupons to the products.

From the Art Cart

Invite your child to create dimensional art with a waffle-type cereal such as Honeycombs™ or Chex™. Let your child glue cereal pieces to a white sheet of paper in the shape of a beehive. Use a water-based ink stamp pad to add fingerprint "bees" around the hive. With markers, add yellow coloring, insect legs, and antennae to each bee. Use the picture to decorate your child's room.

Poetry in Motion

Sing your way into summer fun with a movement song about animals of the sea. Use the following verses to get started; then work with your child to create several more. What a wonderful way to sneak in a little bending and stretching!

Undersea Ballet
To the tune of
"Did You Ever See a Lassie?"

Did you ever see a crab,
A crab, a crab?
Did you ever see a crab
Walk on the ocean floor?
Moving sideways on tiptoe,
Moving sideways on tiptoe.
Did you ever see a crab
Walk on the ocean floor?

Verse 2: Did you ever see the tentacles of an octopus or squid? They wave under-

Mathworks

Use cardboard paper towel tubes and old magazines and newspapers to practice counting skills. Cut bands from the tubes, then slice each band open in one place to make bracelets. Cut numbers from magazines and newspapers. Glue them to the bands in numerical order. Make several bracelets when you count single objects, then double-digit teens, twenties, thirties, etc. Expand your child's knowledge by helping him or her count by 2s, 5s, and 10s.

Picnic Problem

These friends want to have a summer picnic! But where is the food? See if you can find and color the hidden carrot, sandwich, cupcake, watermelon slice and pitcher of lemonade.

by Becky Radtke

291

Story Time

Spark up the summer season with this "sun"-sational array of books!

Summer by Maria Rius (Barron's, 1998) is the perfect book to get everyone in the mood for the new vacation season. This delightful book explores many of the fun-filled activities that are popular during summertime. And that's not all! Also included are directions for youngsters to create their own sun visors, plus helpful guideline questions and ideas for teachers to use with the book.

Snack time will be a breeze this summer with *Snack Art: Eat What You Create* by Elizabeth Meahl (Teacher Created Materials, 1999). This resource book features simple kid-pleasing recipes and crafts. Your children will love creating "edible art" with a variety of animal and seasonal themes. Nutrition activities are also provided, as well as a nifty game idea called Stick the Food on the Food Pyramid.

Sandcastle
by Mick Inkpen
Hodder Children's Books, 1998

Calling all sandcastle fans! Grab your buckets and shovels and head for the beach. You may want to take along this book to inspire you! It's all about a dog named Kipper who has almost created the perfect sandcastle except for something special to go on top. After much searching, Kipper finds a beautiful pointed, pink shell to adorn the top of the castle. However, the shell turns out to be a crab that walks away! Will Kipper ever be able to find just the right castle-topper?

The Seashore Noisy Book
by Margaret Wise Brown
illustrated by Leonard Weisgard
HarperCollins, 1993

Meet Muffin, a little dog with sharp ears, who thinks he has heard everything until he goes to sea in a sailboat. The delighted dog is treated to a variety of unusual sounds from the cries of sea birds flying overhead to the whistles of a gigantic ocean liner passing by. In addition, Muffin is able to experience the sounds of a sandy beach as he encounters a starfish, snail, and crab. Finally, the sea-loving dog gets to hear another noise—his own splashing sound as he takes a swim in the ocean!

by Mary Ellen Switzer

Fish Wish
by Bob Barner
Holiday House, 2000

Come along and join a young boy on an incredible journey through a picturesque coral reef. You will meet a host of sensational ocean creatures such as seahorses, jellyfish, sea anemone, squid, and clownfish. The vibrant, colorful collages bring the beautiful coral reef to life. Also included in the book is fascinating information about coral reefs and the sea animals that inhabit them.

The Ocean Alphabet Book

by Jerry Pallotta
illustrated by Frank Mazzola, Jr.
Charlesbridge, 1986

Did you know that some cod can grow as big as a 10-year-old? Or that the mouth of a goosefish is as wide as its body? Learn some remarkable facts about amazing ocean animals as you "swim" through this unique alphabet book. Be sure this ABC book is on your summer book list!

Boats! Step into Reading Series

by Shana Corey
illustrated by Mike Reed
Random House, 2001

Ahoy, mates! Set sail during the summer with this delightful book featuring a variety of boats. From motor boats and fancy yachts to fantastic ferry boats, this book provides bright colorful pictures and simple rhyming text with a boat theme that will appeal to younger readers.

Grandpa's House

by Harvey Stevenson
Hyperion, 1994

A boy named Woody gets an unforgettable summer vacation when he visits his grandfather who lives near a beach. The two enjoy such fun-filled outings as a canoe ride to a sandbar which his grandfather names "Woody's Island," and picking tasty sweet raspberries along a path. Or course, the two also love splashing around in the sparkling ocean and making a giant airplane in the sand. There will be happy memories galore for Woody and his grandfather this summer! Another appealing book about a boy and his grandfather on vacation is *Jungle Adventure, A Pop-Up Vacation* by Helen Balmer (Simon & Schuster, 1993). It's all about a grandfather who takes his grandson on a "surprise" vacation to a jungle for an action-packed adventure. This humorous, interactive pop-up book is sure to entertain youngsters.

Over in the Meadow

by Jane Cabrera
Holiday House, 1999

Take your students on a captivating counting journey "over in the meadow" this summer! This book's vibrant, eye-popping colors and catchy rhyme is a perfect way to introduce youngsters to the numbers one to 10. They will enjoy meeting an array of colorful animals such as turtles, ducks, frogs, and lizards on this merry countdown.

Summer Camp Crack-Ups and Lots S'more Knock-Knock Jokes
by Katy Hall and Lisa Eisenberg
HarperFestival, 2000

Knock, Knock. Who's there? It's only a group of silly campers with some sensational jokes for you, all with a summer camp theme. Join the kids at Camp Lotsafun for the wackiest summer camp adventure ever!

Elympics
by X.J. Kennedy
illustrated by Graham Percy
Philomel Books, 1999

Attention, sports fans! Don't miss the lively collection of perky poems in this animal's rendition of the Olympic Games. Follow a group of irresistible elephants as they compete for a coveted medal in their own pachyderm version of the Olympic Games. Meet such elephant champions as Trinket, who wins the hundred-meter race by her long nose; or Elijah, who wins a perfect 10 in the diving competition. This book features two sections: Summer and Winter Games.

The Everything Mother Goose Book
300 Favorites Kids Will Enjoy, Again and Again
edited by June Rifkin
Adams Media Corp., 2001

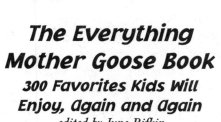

This new book is brimming over with the all-time favorites that we enjoyed as children. Now it's time to share them with our primary youngsters. From the lovable Humpty Dumpty to the tiny Itsy Bitsy Spider, beloved characters are back for lots of reading fun! To further enhance the book, you will find information on the "history" of Mother Goose, and other pertinent facts about nursery rhymes. Also included are activities you can use with the rhymes, as well as a list of Mother Goose-related videos and DVDs.

Computer Corner

Web Sites

Take an exciting trip to Asia without leaving your classroom! Click over to Kids Web Japan at *www.jinjapan.org/kidsweb/index.html* for an introduction to Japanese culture. A map of Japan, games, and coloring activities are included in this site.

Celebrate a panda's birthday! The panda born on August 21, 1999, at the San Diego Zoo is named Hau Mei (pronounced wha-may), and she has received worldwide attention since pandas are such a critically endangered species. Visit the zoo's web site for updates about this panda cutie at *www.sandiegozoo.org*

Follow the journey of Abbey and Addey, two adorable cocker spaniel Beanie Babies®, as they travel around the country visiting other schools. Log on to *www.hobart.k12.in.us/groff/pups2.html*. Abbey and Addey, the Adventurous Pups, is an online project created by Joanne Groff, a teacher in Hobart, Indiana. During their week's visit at each school, the host classrooms discuss good pet care tips and select some of their ideas to share with everyone in the project. The host classes e-mail Joanne Groff giving their pet care tips, along with the pups' adventures that week, and information about their community. That data is then featured on the project web site. Joanne says, "Online projects have brought the world closer to my students, and helped them develop an awareness of the global outreach of the internet."

D.W. the Picky Eater

by Marc Brown
Living Books, Win/Mac CD-Rom, Broderbund

Software

Even your "pickiest eaters" will love Marc Brown's interactive story adventure along with some motivating educational activities. In addition to another of Marc Brown's appealing stories, your youngsters will also enjoy learning about nutrition and the food pyramid.

Other excellent Living Books software featuring the popular Arthur stories include: *Arthur's Birthday, Arthur's Reading Race,* and *Arthur's Computer Adventure.*

Snacktivities

Brighten up your classroom activities with some sunny summer snack ideas.

Burrito Bites

May—Cinco de Mayo

Ingredients

tortillas
cream cheese
sugar
cinnamon

nutmeg
chopped walnuts
raisins
dried apricot bits

Spread softened cream cheese over several tortillas. Mix about 1 tablespoon each of cinnamon and sugar with ½ teaspoon of ground nutmeg in a small bowl. Lightly sprinkle this mixture over the cream cheese. Top the tortilla with chopped walnuts, raisins, and dried apricot bits. Roll the tortilla up tightly and slice the roll into small pieces for snacking.

Wagons Ho-O!

May—Transportation Week

Ingredients

red peppers
cottage cheese
raisins

cucumber slices
celery sticks
toothpicks

Cut peppers into cupped wedges, making one for each child. Show the children how to use toothpicks to attach cucumber slices to the sides of their pepper wedges to create wheels. Remind the children that the toothpicks are not for eating. Mix raisins into the cottage cheese and place a spoonful of this mixture into each pepper wedge. Push a celery stick into the cottage cheese mixture at one end of the pepper wedge to make a handle for each little red wagon.

Sun Snacks

May—Sun Day

Ingredients

English muffins
cheese slices

carrot sticks

Slice and lightly toast the muffins. Give a muffin half to each child. Let the children use a biscuit cutter or blunt knife to cut circles from cheese slices. Top each muffin half with a cheese circle. Place the cheese-topped muffins into a toaster oven or under a broiler just long enough to melt the cheese. Cool each sun muffin on a small plate. Have the children add carrot stick sun rays around their muffin suns before eating.

by Marie E. Cecchini

Banana Caterpillars

June—Summer

Ingredients
- banana slices
- peanut butter
- round crackers

Alternate banana slices with dabs of peanut butter and round crackers to form a caterpillar shape. Begin with the rounded end of a banana for a head.

Tiny Butterflies

June—Summer

Ingredients
- mandarin orange slices
- carrot curls

Have the children place two mandarin orange slices together, back to back, to form the wings of each butterfly. Top each with carrot curl antennae.

4th of July Salad

July—Independence Day

Ingredients
- blueberries
- bananas, cut into bite-size pieces
- watermelon, cut into bite-size pieces
- honey

Place each fruit into a separate serving bowl. Allow children to spoon a little of each fruit into their individual eating bowls or cups. Drizzle a little honey over each, stir to mix, then eat. Optional: Sprinkle with flaked coconut before eating.

297

Pretty May

May is such a pretty month
With lovely garden flowers
That grew so bright and tall
Because of April's showers!
> *(Throughout the poem, pretend to admire, pick, and smell the flowers.)*

Exercise Time

Up and down, up and down;
> *(Raise arms over head, then reach down.)*

Try to touch your toes.
> *(Touch your toes.)*

In and out, in and out;
> *(Spread arms out, then bring them to your chest.)*

Try to touch your nose.
> *(Bring index fingers to your nose.)*

Five Little Peas

Five little peas in a pea pod were pressed.
> *(Show fist.)*

One grew, two grew, and so did all the rest.
> *(Put up one finger at a time as indicated.)*

They grew and grew and grew and never stopped.
> *(Wiggle fingers slowly upward.)*

Until they got so fat the pea pod popped!
> *(Clap hands loudly.)*

A Lovely World

I'm glad the sky is painted blue
> *(Look up and sweep arm back and forth as if painting.)*

And the Earth is painted green.
> *(Look down and "paint.")*

With such a lot of nice fresh air
> *(Take a deep breath.)*

All sandwiched in between.
> *(Clasp hands together making a "sandwich.")*

My Garden

I walk in my garden
> *(Walk slowly around.)*

And what do I see?
> *(Look around.)*

All of the flowers are nodding at me.
> *(Nod head in different directions.)*

by Judy Wolfman

plays

Five Little Bees

One little bee flew and flew.
(Wiggle index finger around.)
He met a friend and that made two.
(Put up another finger.)
Two little bees, busy as could be.
(Wiggle two fingers around.)
Along came another and that made three.
(Put up third finger.)
Three little bees looked for one more.
(Wiggle three fingers around.)
They found one soon and that made four.
(Put up fourth finger.)
Four little bees, going to the hive,
(Wiggle four fingers around.)
Saw their brother, and that made five.
(Put up fifth finger.)
Five little bees, working every hour.
(Wiggle all five fingers.)
Fly away, bees, and find another flower.
(Wiggle fingers to the other hand "flower" and let them rest.)

Summer Storm

The clouds float swiftly by
(With fingers spread, float both hands above your head.)
And block out the bright sun.
(Put hands together to block out the sun.)
Then raindrops fall from the sky,
(Wiggle fingers downward.)
So inside we must run!
(Run in place.)

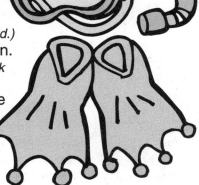

Helping Dad

Today is my day to help,
So first I'll feed my pet.
Then I'll straighten up my room—
I hope I won't forget!
I'll be as good as I can—
Not loud, or mean, or bad.
And I'll be happy all the time
Because I'm helping Dad.

The Beach

I hope I go to a sandy beach
Where I can watch the waves roll in!
(Wave arms back and forth.)
Then I'll go out where they can reach
(Take a couple of steps.)
And splash up over my chin!
(Tap under your chin.)

Swimming

When it's hot, I love to swim
In a pool or ocean blue.
I can dive and stroke and kick.
Can you do these things, too?
(Make appropriate swimming motions.)

4th of July

Bang! Poof! Pop! Crack!
(Flick fingers out on each word.)
Way up in the sky.
(Raise hands higher and do the same thing.)
We watch the fireworks and we shout,
"Happy Fourth of July!"
(Cup hands around mouth and shout this.)

TLC10339 Copyright © Teaching & Learning Company, Carthage, IL 62321-0010

Earth Day 2002

_____
name

is an

Earth Helper!

_____
date

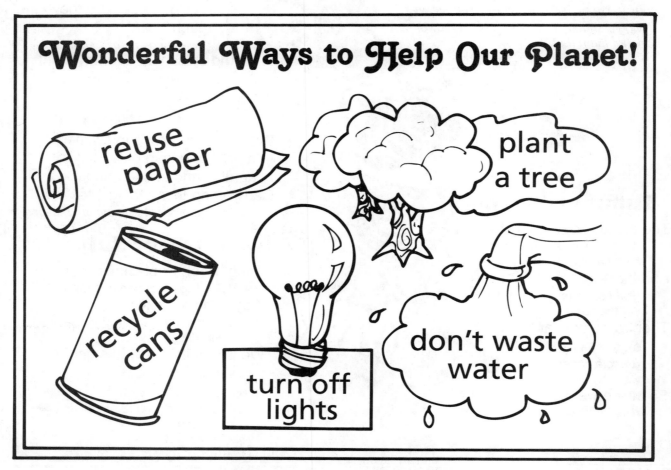

Wonderful Ways to Help Our Planet!

reuse paper

plant a tree

recycle cans

turn off lights

don't waste water

Clip Art for Spring

A **St. Patrick's Day** Reminder:

Happy St. Patrick's Day!

In like a lion . . .

My School
Friends
200_-200_

My Teacher

My Principal

Autographs

304

A Cinco de Mayo Party!

A CINCO DE MAYO REMINDER:

May Day

MAY NEWS

Picnic Reminder:

Enjoy Your Summer!

SUN LOTION

SPF 20

Have a Great **Vacation!**

Happy Birthday, America!

Happy 4th of July

Dear Parent,

It has been a wonderful school year. I enjoyed having your child in my class. Thank you for all of your help and support through the school year. Have a great summer!

To: A wonderful parent

SUMMER

Try to find 6 hidden snowflakes!

January

Sunday	Monday	Tuesday	Wednesday	Thursday	Friday	Saturday

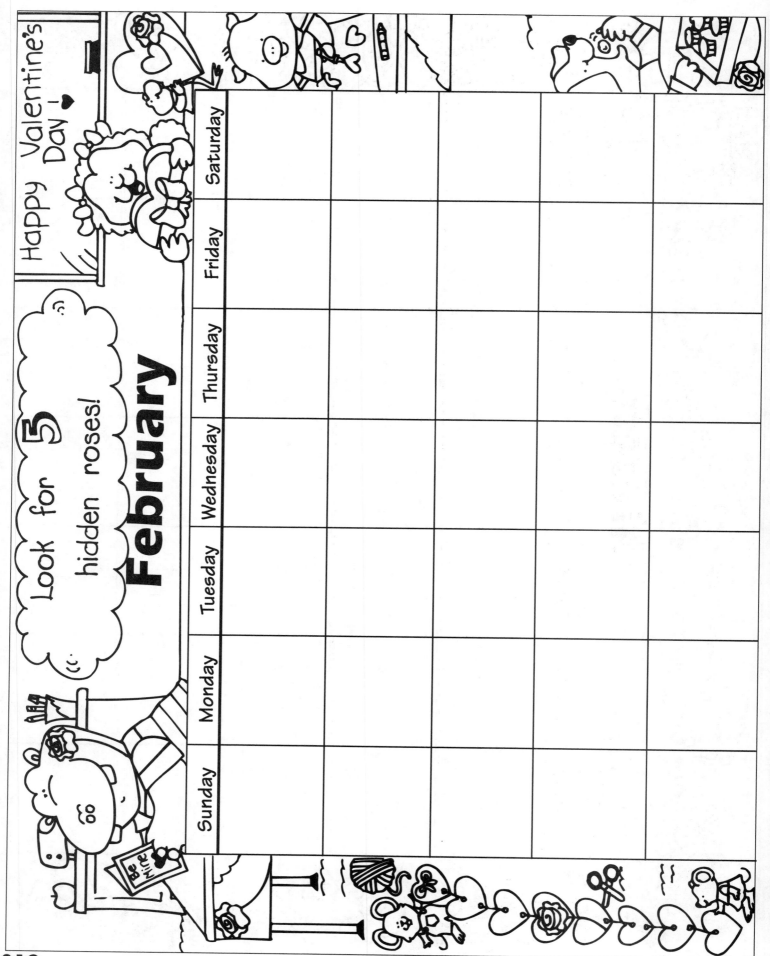

Happy Valentine's Day!

Look for 5 hidden roses!

February

Sunday	Monday	Tuesday	Wednesday	Thursday	Friday	Saturday

March

Sunday	Monday	Tuesday	Wednesday	Thursday	Friday	Saturday

April

Sunday	Monday	Tuesday	Wednesday	Thursday	Friday	Saturday

312

May

Sunday	Monday	Tuesday	Wednesday	Thursday	Friday	Saturday

June

Sunday	Monday	Tuesday	Wednesday	Thursday	Friday	Saturday

July

Sunday	Monday	Tuesday	Wednesday	Thursday	Friday	Saturday

Try to find **4** hidden fish!

August

Sunday	Monday	Tuesday	Wednesday	Thursday	Friday	Saturday

Look for **6** hidden acorns!

September

Sunday	Monday	Tuesday	Wednesday	Thursday	Friday	Saturday

Do you see 3 hidden caramel apples?

October

Sunday	Monday	Tuesday	Wednesday	Thursday	Friday	Saturday

Try to spot
5 hidden leaves!

November

Sunday	Monday	Tuesday	Wednesday	Thursday	Friday	Saturday

December

Try to find 6 candy canes!

Sunday	Monday	Tuesday	Wednesday	Thursday	Friday	Saturday